Praise for
The Japanese Money Tree

"Andrew Shipley has written an enlightening, insightful, and extremely readable book on how the investment and new finance opportunities of post-bubble, post-deflation Japan are being pursued. This book is "must" reading for any student, practitioner, or professional money manager interested in contemporary Japan."

—**Allen Sinai**, Chief Global Economist, Strategist & President,
Decision Economics, Inc.

"Andrew Shipley provides a highly readable account of the new Japan that is finally emerging from a "lost decade" of stagnation, deflation, banking failure, and other problems. While he provides notes of caution when due, this is a tale of exciting new business opportunities that Americans should learn about."

—**Edward J. Lincoln**, Director, Center for Japan-U.S. Business and
Economic Studies, Stern School of Business, New York University

"Andrew Shipley, a true "connoisseur" of the Japanese economy, offers exciting insights into the "New Japan." This new book focuses on the changes that will bring Japan to the forefront of Asia's new century."

—**Håkan Hedström**, senior strategist at Deka Investment,
one of the top 3 German asset management companies

"Japan's lost decade was bound to end, and Andrew Shipley's book describes the efforts of those who had prepared for a new and better decade even before it was clear that the bad times would end. He focuses particularly on the ability to find Japanese companies rich in intangible assets that will give them an advantage as they compete in the global market, especially against new competitors from China and the rest of Asia. This book is important reading for investors everywhere."

—**Rich Mattione**, partner, Grantham, Mayo,
Van Otterloo & Co. LLC (GMO)

"Shipley, who spent 15 years living and working in Japan, writes from an insider's perspective and draws on revealing conversations with the country's key economic players—both foreign and Japanese—to bring readers a knowledgeable, intimate portrait of today's Japanese economy. Both professional money managers and savvy individual investors will gain invaluable insights on how to reap the benefits of Japan's economic rebirth."

—Kirkus Business & Financial Report

The Japanese Money Tree

FINANCIAL TIMES

In an increasingly competitive world, it is quality of thinking that gives an edge—an idea that opens new doors, a technique that solves a problem, or an insight that simply helps make sense of it all.

We work with leading authors in the various arenas of business and finance to bring cutting-edge thinking and best-learning practices to a global market.

It is our goal to create world-class print publications and electronic products that give readers knowledge and understanding that can then be applied, whether studying or at work.

To find out more about our business products, you can visit us at www.ftpress.com.

The Japanese Money Tree

How Investors Can Prosper from Japan's Economic Rebirth

Andrew H. Shipley

An Imprint of PEARSON EDUCATION

Upper Saddle River, NJ • New York • London
San Francisco • Toronto • Sydney • Tokyo • Singapore
Hong Kong • Cape Town • Madrid • Paris • Milan
Munich • Amsterdam

Vice President, Editor-in-Chief: Tim Moore
Executive Editor: Jim Boyd
Series Editor: Bob Webb
Editorial Assistant: Susie Abraham
Development Editor: Russ Hall
Associate Editor-in-Chief and Director of Marketing: Amy Neidlinger
Cover Designer: Chuti Prasertsith
Managing Editor: Gina Kanouse
Project Editor: Andy Beaster
Copy Editor: Stacey Klemstein, Krista Hansing Editorial Services, Inc.
Indexer: Julie Kawabata
Senior Compositor: Gloria Schurick
Manufacturing Buyer: Dan Uhrig

FT Press
FINANCIAL TIMES

© 2007 by Pearson Education, Inc.
Publishing as FT Press
Upper Saddle River, New Jersey 07458

FT Press offers excellent discounts on this book when ordered in quantity for bulk purchases or special sales. For more information, please contact U.S. Corporate and Government Sales, 1-800-382-3419, corpsales@pearsontechgroup.com. For sales outside the U.S., please contact International Sales at international@pearsoned.com.

Printed in the United States of America

First Printing February, 2007

ISBN 0-13-234390-8

Pearson Education LTD.
Pearson Education Australia PTY, Limited.
Pearson Education Singapore, Pte. Ltd.
Pearson Education North Asia, Ltd.
Pearson Education Canada, Ltd.
Pearson Educatión de Mexico, S.A. de C.V.
Pearson Education—Japan
Pearson Education Malaysia, Pte. Ltd.

Library of Congress Cataloging-in-Publication Data is on file

For Laura, Owen, and Elle

CONTENTS

ACKNOWLEDGMENTS

I am very grateful to all the people who cooperated with me during the writing of this book. Scholars such as Akira Furukawa, Masaru Kaneko, Koichi Mera, Hiroyuki Itami, Jun Nishikawa, Thomas W. Roehl, Toshiko Takenaka, Charles Steen, Robert I. Webb, Robert F. Bruner, Eisuke Sakakibara, David E. Weinstein, Peter Duus, Michael Smitka, Christiaan Jörg, Andrew Dewit, Philip Bougen, Anthony P. D'Costa, and Niccolo Caldararo all consented to discuss their research.

I am thankful that extremely busy financiers also agreed to discuss their businesses with me. Frank Jennings, Guy Cihi, Simon A. Ross, Kirby Daley, Gareth Phillips, Sonny Kalsi, Steven P. Thomas, Yusuke Nishi, Nick Ricciardi, Peter Espig, James Fiorillo Ortega, Richard Lemmerman, Takehiro Hashimoto, Richard L. Folsom, Roy Kuan, and Seth Sulkin all kindly provided insight into their enterprises.

Masahiro Kobayashi, Masato Kawasaki, Kenichi Sato, Tatsuo Nishimoto, and Toru Okusa of Mitsubishi Estate Co., Ltd. granted interviews regarding their firm's strategy to develop the Marunouchi area. Marunouchi Heat Supply Co., Ltd. graciously allowed me to visit its underground tunnels. Yasuhiko Sakai at World Public Relations Co., Ltd, coordinated meetings with Mitsui Fudosan Co., Ltd. There I met with Hideyuki Takahashi and Masaki Kamiya, and Takashi Nakayama spoke at length about the Tokyo Mid-Town development. I would like to thank Akira Mori at Mori Trust Co., Ltd., as well. My discussions with John M. Tofflemire have always been interesting, and I appreciate his cooperation with this book project.

Nicholas E. Benes, Tom O'Sullivan, Donald B. Westmore, Abby Pratt, Hiroshi Kadota, Nobuyuki Nagata, Go Kondo, Hiroyuki Tezuka, Kozo Suzuki, Rajeev Baddepudi, Marc Goldstein, Thomas J. Byrne, Brad Glosserman, Carl Haub, Michael D. Kaminski, Masao Igarashi, Kazushi Kaneto, Gemma Kentaro, Shiochiro Chida, Kazuhiro Furuyama, Noriaki Tsuchiya, Genji Tsukatani, Richard Jerram, Takashi Hamada, Holly Bailey, and Suzannah Yip agreed to speak with me.

Robert Babbish of Thomson Financial provided valuable data regarding private equity deals and merger and acquisition activity. The cooperation of Scott Y. Ikeda, Fred F. Hirose, Korendo Shiotsuki, and Masanobu Katoh, of Fujitsu Ltd., is also very much appreciated.

Mika Fukuda in Tama City, Yuji Baba at the Ministry of Finance, and lawmaker Motohisa Furukawa consented to be interviewed. Other officials in the Japanese public sector, who requested to remain nameless, granted interviews that were extremely helpful as well.

I would like to thank my editor, Jim Boyd, for giving me the opportunity to write this book.

A special thanks goes to Brutus Cornelius, Yasunao Nakano, Masumi and Machiko Kizuka, and Hamish Ross. Chin Ong, Robert Tomkin, Paul Summerville, Andrew Morse, Herbert Donovan, Katherine Proctor, Cameron Umetsu, and Leslie Norton provided assistance.

This book would not have been possible but for the support of my wife, Laura, and our family. Patricia, Herman, Chan Ah Mui, and Josephine Goh all helped with this book. My brother Howard, a patent attorney, shared his thoughts on intellectual property.

ABOUT THE AUTHOR

Andrew H. Shipley lived in Japan for fifteen years. He has worked as an economist at Lehman Brothers Japan Inc., Schroders Japan Ltd., Credit Suisse First Boston Securities (Japan) Ltd., and Westdeutsche Landesbank Girozentrale (West LB). He graduated from the University of Virginia and received a Japanese government scholarship when studying for his graduate degree at Waseda University in Tokyo. His writing has appeared in the *Asian Wall Street Journal* (op-ed page), *Institutional Investor*, *The Nikkei Weekly*, and *The Daily Yomiuri*. This is his first book.

Introduction and Executive Summary

"When the wind blows, barrel makers earn money."

This old Japanese proverb reflects the enigmatic nature of Japanese markets. To decipher this puzzle, one must follow an obscure series of events unfolding in premodern Japan. When wind blew, dust got into people's eyes. More people went blind and could no longer work, and thus became destitute. Sightless beggars during the feudal period often played the *shamisen,* a string instrument with a banjo-like hide covering its body. Feline skins were used to make a *shamisen,* so when sales took off, cats started disappearing from city streets.

With their natural predators gone, mice quickly overran towns, getting into rice-storage warehouses and gnawing through barrels to get to the grains. Merchants then bought more casks, to prevent their precious rice from being devoured by swarms of rodents. Thus, the cooper was a happy man indeed.

If local merchants were baffled by the disjointed events that moved prices in premodern Edo, foreign investors today face even greater challenges in assessing Tokyo markets. Yet they cannot ignore them; Japan is simply too important. The world's second-largest economy outperformed all other major markets in 2005. Japan has a seat at the highest-stakes game in global finance: underwriting the growth of the sprawling and densely populated Asian region. Japan's corporate giants are among the fiercest competitors in the world, and even ordinary households are sitting on legendary hoards of savings. Indeed, many experienced foreign financiers of all stripes—value investors, hedge fund advisors, and private equity turnaround engineers—are now convinced that this country offers better opportunities than anywhere else in the world.

This book explores how foreign investors today are trying to make money as Japan enters the twenty-first century. Chapter 1, "From Ultimate Capital Destruction Machine to the Best Value in the World," explores why Japan is suddenly back on the radar screen of large institutional value investors. Convinced that they were snapping up top-drawer companies at bargain-basement prices, many such investors have poured money into Japan in recent years. As the nightmarish prospect of a deflationary spiral receded and the twin engines of the U.S. and Chinese economies powered faster economic growth, Japanese share prices took off, more than doubling from those of 2003.

Foreign value investors now must sniff around much longer for deals. The easy money has probably already been made by those buying deeply discounted tangible assets, such as plants or equipment, that typically appear on balance sheets. Some analysts point to a recovery in domestic demand to support further across-the-board gains of Japanese share prices. The verdict is still out on this assertion; twice in the last decade, slowdowns overseas have weighed heavily on Japanese stocks. No compelling evidence suggests that the economy, which is continuing to experience wrenching restructuring, would be resilient in the face of an another downturn overseas.

Instead of betting on continued upside economic surprises, the foreign researchers interviewed in Chapter 2, "Intellectual Property Wars," are focusing on an exciting new field in investment analysis. They are trying to cherry-pick firms with undervalued *intangible* assets, such as intellectual property (IP) or corporate brands, whose full values do not typically appear on financial statements. Such a strategy could be extremely promising: Many Japanese firms are beginning to milk their intellectual assets, such as patents, for more money. Indeed, some scholars argue that Japanese firms have a competitive advantage in cultivating such assets because of their unique management style. The government has launched extensive policy initiatives to safeguard IP at Japanese firms and promote its cultivation.

Hedge funds are proliferating in Japan, as elsewhere. Chapter 3, "Cultural Arbitrage," reveals that managers and advisors of hedge funds in Tokyo appear to be facing both challenges typical to this highly secretive industry and uniquely Japanese ones as well. One pioneering foreign hedge manager discusses his initial efforts at targeting Japanese high-net-worth individuals for fund raising. However, this manager found such marketing efforts to be singularly unproductive and had to shift gears. Others find Japanese regulation in the industry cumbersome and see costs rising because of increased demand for risk management and compliance controls. Foreign talent in Japan may be insufficient to manage all the money flowing into the country as well.

Private equity funds are the vanguard of Japanese corporate-restructuring efforts. Credited with improving corporate governance and boosting the profitability of many firms, such operators are increasing the independence of managing boards and forcing firms to disgorge loss-making enterprises. Many believe this market remains tantalizingly underdeveloped. Chapter 4, "The Future of Japanese Management," chronicles the experience of one of the founders of the first private equity fund in Japan in his efforts to rescue Daiei. The supermarket chain hemorrhaged money until his fund took it over in spring 2005. Meanwhile, the head of the first infrastructure fund in Japan talks about his desire to help revitalize the Japanese economy, starting with a sleepy toll road in the mountains of Hakone.

Inspired by such examples, Japanese public corporations are now actively buying and selling businesses. Morning TV shows scrutinized the takeover battle between Livedoor Co., Ltd., and Fuji Television Network Inc., increasing public awareness of and lessening resistance to these transactions. The government and the courts have also become more supportive of shareholder rights. Although international deals remain few in number, M&A negotiations among domestic firms are becoming increasingly common, observes an investment banker in Chapter 5, "Barbarians at the *Genkan.*" Some foreigners complain that Japan is still closed, but others argue that the government has done virtually all it can to promote deal-making. In some respects, Japan resembles the U.S. market in the 1980s, which also witnessed limited international activity. One M&A scholar notes that foreign deals are often driven by different factors than domestic ones, including a desire to capitalize on intangible assets. As Japanese firms become more aggressive in attempting to extract value from their intellectual property, M&A deals involving foreign partners will likely increase as well.

Even the most jaundiced of observers are stunned by the construction activity that has erupted in previously sleepy Tokyo neighborhoods and the numerous skyscrapers bursting onto the city's fragmented skyline. Real estate tycoon Akira Mori, interviewed in Chapter 6, "The Manhattan of Asia," says that businesses and residents are flocking to new developments in areas blessed with good transportation and communication links. Low interest rates, newly available financing tools, and the relative ease at which land can be redeveloped in Tokyo are all sparking an urban renaissance. Developers say they are looking past the day when interest rates start to creep back up and are striving to add value to their properties. The Marunouchi business district has gone from a low-tech holdout to a cutting-edge nerve center for corporate headquarters by a fluke in industrial design; Mitsui Fudosan Co., Ltd. aims to make Tokyo Midtown in Roppongi a global showcase of Japanese creativity. Indeed, one politician anticipates Japan and Tokyo playing a "New York" role in the Asian region, as a center for the arts and business.

Many have written off Japan as a rapidly aging society destined to stumble under the weight of its oppressive debt. However, some market watchers assert in Chapter 7, "Birthrates and *Bushido*," that the dire population forecasts of the government are unrealistic. Meanwhile, even though the Ministry of Finance and some bond analysts fret about debt ratios, one scholar further argues that Japan's fiscal solvency is virtually assured over the long term. Others point to a revolution in corporate governance as a new generation of Japanese executives takes the helm. New ideas are already percolating through policy-making circles as the first generation of political leaders born after World War II moves into ascendancy. Civil society is Japan is also found to be rapidly evolving.

Chapter 8, "The Chinese Paradox," examines Japan's trade relations with China, its rival for influence in East Asia. One researcher argues that Japan's long experience competing with mainland factories has trained Japanese firms to focus on high-value-added products and services. Such an orientation is likely to be a competitive advantage in the post-industrial age, as Chinese firms increasingly commoditize anything that can be replicated quickly. The new generation of political leadership is likely to take a firm stance with China, especially regarding intellectual property rights. This leads to a paradox for Japanese corporations: How can they effectively fence off their intellectual property while at the same time engender the goodwill needed for their products to become the *de facto* standards in the increasingly important Chinese market?

Finally, many foreign investment advisors are convinced that recent policy reform implemented by the Koizumi administration will grease the wheels of profit-making firms. Some even have quit investment bank posts to set up firms to take advantage of these new opportunities. Chapter 9, "High-Speed Capitalism," explores the revision of the Commercial Code, deregulation, and the privatization of Japan Post. Many believe these will result in an evolutionary development of Japanese financial markets that will not likely be reversed by stock-market downturns or economic slowdowns. The Japanese themselves are bracing for an era of "high-speed" capitalism.

1

FROM ULTIMATE CAPITAL DESTRUCTION MACHINE TO THE BEST VALUE IN THE WORLD

Japan Is Back in Favor Among Global Investors

The ivory gavel dropped with a bang, establishing yet another world auction record. The price of the wood block print *Foxfires*, from Hiroshige's *Hundred Famous Views of Edo*, soared to £81,600 in the auction room of Sotheby's in London in fall 2005. The winning bid was fully triple the house's estimate. *Ohashi*, from the same series, commanded bids of up to £90,000 earlier in the day, close to twice the auction house's projections.

After more than a decade, Japan is back. The Nikkei 225* closed the year 2005 above 16,000 for the first time since 1999, making the Tokyo market the best performer of any major developed economy for the year. Interest in Japanese culture is rebounding, driving up demand for antiques and other collectables. *Memoirs of a Geisha* opened in theatres across the United States. After dropping off in the

* © Nihon Keizai Shimbun, Inc.

1

early 1990s, the number of students registering to study Japanese at U.S. colleges is again on the rise. Japan appears to be on the verge of being trendy for the first time since the 1980s.

Some global investors are shaking their head in wonder. Many have long viewed Japan as the sick man of Asia. In a reversal of fortune rivaling the collapse of Soviet Russia, asset values in the world's second-largest economy virtually imploded in the early 1990s. Businesspeople across the globe wrote it off as a disaster zone, and foreign investors deserted Tokyo in droves. In the mid-1990s, Frank Jennings, now portfolio manager of the $4 billion Global Opportunities Fund at Oppenheimer Funds, referred to the Japanese markets as "the ultimate capital destruction machine." Some privately speculated that there would be "blood in the streets" as a result of what was regarded to be horrible mismanagement of the economy. The Nikkei 225° tumbled from almost 40,000 at the end of 1989 to a low of 7,607 in 2003, while commercial real estate in Tokyo lost about 70% of its value from its peak in the early 1990s.

What went wrong is not the focus of this book—I examine what some investors believe is finally going right. A debate continues to rage regarding why the Japanese economy slid into an apparently intractable recession, a debacle experienced by no other developed economy since World War II. While commentators in both the financial markets and academia agree that the tardiness of the government in addressing bad debts at Japanese banks delayed any rebound in share prices, views on the overall role that economic policy played in the downturn remain sharply divergent. Some analysts view the recession as typical of a business cycle downtrend and argue that fiscal and monetary policy was insufficiently stimulatory; others focus on perceived unique rigidities in the Japanese economy that prevented a reallocation of resources to more profitable industries. Happily for investors, they do not need to take sides in this ongoing discussion. Nonetheless, it is clearly to time to reassess what is going in the Japanese financial markets.

° © Nihon Keizai Shimbun, Inc.

The sheer magnitude of gut-wrenching and painful price declines in Tokyo has prompted sweeping comparisons with epochal events of the past. Alex Kerr wrote in *Dogs and Demons* that Japan lost more money than any nation in human history, surpassing even Rome's losses when it was sacked in 455 A.D. Perhaps, although no Vandals were seen helping themselves to finery in Ginza department stores following the collapse of the bubble economy. To be sure, fans of the eighteenth-century English historian Edward Gibbon and other such connoisseurs of decline find such parallels irresistible. But the legacy of Japan's so-called lost decade should not blind investors to the present.

"This spectacle of the world, how is it fallen! How changed! How defaced! The path to victory is obliterated by vines, and the benches of the senators are concealed by a dunghill." Poggius' words as he surveyed Roman ruins on the Capitoline Hill in the fifteenth century resonate strongly in Tokyo in the wake of the disastrous '90s. Nonetheless, in the rubble of the Japanese economy, a new plant has taken root. An exceedingly rare species, it flourishes in times of uncertainty and change. It also grows only where hard work is rewarded and property rights are respected. The prospect of finding such a botanical specimen is prompting foreigners to flock to Tokyo. This highly coveted prize is the Japanese money tree.

Many foreign hedge fund managers and advisors, private equity turn-around specialists, property developers, and value investors now see the country as fertile ground to grow businesses and create value. Japan's restructuring is perceived to be a once-in-a-lifetime opportunity, offering returns unavailable in other markets. This book focuses on where such foreigners are finding opportunities in Japan, how they are trying to make money, and the risks that still plague investors today.

This revaluation by the markets of the country's prospects has been sudden and dramatic. Indeed, 3 short years ago, traders in Tokyo nervously eyed the nation's fifth-largest banking group, which was teetering on the edge of bankruptcy.

By June 10, 2003, many foreigners viewed Japan as the Death Star of financial assets, blowing up funds and zapping the performance of any manager who had the temerity to overweight the country in global portfolios. The yield on Japanese 10-year government bonds fell that day to 0.46%, or effectively zero. People snapped up bonds that offered nothing but the assurance that they would get their original capital back in a decade. The Nikkei 225* had plummeted to a 20-year low of 7,607 a few weeks earlier.

Stock market participants were panicking, remembers Nick Ricciardi, a founder at Light Year Research (Japan) K.K. Unlike many brash, loud traders who appear to have the reflective capacity of race-car drivers rounding a curve in fourth gear, it is easy to picture Ricciardi enjoying a quiet chess match in the park. With dark eyes and an unruly head of brown hair, he lacks the hulking physique and stentorian voice often used to dominate discussions by the computer screens at derivatives desks. One should not be fooled, however. A grand master at market strategy in his 40s, he has little need to intimidate in debates, using instead sharp-edged logic and seamless mathematical reasoning.

Having headed the Asian Equity Derivatives business at Goldman Sachs until 1997, Ricciardi was originally banished to Tokyo by Robert Rubin when the former treasury secretary was still co-running the firm. Rubin interviewed him for a position managing Goldman's structured equity products business in Japan in 1990.

"I'm 24 years old, I am looking across at this senior guy, I can't believe I am even meeting him, and he is offering me this job," he reminisces years later. The only catch was that the chairman was stipulating that Ricciardi could not return to the United States for years.

Suddenly Ricciardi realized the droll investment bank head was joking. He deadpanned, "Sure, I can stay there for 5 years; I never have to see my family again."

* © Nihon Keizai Shimbun, Inc.

Following his years at Goldman, Ricciardi settled in Kyoto and started scouting firms overlooked by others. He scrutinized balance sheets and found amazing deals. "A couple of years ago, a great way to make money was to identify companies that had undervalued tangible assets," Ricciardi notes, pointing to property, cash, and securities held by firms. Companies in aggregate on the First Section of the Tokyo Stock Exchange were priced below their book value, and many of these had a great deal of hidden assets.

"It was a relatively straightforward trade to identify those companies that were trading at the largest discounts." Whole swaths of the Japanese market were made up of such bargains—companies trading below their net current asset value. This is a fire-sale price of a firm— what an investor could, in theory, take home from a firm's safe and bank accounts after quickly shutting it down. To get this value, Riccardi subtracts total liabilities from the total amount of cash listed on a firm's balance sheet. He then adds back cash equivalents, marketable securities, and tax-adjusted long-term shareholdings, and compares the result to the firm's market capitalization.

"The situation was unparalleled in recent financial history in any real market. You probably had to go back the post-Depression 1930s in the States to find chunks of the market that were comparably undervalued," Ricciardi points out.

The deep price declines in Japanese share prices prompted many institutional investors to give Japan another look. Much of corporate Japan was up for sale at bargain-basement prices. "I would say a year ago, many people would have argued Japan was the best-value market in the world," remembers Jennings at Oppenheimer in early 2006.

Stocks selling below their net current asset value may well be bargain issues, observed the two pioneers of value investing, Benjamin Graham and David Dodd, in their classic *Securities Analysis*. One reason is that net current asset value "may be considered a conservative measure of liquidating value," they wrote, but added that diversification of such stocks is desirable to ensure good performance.

Ricciardi saw even more Japanese companies trading below their net *tangible* asset value. This he defines as his calculation of net current assets (which subtracts total liabilities) plus conservative values for tangible assets, such as land, plant, equipment, and inventories. In isolated cases, there may be a good reason a company is trading at a deep discount relative to net tangible asset value. For example, if managers are corrupt and are not running the company in the interests of shareholders, a low stock price could be warranted. "But when you see it across thousands of companies, then it is highly unlikely that there are that many fraudulently run companies," observes Ricciardi.

Although Japanese stocks in 2003 did not approach 1930s Depression-level prices in the United States, there were comparably undervalued parts of the market that Graham and Dodd "would be in heaven over if they were picking stocks today," says Ricciardi. He points to Japan Maintenance Co., Ltd. (9787), and Toei Labo Tech Co., Ltd. (9732), as two companies that subsequently went through the roof. Japan Maintenance rose from a low of ¥250 in January 2001 to ¥3,040 by May 2006, a stunning elevenfold increase. Toei Labo Tech jumped from ¥122 in December 2002 to ¥688 in February 2006, a dramatic 463% gain.

"One of the big explanations for this undervalued situation was deflation," points out Ricciardi. Wrenching price declines for years had led many investors to expect to lose money if they held on to assets in Japan. "To the extent that deflation is expected to persist permanently or for the foreseeable future, then you can get hurt buying companies below their net tangible asset value," he warns. To illustrate his point, he uses the example of a company that owns $100 million of property and has a market capitalization of only $50 million. Under grinding deflation, the property holdings of the firm could ultimately lose 50% of their value. Under this scenario, the market could be pricing the firm correctly, assuming that investors had no ability to hedge.

June 2003 marked the height of such fears. Ricciardi attributes much of the rise in share prices since then to the end of deflationary paranoia. About this time, the government agreed to bail out Resona Holdings, Inc., a major banking group. The government pumped about ¥2 trillion into the beleaguered institution, convincing many investors of its determination not to allow a full-fledged crisis in the banking sector, one that would have led to a credit crunch and, ultimately, a deflationary spiral. The outlook for banks was still far from rosy. The public was dismayed to learn in September that Resona Holdings was still hemorrhaging money at an alarming rate—it had lost more than ¥1 trillion during the previous 6 months. Indeed, it still took bravery to buy into Japanese stocks. Capital destruction was continuing. However, many foreigners decided it was safe to buy deeply discounted Japanese assets.

Investors heaving a sigh of relief at the government's intervention, however, were only part of the story. Foreign shipments at Japanese firms began to pick up, supporting earnings. Exports climbed 12% year-on-year in 2004, their fastest rate of increase since the heady days preceding the Asian crisis in 1997. U.S. consumers packing shopping malls and Chinese factories running at full-throttle resulted in another 7% gain the following year. Fear receded in Tokyo, and, at some point, greed took over.

With the Nikkei ending 2005 over twice as high as it was during the grim days before the government's announcement of the Resona Holdings bailout, Ricciardi is convinced the large move in the market due to tangible asset repricing has already occurred. A new strategy is needed to find value in Japan.

Some observers, convinced that the Japanese economy is finally back on track, argue that the stock market will be supported by across-the-board strong earnings growth for years to come. Such siren songs repeatedly seduced investors in the previous decade, but they often found share performance crashing on the rocks as Japan's economy repeatedly stalled. "Ah, but this time it is different," runs the argument. Jobs are being created, and wages are rising. Such income growth will fuel consumer demand, boost sales growth, and

support earnings, proclaim these bullish commentators. In 1997, jobs
grew, and wages were also climbing at over twice the rate recorded in
2005. Nonetheless, the stock market imploded in the autumn, when
exports collapsed during the Asian meltdown.

Is it really different this time? This is the question I put to Akira
Furukawa, former Deputy Director General of the Economic Planning Agency's (EPA's) Economic Policy Bureau, in summer 2005. The
EPA was folded into the Cabinet Office in 2001. The bespectacled
scholar, whose hair is salted with gray, has the kindly presence of a
gentlemanly diplomat. Furukawa enjoys an encyclopedic knowledge
of economic trends and is one of the country's leading experts on the
business cycle. He has written numerous surveys of the Japanese
economy published by the government, and regularly helped brief
Cabinet members during his stint at the EPA. He retired from the
government in 2000 and took a position with Ritsumeikan University,
where he teaches courses in economic policy and statistics.

Ritsumeikan was initially founded by Prince Kimmochi Saionji on
the site of the Kyoto Imperial Palace. Saionji was the last of a group
of elite elderly statesmen, known as *genro,* who held tremendous
sway over Japanese politics until the beginning of World War II. The
current university adopted this name in 1913 and has campuses
throughout the Kyoto area, including one across the street from the
Ryoanji Temple, known throughout the world for its elegant rock garden. The economics department is located 15 minutes from nearby
Otsu City, an ancient capital of Japan that predates the sixth-century
Nara Period.

Furukawa's office overlooks the imposing gray mass of Mt. Hiei
and glittering Lake Biwa in nearby Shiga Prefecture. Mt. Hiei, home
to the Enryakuji Monastery, was the site of one of the bloodiest mas-
sacres in Japanese history. The Japanese credit Oda Nobunaga, along
with Toyotomi Hideyoshi and Tokugawa Ieyasu, with unifying their
country after the destruction of the Ashikaga shoguns. He had a

complete lack of regard for tradition. In 1571, Nobunaga and his troops surrounded the mountain, whose 800-year-old Buddhist center opposed him, and he gave the order to kill every inhabitant and burn every building.

"Nobunaga was a reformist," observes Furukawa when asked about the warlord's role in Japanese history, over dinner in a French restaurant in Marunouchi OAZO, one of the high-rise office buildings recently built near Tokyo Station. On further reflection, he adds, "Perhaps he was a destroyer."

Nobunaga is a favorite historical figure of Prime Minister Junichiro Koizumi. Referring to the current ambitious prime minister, Furukawa notes, "Koizumi is also a reformist, but he lacks Nobunaga's power." Nonetheless, he argues that progress has been made under previous administrations, and the outlook for the economy is brighter than it has been in more than a decade.

Furukawa wrote a segment of the *Economic Survey of Japan (1996-1997)* that attracted much attention—a simple, common-sense explanation of the stagnation the economy had experienced since the collapse of the bubble in the early 1990s. At the time, his analysis was a useful tool in interpreting the outlook for monetary policy.

In the wake of the stock market and real estate market collapses, the Bank of Japan (BoJ) aggressively slashed rates, ultimately cutting them next to zero in February 1999. Central bankers in Tokyo then were clearly uncomfortable; since interest rates had hit rock bottom, monetary policy options in the event of further economic shocks were limited to controversial quantitative easing measures. Such measures, which essentially involved flooding the banking system with excess funds, were feared by some to be excessively inflationary; others doubted the effectiveness of such measures because banks at the time were trying to shrink their balance sheets. Many investors sensed that the BoJ was on a hair trigger, eager to raise rates at the earliest opportunity. Indeed, in summer 2000, the central bank started draining excess liquidity in the overnight call market, putting

upward pressure on rates, a move that turned out to be premature as
the economy slowed abruptly in the winter. The BoJ reversed course
in March 2001.

With the central bank clearly eager to tighten, investors needed
to know what conditions the central bank considered necessary for a
lifting of the zero-interest-rate policy. The central bank gave some
clues regarding what it was looking for. For example, the BoJ repeatedly mentioned in its economic reports that accommodative monetary policy was necessary until the economic entered a sustainable
recovery. However, it was unclear what the central bank meant by this
vague phrase.

Furukawa's elegant, simple model explained what a sustainable
recovery would entail for Japan in the wake of the chronic asset deflation that the country has experienced since 1990. He noted that the
basic mechanism engine for growth—production increases—was
usually triggered by either rising demand for Japanese exports abroad
or boosted public works spending. In a healthy economy, production
increases jumped started two virtuous cycles. First, among Japanese
households, rising production usually sparked additional hiring by
industrial firms, thus supporting income growth. The rising demand
for workers resulted in wage increases and bonus gains, also supporting rising incomes. Such income gains boosted consumer spending,
further increasing demand for consumer goods, and production
increased further.

In the corporate sector, production led to a second self-sustaining
dynamism through increasing profits. In addition to hiring more
workers, firms invested in plant and equipment as returns on real
assets rose. Such demand for machinery triggered more production,
thus restarting the cycle again. If the Japanese economy was functioning normally, an export-led recovery, or one triggered by public works
spending, was possible because of the boosted spending by both
households and corporations in the wake of rising production levels.

However, Furukawa went further and noted why a sustainable recovery was not materializing. Several wrenches were being thrown into the growth mechanism. Payrolls were bloated in the 1990s. Managers aged and swelled the executive ranks, resulting in firms top-heavy with white-collar workers. Personnel costs as a percentage of sales climbed to a record high by 1999. Even when production levels rose, firms refused to hire more workers, as they attempted to rein in spending on salaries. As a result, many households witnessed neither wage gains nor new job offers even when factories revved up production activities. In addition, worries about the economy kept the savings rate relatively high. Meanwhile, corporate-sector profit gains were meager even when production levels rose because of the intense deflation in the economy. Falling prices limited nominal sales gains even when real output levels climbed. Depressed profits meant firms had little to spend on additional investments in plant and equipment, and no further boost to production was experienced. Firms were also shifting production to lower-cost centers overseas.

The decade-long banking crisis also weighed heavily on the corporate sector. Furukawa noted in 1997 that banks were adjusting their balance sheets in response to damage sustained during the collapse of the stock and real estate bubbles earlier in the decade. Financial institutions scaled back lending dramatically twice since the early 1990s, according to BoJ surveys. When concerns about a series of bank collapses in 1997 resulted in major banks facing a rising cost of capital, the so-called Japan premium, banks suddenly became much more tight-fisted. Later, when banks faced a deadline to achieve capital adequacy ratio goals dictated by the government in 2001, funds for some corporations dried up again.

Furukawa's analysis suggested that when external stimuli to the Japanese economy—the previously noted export increases and public works spending—ran their course, the economy would sink back into recession. Indeed, this happened repeatedly. Large-scale downturns were twice triggered by collapses in foreign demand—once in 1997, in the wake of the Asian crisis, and a second time in 2001, when the NASDAQ shock triggered a slowdown in U.S. demand. Without export growth, there was no trigger for economic activity—public works spending has been a drag on growth since 1999. Despite optimistic forecasts to the contrary, domestic demand proved neither sustainable nor resilient, and the economy grew only 0.1% in 2002.

Bolstered by strong demand from China, Japanese production is once again rising. The capacity utilization rate of manufacturers, after bottoming out at an abysmal 64.9% in December 2001, had risen to 79% by January 2006. Although the economy overall is far from overheating, in industries most directly linked to the Chinese market, such as steel, the recovery has been even more dramatic; JFE Steel Corp. usage rates have jumped from 83% to more than 100% on the back of strong shipments to China. The most closely watched measure of cyclical activity in Japan, the sentiment of business managers' index in the BoJ *Short-term Economic Survey of Enterprises in Japan*, more commonly known as the *Tankan*, bottomed out in the winter of 2001–2002. The GDP report has also strengthened in recent years, with real output rising 1.8% in 2003, 2.3% in 2004, and 2.7% in 2005.

Importantly, the return on real assets in Japan has started to tick up as well. Rising returns suggest that business operations are becoming more profitable and thus could fuel investment. Returns on real assets have declined for decades in Japan, reflecting not only the maturing of the Japanese economy, but also the rigidity of its markets. If managers do not reallocate resources in response to changes in demand over time, returns drop as sales dry up. Over-regulation, particularly in the services sector, has often prevented companies from taking advantage of new opportunities in the past. In the 1970s, return on real assets was about 18%. In the 1980s, returns remained a respectable 16%. During the deflationary decade of the 1990s, returns halved to only 8%. Although returns have fallen further in the last 5 years, they appear to have bottomed out in 2002 when they hit a

near-record low of 5.3%. They have since climbed back to more than
7.6% in 2005. The growth rates of the 1970s and 1980s are likely never
to be repeated, but the declining trend, which has been accompanied
by severe asset deflation and economic stagnation, must be broken.

Are the twin engines for sustainable growth in Japan—the virtuous
cycles in the corporate and household sectors outlined by
Furukawa—still misfiring? Clearly, the first emergence in more than
a decade of a sustainable, private demand–driven recovery in the
world's second-largest economy is not an event that global asset allocators can afford to miss.

Furukawa notes that some data suggests that a few hurdles to
growth have been lowered. After years of wrestling with bloated payrolls, many firms are finally hiring again as they pump up production.
The BoJ surveys of labor market conditions have been improving
since the second quarter of 2002. The effective-job-offers-to-
applicants ratio hit its highest level in more than 10 years in 2005 and
has finally reached 1, which means there is a job for every applicant in
the market (although not necessarily the right one, in the eyes of the
unemployed). Ongoing retrenchment may have finally brought
employee numbers in line with production levels. In recent years,
companies have shed full-time workers and hired part-timers, to trim
expensive benefits and increase control over their labor costs. In
2002, for example, when the number of full-time employees fell by
2.5% YoY, the number of part-time workers jumped more than 6%.
This trend appears to be abating. In 2005, firms began to hire full-
time workers again, which the International Monetary Fund con-
tends supports consumption. Total cash earnings of workers had
fallen since 2001, but these stabilized in 2005—a lukewarm endorsement of improvement, to be sure, but Furukawa sees evidence that
the long process of restructuring the Japanese workforce is coming to
an end.

In addition to improving conditions in the labor market, households save less. Savings rates have declined in recent years. The renewed drop apparently stemmed from a collapse in income during the downturn in 2002. However, now Furukawa and other economists look for demographic trends to push savings rates lower. As Japanese society ages, a greater proportion of the population will enter retirement. Retirees tend to dissave. In any case, the savings rate is unlikely to climb higher.

In the corporate sector, the rebound in exports has bolstered profits and led to further investment in plant and equipment. Rising capacity ulization rates and increasing returns on investment point to renewed demand for such spending. Banks also have become more eager to make loans; recent surveys show a continued decline in firms complaining about frugal lenders. The central bank stopped citing balance sheet restructuring in the banking sector as a risk for the first time in recent memory in its biannual *Outlook of Economic Activity and Prices* of October 2004. Banks achieved the government's goal of halving the amount of nonperforming loans on the sector's balance sheets by the end of fiscal 2004. The fallout of the banking crisis on the real economy (at least, in the opinion of the central bank) has come to an end.

Such developments are promising, to be sure, but deflation remains chronic among many goods makers and service providers. Falling prices weigh heavily on nominal sales growth and suggest that cost-cutting pressures will remain intense. Large retail store sales are falling and widely expected to remain weak. Still, the outlook for the economy is better than the markets have enjoyed in years, Furukawa concludes.

In Japan's worst train disaster in 4 decades, two West JR train cars smashed into a condominium building edged on a curve after five carriages derailed, killing 107 people in Amagaseki, Hyogo Prefecture, on April 25, 2005. Transport Minister Kazuo Kitagawa later said that the cause was undoubtedly speeding, which could have been avoided if a new automatic train stop (ATS) system had been installed.

Masaru Kaneko, an economics professor at Keio University, noted in an *Asahi Shimbun* newspaper column the following June that industry watchers had observed that investment in ATS systems had been low, even though profits had risen at JR West since FY 1999. The lightening of the train cars, a cost-reduction measure, also contributed to the number of fatalities. Kaneko is an outspoken critic of the Koizumi administration and has written many books, including works on public finances and globalization. In his book *Chouki Teitai* (translated as *Long-Term Economic Stagnation*), published in 2002, he outlined problems his country faces in achieving sustainable growth.

Many TV viewers instantly recognize this avuncular scholar. With long, grayish hair parted in the middle and a down-to-earth, affable demeanor unlike the cold aloofness cultivated by many intellectuals, he often finds a receptive audience for his pointed jabs at the Koizumi administration. I met him in his office, which was lined with floor-to-ceiling bookcases stuffed with economic texts.

West JR spun off when Japan National Railways was privatized and divided in 1987. Throughout the 1990s, Kaneko was critical of policymakers promoting deregulation and privatization while the country was grappling with entrenched deflation. He observes that Japanese policymakers often argue that such policies introduced by U.S. President Ronald Reagan and U.K. Prime Minister Margaret Thatcher are necessary to tackle Japan's economic stagnation. However, Kaneko also notes that in those countries, deregulation and privatization measures were introduced to fight inflation in the wake of the second oil shock. In Japan's case, deflation, not inflation, is the problem. Such initiatives can only lead to higher unemployment and a further downward pressure on prices, he warns.

Kaneko observes problems with the adoption of what he calls "market fundamentalist" policies being promoted by the current and previous administrations. He dates the move to deregulation and "American standards" to the defeat of the Liberal Democratic Party in 1994. By measures forced through the Diet to align Japanese bank requirements with global standards for reserves, banks and their corporate customers were forced to dump shares to raise capital. This led to stock price declines, further worsening the condition of the banking sector. Instead of a rational restructuring of the corporate sector, small and medium-size companies were starved of capital—and still are.

He also points to ongoing stagnation of consumption. The seniority-based system in many corporations leads to an upward-sloping curve in wages when plotted against worker age. However, rising pressure on firms to boost profits is leading to an increasing number of older, better-paid workers getting let go, he notes. This flattens the lifetime earnings curve and lowers income at households. Kaneko is skeptical that a recovery can be sustained in the event of slowing overseas demand.

Even as Japan remains dependent on exports for growth, Kaneko warns that the global economic system is becoming increasingly unstable and is characterized by sharp cyclical swings and financial bubbles. He argues that Japanese market-fundamentalist policymakers are not coordinating domestic policies with overseas risks. He cites the Economic Package and other policy initiatives announced in spring 2001 as insufficiently responsive to the NASDAQ downturn the previous year, which, as a result, led to further deterioration of the banking system. Looking ahead, he worries that the global economy is increasingly dependent on asset inflation in the United States because the United States needs to attract overseas capital to finance its huge fiscal and trade imbalances. However, he doubts the sustainability of such capital and trade flows, and argues that adjustment will proceed during a protracted period of "slow panic."

He also points to a bubble in the Chinese economy, one that requires policy coordination among China and its trading partners. In particular, growth of the Chinese Western and Northeastern regions needs to be promoted to offset the impact of tightening credit in China's urban areas, he argues. Against the backdrop of anti-Japanese demonstrations in Shanghai and other cities in spring 2005, the Japanese government is unable to play a constructive role in encouraging a more balanced Chinese regional policy. This raises the specter of a hard landing, rather than a soft landing, for East Asia.

Interestingly, Kaneko sees parallels in Japan's current deflationary period and the policy mistakes in the period leading up to and during the Great Depression. In the early 1920s, following the decline in demand at the end of World War I, the BoJ extended aid to threatened banks. The banking system weakened further after the Great Kanto Earthquake of 1923. The central bank responded to this disaster by extending emergency loans to banks through rediscounted commercial bills. Eventually, the central bank reached its financing limits, and the bankruptcy of Watanabe Bank in 1927 plunged the financial system into crisis, fueling a sharp increase in bad debt.

Kaneko notes that the 1990s were also marked by a decline in demand early in the decade, this time because of the collapse of the bubble economy. The last decade also witnessed bank runs and a major earthquake in Kobe in 1995. Kaneko observes that there was a run-up in U.S. share prices during both the 1920s and 1990s.

In July 1929, Prime Minister Gi'ichi Tanaka was forced to resign when he was unable to punish army officers involved with the assassination of a Chinese warlord in Manchuria. The opposition administration of Osachi Hamaguchi thus took the reins of power as the global economy sank into depression. Hamaguchi appointed Junnosuke Inoue, who previously served as head of the central bank, as finance minister.

The policies of the Hamaguchi government resemble those of the Koizumi administration in three important ways, Kaneko maintains. First, corporate restructuring was encouraged because of a surfeit of bad debt. Second, a contractionary fiscal stance was urged. Finally, the Hamaguchi government insisted on a return to global standards in Japanese finance, which consisted of shifting Japan to the gold standard. During the current slowdown, the government forced banks to meet the capital requirements of the Basel Accords. Although the central bank has become more sophisticated in providing liquidity to the banking system in recent years, fundamental policy errors are being repeated, he observes.

Kaneko suggests that an over-reliance on the market mechanism could raise havoc in the Japanese financial system. A too-narrow focus on shrinking bad debt balances (because many banks labor under them) could raise doubts about the survival of both banks and their client firms. Meanwhile, if companies lose their trust in banks and each other, overall trading on credit will contract as well.

As a solution to what Kaneko calls "Koizumi deflation," Kaneko argues that banks must undertake strict audits, and bad debts should be offset with government funds. Meanwhile, Kaneko advocates that the national pension system be changed from an insurance style to a tax-payment style. As labor market mobility increases, Kaneko advocates a standardization of corporate pension and health insurance plans to provide a safety net for workers.

Decentralization of authority to the regions is also critical, he urges. Some tax revenue collection should be transferred from the central to the prefectural local governments, to encourage self-sufficiency as well as provide security to local residents. The Koizumi administration should also undertake small-scale public works and welfare projects to underpin sustainable economic growth in the countryside, Kaneko argues. Finally, to insulate Japan from what he sees as excessive dependency on increasingly volatile U.S. markets, the Koizumi administration should foster a framework for cooperation among East Asian nations in trade and monetary affairs. Kaneko is not alone among Japanese scholars in criticizing the direction of government policy; Takamitsu Sawa, director of the Institute of Economic Research at prestigious Kyoto University, noted critically in a recent newspaper editorial that the Japanese government supports neoclassical economics and conservatism. Such policies contravene modern Western philosophies and even *bushido,* the way of the samurai, he caustically observed.

Despite Koizumi's landslide victory in September 2005—ostensibly a referendum on the privatization of Japan Post —support for market opening, deregulation, and globalization, while increasing, is not as deeply rooted in East Asia as in the United States or even Europe. Kaneko raises concerns about the need for a safety net for Japanese households as the government attempts to restructure the economy. Others worry that on a pan-Asian basis, economic integration has limited institutional underpinnings. Eisuke Sakakibara, known as "Mr. Yen" in his days at the Ministry of Finance for his perceived ability to manipulate the exchange markets, observes that " the origins of integration in Europe were institutional in nature, and the regional institutions that were created have become a driving force for the deepening of that integration." On the other hand, the former Vice Minister for International Affairs notes, "East Asia's efforts to formalize regional cooperation into a workable arrangement for the promotion of trade, investment, and security in the region have been varied but not very successful."

The bureaucracy in Kasumigaseki has been deeply suspicious regarding the reliability of markets to allocate resources fairly since the early 1950s. John Dower's study of the occupation period in his Pulitzer prize–winning book *Embracing Defeat* underscores the traumatic experience many families faced securing food following the end of the war. When Americans think of free markets, they take a functioning legal system for granted. What some Japanese senior bureaucrats may have in mind are the lawless black markets that thrived under the train tracks of Ueno in the later 1940s. As a new generation emerges to replace the old guard in the ministries and the Diet, running turf battles over liberalization efforts are likely to continue.

Strong overseas growth, especially in China and the United States, has resulted in a recovery in the Japanese economy in recent years. Twice in the past 10 years, overseas downturns have resulted in Japanese slowdowns, and there is no compelling evidence that Japan is strong enough to go it alone if exports plunge again. However, just because top-line growth in Japan remains heavily dependent on overseas demand obviously does not mean there are no opportunities for foreign investors. Foreign investors looking for exposure to the rapidly growing Chinese economy can invest in Japanese firms operating in the country, benefiting from the legal safeguards and deep liquidity of Tokyo markets, which are unavailable when buying directly into firms listed in Shanghai. Meanwhile, as market liberalization and deregulation proceeds, albeit at a halting and sometimes disappointing pace, investors can also look for arbitrage opportunities as inefficiencies in the economy are eliminated.

The most exciting opportunities in Japan, however, may well be invisible. In the future, astute value investors, both foreign and Japanese, will likely shift their attention from discounted tangible assets to intangible ones. Assets such as patents, licenses, and corporate brands, also sometimes referred to as invisible assets, are likely to account for an increasing amount of corporate value in the twenty-first century. Because intangibles are extremely hard to evaluate, investors have rarely explicitly focused on them when deciding whether to buy companies in the past. On the other hand, companies have been hesitant to share information on their holdings of such intellectual property, carefully guarding such knowledge as a vital secret. Such days may be ending. Indeed, the age of intellectual property wars has already dawned.

References

"Price of the wood block print …." Sotheby's, Sale Results. 10 November 2005.

"After dropping off in the early 1990s …" "Foreign Language Enrollments in United States Institutes of Higher Education." *ADFL Bulletin* 35, nos. 2–3 (2004).

"… while commercial real estate in Tokyo lost about 70% … ." *Nikkei Net Interactive*, Nihon Keizai Shimbun, Inc. "Urban land prices turning up, signaling end of asset deflation." 27 March 2006.

"In the mid-1990s, Frank Jennings … ." Interview conducted by the author on 10 January 2006.

"Alex Kerr wrote in *Dogs and Demons* … " Kerr, Alex. *Dogs and Demons: Tales from the Dark Side of Japan.* Hill & Wang, 2001. See esp. p. 97.

"This spectacle of the world, how is it fallen!" Gibbon, Edward. *The Decline and Fall of the Roman Empire.* Penguin Classics edition. Penguin, 1994. See esp. vol. 3, p. 1062–1063.

"Nick Ricciardi, at the time a private investor in Kyoto …." His comments in this chapter are from an interview conducted by the author on 29 November 2005.

"I would say a year ago, many people would …." Interview conducted by the author on 10 January 2006.

"Stocks selling below their net current …." Graham, Benjamin, David L. Dodd, and Sidney McCottle. *Security Analysis Principals and Technique,* 1962 edition. McGraw-Hill, 1962. See esp. p. 561–562.

"Japan Maintenance rose …." Stock price quotes from *Nikkei Net Interactive.* Nihon Keizai Shimbun, Inc.

"About this time, the government agreed to bailout Resona Holdings …." *Nikkei Net Interactive.* Nihon Keizai Shimbun, Inc. "Resona to get ¥1.96 trillion in aid." 2 June 2003.

"… the public was dismayed to learn in September …." *Nikkei Net Interactive.* Nihon Keizai Shimbun, Inc. "Resona Group's net loss likely to top ¥1 trillion." 24 September 2003.

"In 1997, jobs grew, and wages were also climbing…." Total cash earnings rose 1.6% YoY in 1997, versus only 0.6% YoY in 2005. Refer to Ministry of Health, Labor and Welfare statistics. wwwdbtk.mhlw.go.jp/toukei/kouhyo/data-rou1/jikei/t07.xls.

"This is the question I put to Akira Furukawa …." Interview conducted by the author on 9 July 2005.

"He had a complete lack of regard for tradition …." Jansen, Marius B. *The Making of Modern Japan.* The Belknap Press of Harvard University Press (2000). See esp. p. 12–13.

"Furukawa wrote a segment of the 1997 Economic Survey of Japan …." Economic Planning Agency. *Economic Survey of Japan (1996–1997).* See esp. Chap. 1, "Self-Sustained Recovery after Settling the Legacy from the Bubble Economy."

"… accommodative monetary policy was necessary until the economic …." Bank of Japan. *More Detailed Description of the Commitment to Maintaining the Quantitative Easing Policy.* October 2003. It says, "With the aim of laying the foundation for sustainable growth of Japan's economy, the Bank is currently committed to maintaining the quantitative easing policy until the consumer price index …."

"Personnel costs as a percentage of sales climbed …." Author's calculations from Ministry of Finance. Financial Statements of Corporations by Industry, http://www.mof.go.jp/english/e1c002.htm

"Despite optimistic forecasts to the contrary…" National Accounts, Cabinet Office, www.esri.cao.go.jp/jp/sna/qe054-2/kiyo-jcy0542.csv.

"The capacity utilization rate of manufacturers, after bottoming out at an abysmal 64.9% in December 2001, had risen to 77.3% by May 2005." Ministry of Economy, Trade and Industry reports.

"The GDP report has also strengthened in recent years ...." National Accounts Data, Cabinet Office. www.esri.cao.go.jp/jp/sna/qe054-2/kiyo-jcy0542.csv.

"In the 1970s, return on real assets was about 18% ...." Author's calculations, based on Ministry of Finance *Financial Statements of Corporations by Industry*, http://www.mof.go.jp/english/e1c002.htm data, using formula of operating profit/(total assets-financial assets)

"The effective-job-offers-to-applicants ratio hit its highest level ...." Ministry of Health, Labor and Welfare. wwwdbtk.mhlw.go.jp/toukei/kouhyo/data-rou16/jikei/jikeiretu03.xls.

"In 2002, for example, when the number of full-time employees declined ...." Ministry of Health, Labor and Welfare statistics. wwwdbtk.mhlw.go.jp/toukei/kouhyo/data-rou1/jikei/t03.xls,   and wwwdbtk.mhlw.go.jp/toukei/kouhyo/data-rou1/jikei/t05.xls.

"In 2005, firms are beginning to hire full-time workers again ...." IMF. *World Economic Outlook 2005*. See esp. p. 30.

"Total cash earnings of workers have fallen since 2001, but these ...." Ministry of Health, Labor and Welfare statistics. wwwdbtk.mhlw.go.jp/toukei/kouhyo/data-rou1/jikei/t07.xls.

"Furukawa noted in 1997 that banks ...." Economic Planning Agency. *Economic Survey of Japan (1996–1997)*. 1997. See esp. p. 2

"Financial institutions scaled back lending dramatically ...." Bank of Japan. *Short-term Economic Survey of Enterprises in Japan*, or *Tankan*. Survey of financial institution lending attitudes.

"Savings rates have declined in recent years ...." National Accounts, Cabinet Office. www.esri.cao.go.jp/en/stat/data/p028en.pdf.

"Banks as well have become more eager ...." Bank of Japan, *Short-term Economic Survey of Enterprises in Japan*, or *Tankan*. Survey of lending attitude of financial institutions. March 2006.

"The banking sector achieved the government's goal ...." *Nikkei Net Interactive*. Nihon Keizai Shimbun, Inc. "With bad-debt cleanups complete, top banks' earnings recover." 2 August 2005.

"In Japan's worst train disaster in 4 decades ...." *Nikkei Net Interactive.* Nihon Keizai Shimbun, Inc. "Death toll rises to 104 in Amagasaki train accident." 28 April 2005.

Nikkei Net Interactive. Nihon Keizai Shimbun, Inc. "Train was traveling at 126 kph before derailment." 7 May 2005.

"Transport Minister Kazuo Kitagawa later said ...." Kaneko, Masuru. "Mineika to iu bousoudensha." *Asahi Shimbun.* 28 June 2005.

"Masaru Kaneko, an economics professor at Keio University ...." Kaneko, Masuru. "Mineika to iu bousoudensha." *Asahi Shimbun.* 28 June 2005.

"In *Chouki Teitai (Long-term Economic Stagnation)*...." Kaneko, Masuru. *Chouki Teitai.* Chikuma Shinsho, 2002.

"Throughout the 1990s, Kaneko has been critical ...." This quote and following statements are from an interview conducted by the author on 29 June 2005.

"Looking ahead, he argues that the global economy ...." Kaneko, Masuru. *Chouki Teitai.* Chikuma Shinsho, 2002. See esp. Chap. 3, p. 97–129.

"Interestingly, Kaneko sees parallels in Japan's current deflationary period ...." Kaneko, Masuru. *Chouki Teitai.* Chikuma Shinsho, 2002. See esp. Chap. 1, p. 57–65.

"As a solution to what Kaneko calls "Koizumi deflation," Kaneko argues that banks must undertake strict audits ...." Kaneko, Masuru. *Chouki Teitai.* Chikuma Shinsho, 2002. See esp. Chap. 1, p. 186–195.

"Kaneko is not alone among Japanese scholars ...." Sawa, Takamitsu. "Denial of a philosophical root." *The Japan Times,* 4 July 2005.

"Eisuke Sakakibara, known as 'Mr. Yen' in his days ..." Sakakibara, Eisuke. *Regional Economic Integration in a Global Framework.* European Central Bank, 2005. See esp. p. 37, 39.

"John Dower's study of the occupation period ...." Dower, John. *Embracing Defeat.* W.W. Norton & Company, 1999. See esp. Chap. 3.

2

INTELLECTUAL
PROPERTY WARS

Investors to Increasingly Focus on the Hidden Strengths of Japanese Firms

Forget bank cards. Those are so twentieth century. Suruga Bank customers with Bio-Security Deposit accounts just hold out their palms to get cash.

"I thought that was a really great product; I think it might be superior to fingerprint-verification systems," Minsuk Kim tells Masanobu Katoh, president of the Law & Intellectual Property unit of Fujitsu Ltd. Kim, a founder of Light Year Research (Japan) K.K., is referring to the cutting-edge technology of palm vein recognition used by Suruga Bank, whose global launch was announced by Fujitsu in June 2005.

"In some U.S. banks, a lot of fingerprint verifications are used, and some of your competitors, like IBM, NEC, Dell, have fingerprint authentication on their PCs," Kim continues, leading to what he really wants to ask.

"Have you gotten the patents for the palm vein–authentication system? How are you doing with the production costs and downsizing? How much sales are you looking for in the future?" Kim is eager to learn more about Fujitsu's plans, but he cautiously notes that palm vein technology is relatively large compared to fingerprint sensors.

Investors have long held dialogues with the firms that they own, visiting plant facilities and talking with managers and executives. Such discussions will likely increasingly focus on intellectual property in the future. Fujitsu managers are trying to enlighten Kim and Nick Ricciardi, another founder of Light Year Research, about the value of the firm's huge global portfolio of 80,000 patent applications and patent grants in this conference call during March 2006.

Katoh acknowledges that Fujitsu has many patents relating to the palm vein technology, filed both in Japan and overseas. He also has good news to report.

"We have just announced the new type, much smaller-size palm vein–recognition system," he declares, noting the new technology is only 1.3 by 1.3 inches wide.

Kim is impressed.

"We think we have unlimited opportunity [to expand sales]," Katoh adds pointing to recent increased worries about security risks. In addition, palm vein technology is much more hygienic than fingerprint-based technologies because it is no-contact, he notes.

"Young women do not like to touch those [fingerprint] sensors after old men like me," Katoh jokes.

Ricciardi probes the extent of legal protection of Fujitsu's intellectual property. "Do you find you are dealing more with patent trolls or submarine patent issues, than, say, 2 or 3 years ago?" he asks. He is referring to unorthodox and abusive uses of the protection that patents offer their holders. Patent trolls are firms that quietly acquire patents, aiming solely at filing patent-infringement claims. Submarine patents are published long after the original application was filed, thereby surprising the marketplace and opening up companies to charges of infringement if they used such technology, unaware that it was patented.

"We see more patent trolls, and that is becoming more problematic for many large companies," Katoh says. He adds that patent trolls do not make products, so it is very difficult to negotiate with them. Usually, when a large company such as Fujitsu wants to use another firm's technology, it can offer that firm rights to use some of its own extensive technology holdings. Patent trolls are simply not interested.

Ricciardi and Kim will use information revealed on this call to size up whether Fujitsu will meet medium-term earnings and revenue projections. Light Year Research, scheduled to be launched in fall 2006, is at the cutting edge of both commercial technologies and investment strategy. Ricciardi and Kim fully intend to race—at the speed of light—ahead of their competitors. They focus on intangible assets, such as brands, trademarks, copyrights, research and development (R&D), and trade secrets.

Ricciardi and Kim believe the equity markets undervalue many of these assets in systemic, predictable, and scalable ways, and argue that as Japan's economy normalizes, IP-intensive firms should outperform. They have developed a proprietary method to exploit this perceived market inefficiency. Their analysis includes quantitative factors to rank the potential value of intangible assets across industries, qualitative measures to assess the capability of corporate management to cultivate such assets, and valuation conditions for initiating positions.

At their Kyoto research offices, they are developing detailed databases on intangible asset holdings in various industries, including information such as patent totals, patent references in leading scientific journals, frequency of patent citations, and projected licensing revenues. They are not alone in attaching importance to such variables. Sadao Nagaoka, professor at the Institute of Innovation

Research of Hitotsubashi University, published a working paper entitled *Patent Quality, Cumulative Innovation and Market Value* in February 2005. He found that empirical evidence suggests that indicators of patent quality, such as number of citations, affect the market value of the Japanese firm holding such intellectual property.

Ricciardi is eager to launch his research firm, convinced that the inherent value of corporate intellectual property in Japan has been masked for the past 16 years because of the country's disastrous economic performance. "I believe firms with high levels of intangible assets should be able to maintain or grow revenues for a considerably longer duration than is presently implied by many of their share prices."

"I am especially excited to develop, test, and apply this idea to the market here because—to the best of my knowledge—*almost nobody else is doing this.*"

In the post-industrial age, intangible assets are expected to generate the bulk of value for many firms. Researchers such as Ricciardi and Kim believe that Japan holds tremendous strengths in this area and search for opportunities at Japanese firms that are still overlooked by the investment community.

"Japanese companies spend a great deal of time thinking about the value of their intellectual property, making sure it is properly guarded and cultivated," argues Ricciardi. "Investors don't nearly focus on it to the same degree. I would argue it is the companies that are correct, and the investors will catch up."

The importance of intangible assets to firms has also caught the eye of the government. The share of intangible assets in total market capitalization rose from 17% in 1978 to 69% in 1998 at U.S. corporations, noted the *White Paper on International Economy and Trade 2004*. The paper observed that the share of intangible assets in Japan fell from 59% in 1996 to 38% in 2003 because of the decline in share prices, but this still represents a significant portion of enterprise value.

A disparity between market valuations of various IP-intensive firms is shown by Nobuyuki Nagata, a CPA and a senior manager in the Intellectual Property Group at Deloitte Touche Tohmatsu in Tokyo. In early 2006, the price-to-book ratio (PBR) of Japanese top patent holders was lower than that of their American counterparts. The no. 1 patent holder in the United States, IBM, had a PBR of 4.34; no. 2, Canon, Inc., had a PBR of only 2.57. Overall, Japanese firms, which occupied five of the top ten slots, had an average PBR of 2.1, whereas non-Japanese firms, excluding Samsung, had a value of 3.1.

This analysis is too primitive to come to any conclusion, Nagata notes. However, he adds that awareness in Japan regarding intellectual assets is still underutilized, a deficit that the government is attempting to address.

Unfortunately, financial statements are often little help in assessing the value of intangible assets held by a firm. For the most part, neither Japanese nor U.S. firms capitalize their internally developed intangible assets on their balance sheets, notes Kozo Suzuki, a managing director of Economic and Valuation Services in the New York office of KPMG. Most intangible assets that do show up in financial statements are those acquired from other firms.

Japan has been trying to internationalize its accounting principles and is striving to reach equivalency with International Financial Reporting Standards (IFRS), used by many global companies. Japan will require the application of a new accounting standard for business combinations from April 2006, similar to IFRS and U.S. Generally Accepted Accounting Principles (GAAP), notes Suzuki. A government study group on international business accounting noted that Japanese accounting standards use acquisition case as the basis for recognition of intangible assets and are thus similar to IFRS. This suggests that it will still be a challenge for investors to assess the value of such assets at Japanese firms, even with reforms.

"In the last 3 years, the government is shaking the flag, and people were talking, people were discussing [intellectual property] in general terms," says Nagata. Now he notes a difference in attitudes. "In the last 12 months or so, I feel that people have become more serious about improving intellectual asset management."

Over the last 10 years or so, Japanese firms have restructured, struggling with debt and financial weakness, and tried to consolidate their businesses. More recently, Japanese companies have been able to pay more attention to growth strategies, which inevitably involves looking at R&D and technology development, Nagata notes.

Nagata's firm values intellectual assets for their clients. "The inquiries we have received to support intellectual asset management or transactions related with intellectual assets have increased considerably," he notes.

His firm primarily uses three major methodologies to value intellectual assets.

Under the cost approach, the replacement cost of a firm's intellectual property, such as administrative software, is estimated. In some cases, such as with copyrights or entertainment cases, a market approach is attempted. In this methodology, comparative valuations of similar products in the market are sought out. Meanwhile, under several income approaches, royalty savings or excess earnings are often deployed to determine the value of intellectual assets.

"We are trying to raise awareness of the market," he notes, but adds that many market analysts still do not use assessments of research and development and intellectual property in forecasting. There is "still a long way to go" before many investors use intellectual asset valuations in their investment models, he notes. Institutional investors qualitatively evaluate R&D and intellectual property at target firms but rarely use quantitative approaches.

Japan has a long history in the cultivation of intellectual property. The Japan Patent Office opened in 1885, four years before the adoption of the Meiji Constitution.

The Japanese government received about 3.71 million patent applications from 1885 to 1982, and 1.04 million were granted.

Japan gained a reputation as a copy-cat nation abroad as it made inroads into various industries, but its track record in innovation should not be disregarded. Kenjiro Takayanagi, a teacher at Hamamatsu Technical High School in Shizuoka Prefecture, perfected the world's first electronic television in 1926. However, he waited a year to file for a patent and thus lost the right of commercial production to Dr. V. K. Zworykin of RCA in the United States. Sakichi Toyoda, the father of the founder of the Toyota Group, invented an automatic loom that was "crucial to Japan's development and a major impetus for its industrial revolution," according to Hisamitsu Arai, a former vice minister for international affairs at the Ministry of International Trade and Industry. This ministry was reorganized into the Ministry of Economy, Trade and Industry in 2001.

In the hall of the Japanese Patent Office in Kasumigaseki, memorial plaques to the country's ten greatest inventors line the wall. Umetaro Suzuki, who lived from 1874 to 1943, succeeded in isolating Vitamin B_1 and obtained a patent for it, the world's first vitamin to be extracted. Kikunae Ikeda (1864–1936) developed a method to manufacture monosodium glutamate, which eventually become used worldwide as a food condiment. Hidetsugu Yagi (1886–1976) studied radio transmission extensively and invented a method for directional radio waves on which the "Yagi antenna" was based.

Following World War II, Japanese firms actively applied for patents for invention in the United States and received 94,400 between 1963 and 1983, more than any other country except Germany. Some firms, such as Hitachi, worked hard to improve basic technologies, notes Arai in *Intellectual Property Policies for the*

Twenty-First Century. Hitachi filed 20,000 patent applications in 1970 alone, he notes. From 1963 through 2004, Japan received 591,683 patents for invention in the United States, more than twice than those received by German firms and 27% of the total received by U.S. residents.

"In general, Japan has a large number of patents, but many people say the patents are not original, so patents are not significantly linked to sales," acknowledges Kim, but he stresses that he does not subscribe to that view. Regardless of such debate, by the late 1980s, Japan challenged U.S. supremacy in several high-tech fields and took the lead in others. In a 1986 survey by *Fortune*, Japanese firms were recognized as industry leaders "hands-down" in optoelectronics and were gaining ground rapidly in advanced materials. The survey noted that the United States had lost leadership in seven of nine critical emerging technologies in electronic and optoelectronic materials.

However, during the 1990s, Japan appeared to stumble. Newly emerging competitors from South Korea and Taiwan made inroads in information technology industries such as dynamic random access memory (DRAM) chip production. With the possible exception of Softbank Corp., few Japanese firms were major contenders in the battles for market share of the global software industry. In addition, the number of domestic patent registrations peaked in 1996.

Perhaps worried about technological complacency, Prime Minister Junichiro Koizumi announced he was aiming to create a "nation built on the platform of scientific and technological creativity" in his policy statement to the Diet in February 2002. He launched the Strategic Council on Intellectual Property, which met the following month. By the end of the year, the Basic Law on Intellectual Property was issued, and it went into force March 2003. The same month, the Intellectual Property Strategy Headquarters, headed by the prime minister, was founded.

The headquarters immediately went into action and announced the Intellectual Property Strategic Program within 4 months. Among the 270 measures promulgated were steps to accelerate the process of patent examination and the establishment of an Intellectual Property High Court. Ichiro Nakayama, secretariat of the Intellectual Property Strategy Headquarters, noted in August 2003 that there was a huge backlog of 800,000 applications at the patent office.

The Tokyo High Court already had special chambers focusing on intellectual property, so the creation of a quasi-independent high court in June 2004 was primarily a symbol of the Japanese government's commitment to strong enforcement of intellectual property rights, says Toshiko Takenaka, professor of law at the University of Washington. She is also director of the Center for Advanced Study & Research on Intellectual Property.

That is not to say that the government initiatives were all spin; the process of patent application had already been improved over the last 5 years, Takenaka notes. The Japan Patent Office was previously restrained from hiring more examiners because of a general policy of downsizing government. With the decision of the Koizumi administration to actively cultivate and promote intellectual property, the government decided to make an exception to the general policy of reducing civil service staff and allowed the Japan Patent Office to hire examiners with limited appointments, she notes.

Although there has been limited progress in reducing the application backlog to date, the government hopes to cut the waiting time for new applications from the 26 months in early 2005 to 11 months by 2013.

The Japanese equivalent of the U.S. Bayh–Dole Act is expected to help support technology transfer from universities to the private sector, Takenaka says. The Patent and Trademarks Law Amendment Act in the United States was enacted in 1980. This act, widely known as Bayh–Dole, enabled universities to keep ownership of intellectual

property developed in government-financed research and greatly stimulated patent applications by universities. Before the act, ownership of
such research went to the government. Newly incentivized to develop
intellectual property, universities created technology-transfer offices
and worked hard to find licensees and commercialize technology.

The impact of this legislation has been far reaching and is widely
credited with helping to reverse America's decline in technological
competitiveness. More than 3,800 patents were awarded to U.S. universities by the U.S. Patent and Trademark office in fiscal year 2004,
a more than tenfold increase on the 250 issued in 1980. Since that
year, more than 4,500 companies have been created to commercialize
technology created by U.S. universities and research institutes, and
two-thirds remain in existence. More than 3,100 new products have
been introduced into the commercial market since 1998.

Japanese policymakers are hoping that the Law on Special Measures for Industrial Revitalization Article 30, enacted in October
1999, will have a similar impact. "Assistance is even greater than in
the U.S., where the government did not give money," argues Takenaka. "The Japanese government gave a lot of money to create technology-transfer offices." Former examiners and ex–patent attorneys
now work as technology managers at the universities, and almost all
major universities in Japan now have technology-transfer offices.

As a result of government efforts, patent applications at national
universities and institutions have risen steadily, from only 220 in fiscal
year 1999 to more than 900 in fiscal year 2003. The Patent Office also
is creating a Patent License Database, in which licensable patents of
companies, research institutes, and universities can be searched on
the Internet. As of the end of May 2005, about 59,000 patents were
included.

Nonetheless, some, including Professor Hiroyuki Itami at Hitotsubashi University, are skeptical that the Japanese university system
will have a major impact on innovation in the short run. Even in the

longer run, its support will be limited, Itami argues. Japanese universities are simply not as well financed as their U.S. counterparts, he notes. The University of Tokyo has the same number of students as Harvard and MIT together, but its budget is only one-third of the U.S. institutions' combined, he adds.

However, the American university system is a public asset to the whole world, Itami notes. Japanese firms can easily access research at U.S. schools. Technology transfer is probably one reason Japanese firms are donating generously to American universities. More than 20 Japanese firms participate in the Industrial Liaison Program at MIT, including Canon Inc.; Matsushita Electric Industrial Co., Ltd.; and Fujitsu Ltd.

The government is not alone in refocusing on intellectual property as a mainstay of future growth. Japanese businesses spent 3.2% of their added value generated on research and development in 2003, a higher percentage than any other OECD country except Sweden and Finland.

Indeed, Japanese industry leaders see intellectual property protection as a life-and-death issue. "The industry has entered the era of intellectual property wars … the firm must arm itself in order to survive," Matsushita Electric Industrial Co. president Kunio Nakamura told Nihon Keizai Shimbun, Inc. He ordered the company to increase patent registrations in Japan, the United States, and Europe as a result.

Some see Japan's loss of market share in dynamic random access memory (DRAM) chips caused by insufficient protection of intellectual property rights. Toshiba Corp. president Tadashi Okamura, whose company has withdrawn from such production, attributes this defeat to the outflow of patent rights.

Ten years ago, Japanese firms obtained patents but never enforced them, notes Takenaka at the University of Washington.

Now, however, "things have changed," she says. Serious competition from emerging economies such as South Korea and Taiwan was the catalyst, she adds.

The new aggressiveness of Japanese corporate giants in protecting what they perceive as their lifeblood could be seen in a battle between Fujitsu Ltd. and South Korean giant Samsung Electronics Co. over plasma display panels (PDPs).

"We don't like to litigate if we can settle amicably on any dispute," notes Masanobu Katoh of Fujitsu. However, if Fujitsu cannot settle with a reasonable effort, the firm does not hesitate to act, he adds.

Fujitsu filed suit in April 2004, charging Samsung SDI Co. with patent infringement on basic technologies for PDPs. Fujitsu's joint venture with Hitachi, Fujitsu Hitachi Plasma Display, Ltd., was the world leader in PDPs, but Samsung was coming up fast, boosting its market share from a mere 1% to 20% in only 2 years. The stakes were large for both firms; the PDP market was expected to grow to ¥1 trillion within a few years.

Fujitsu apparently felt that it could not afford to allow Samsung a pass on this issue. "It is no exaggeration to say that for Fujitsu and other firms that own intellectual property, technology represents corporate value. Claiming ownership of the property is not only a precondition for our existence, but also justifiable behavior," Fujitsu chairman Naoyuki Akikusa told Nihon Keizai Shimbun, Inc. at the time. Fujitsu started developing PDPs back in the 1960s and holds some 800 related patents globally. Fujitsu decided to sue when negotiations with Samsung to sign a licensing contract broke down.

Within a few weeks of the filing, Tokyo Customs blocked imports by the South Korean firm. Tension escalated as the Minister of Commerce, Industry, and Energy, Lee Hee-Boem, in Seoul, summoned the Japanese ambassador to express concern over the move. However, the decision by Tokyo Customs to block shipments apparently helped influence Samsung to settle by June, and the firm entered into a cross-licensing agreement, under which the South Korean maker agreed to pay for using PDP technology.

This new focus by Japanese industry on the value of its invisible assets can also be seen in current account statistics measuring cross-border trade and capital flows. Japan's patent revenue balance turned positive for the first time in 2003 and grew to ¥316.3 billion by 2005. This does not necessarily mean that Japan's competitiveness has improved because the bulk of payments could well be from overseas subsidiaries of Japanese firms. However, the increased payments suggest that more companies are becoming aware of the value of their intellectual property holdings.

As more Japanese firms focus on extracting financial value from intangible assets, they are increasingly using intellectual property as a source of financing. The Development Bank of Japan has loaned more than ¥16 billion secured by patents, software-related copyrights, and business models, the Nihon Keizai Shimbun, Inc. reported in February 2006. Now other banks are getting into the act. Saitama Resona Bank, Minato Bank, and Bank of Tokyo–Mitsubishi UFJ all put loans on their books collateralized by intellectual assets in 2005.

With graying temples, but surprisingly young-looking for one who helped establish a new field of study almost 2 decades ago, Hiroyuki Itami speaks with an animated candor unusual among scholars. Perhaps his directness and practicality come from his many discussions with policymakers; Itami serves on the Information Technology Strategic Headquarters and the Biotechnology Strategy Council of the prime minister's office. He can flip conventional wisdom regarding Japanese management on its head with the careless ease of a grizzly bear toying with its prey. Never shying from an argument, he appeared to relish rebuking views held by many overseas investors about Japanese firms when I met him in March 2006.

The second edition of his classic 1980 treatise *Keiei Senryaku no Ronri* (translated as *The Logic of Corporate Strategy*) was translated and adapted with the collaboration of Thomas W. Roehl and published in 1987 as *Mobilizing Invisible Assets*. It established his reputation as the father of invisible asset management.

"My concept of invisible assets is broader than the usual concept of intangible assets, which tends to be colored by the accounting concept of the same name," Itami notes. He refers to information-based assets such as consumer trust, brand image, technology, corporate culture, and management skill as invisible assets. Arguing that they are the most important resources for the long-term success of a firm, Itami compares visible assets to the brushes, canvas, and paint of a painter, and invisible assets to the ability to create a masterpiece.

Japan has a competitive advantage in the cultivation of such assets, which will enable it to prosper even when faced with low-cost Chinese production, he argues. In fact, many Japanese firms are rethinking a widespread shift to production on the mainland.

"Canon is already bringing factories back from China," he says. This firm is investing about ¥80 billion in a domestic toner cartridge plant in Oita City, Japan to start production from January 2007. Previously, Canon's main plant for such products was in Dalian, China. Canon president Fujio Mitarai has repeatedly voiced his commitment to relocating plants to domestic locations.

"In the field of advanced technology, it is often very inexpensive to do production in Japan," Itami notes. Much of the work is automated, driving down labor expenses. In addition, Japan enjoys a highly developed network for the supply of advanced parts. Because many firms order such parts, even if individual orders are of a small quantity, parts suppliers can boost production and keep costs down, he adds.

The ratio of research and development to sales is a good indicator of the level of a firm's commitment to the cultivation of invisible assets, notes Itami. However, he uses another, more unique measure—the portion of very clean toilets in a firm's offices and factories.

"There is no firm that can do a huge accumulation [of information-based assets] with dirty toilets," he wryly comments. Whether in China, South Korea, or Japan, whenever Itami visits a factory, he checks the cleanliness of the firms' bathrooms.

Itami cites increased discussion of corporate brand management as evidence of rising interest in invisible assets at Japanese firms.

From April 2000, Hitachi, Ltd., embarked on such a strategic effort, announcing a slogan: "Inspire the next." Acknowledging that Hitachi brand awareness had weakened among young Japanese, the firm launched a direct-mail and newspaper advertisement campaign to raise its profile. The firm stressed its origin as a venture capital firm and its possession of cutting-edge technology. The results were dramatic. Its ranking among engineering students as a desirable place to work jumped from 72 in a 2004 Nihon Keizai Shimbun, Inc. survey all the way to 14 the following year. Hitachi also held symposiums in three Chinese cities in 2004 to raise awareness of its brand in this crucial market.

Invisible asset management among Japanese firms is much different than at U.S. firms, Itami notes. Japanese firms try to nurture invisible assets within the firm. U.S. firms cultivate internally much less, relying instead on the market. "The notion you can buy invisible assets from outside is very foreign to Japanese firms," he says.

Not all U.S. firms neglect cultivation of invisible assets, he concedes, citing IBM Corp. and Intel Corp. as two examples of firms actively trying to nurture and develop invisible assets internally. However, many U.S. firms do not give such activities a high priority, he notes.

On the other hand, Itami points to Matsushita Electric Corp., which has developed its own large scale integration (LSI) for its plasma TV within the firm. "The technology they used in designing this has been nurtured, developed, and cultivated with the firm for the last 20 years," Itami says.

Not just large firms are accumulating invisible assets, he adds. The only strength of many small and medium-size firms is their know-how and craftsmanship, says Itami, who serves as chairman of a council on the management and assistance of smaller firms at the Ministry of Economy, Trade, and Industry. Itami just headed a committee to select the best 300 small companies in Japan.

He points to Okano Industrial Corp., a very small operation specializing in pressing technology, as a success story. The firm supplies needles to Terumo Corp., a major medical-equipment maker. Okano Industrial has succeeded in manufacturing needles so small that pain is greatly eased during injections. Many small Japanese firms have 70% of the world market in specified, minute niches, he adds.

Attention to minor details by workers on the factory floor or by salesmen in the marketplace gives Japanese firms a competitive advantage. "The basic conviction, sometimes very implicit, of many Japanese managers is that invisible assets are cultivated by doing things correctly day after day."

Itami even argues that traditional Japanese corporate governance, long criticized by many foreign investors because of its emphasis on worker interests, is well suited for managing invisible assets. "Managing a firm for the sake of employees first and for shareholders second, that's the best practice," he provocatively declares. What is the incentive of workers to accumulate invisible assets "if they know the company is run for shareholders?" Itami asks.

Employees are also more likely to cooperate and share information if they are assured of keeping their jobs. Long-term employment and limited labor market mobility influence the behavior of Japanese workers; therefore, it is much easier for the Japanese firms to accumulate invisible assets internally. This advantage will be maintained into the future, Itami argues.

Indeed, by focusing on invisible asset cultivation, Japanese firms will be able to develop new products that Chinese firms cannot immediately replicate, so Japan will not lose as many manufacturing jobs to China as the U.S. has, Itami argues. Because the U.S. has decided not to keep manufacturing operations at home, the country is losing its ability to develop new products, Itami adds.

Japan has lagged in some industries, such as software development, but Itami points to language rather than mistaken management techniques as the reason for Japan's weakness. The Japanese language, with its hundreds of Chinese characters, demands much more computing power than English. At the early stages of personal computer (PC) development, PCs that could handle Japanese were much more expensive than ones built to use English software. This price differential resulted in a much slower diffusion rate for PCs in Japan. A computer with Japanese software cost three times more than a computer with English software with the same functions at the beginning of the 1990s, Itami notes. Although there is no price difference now, he argues that it will be difficult to overcome the advantages enjoyed by U.S. software makers because of their huge market shares. One exception he points to is gaming, in which language is not an issue.

Japanese software has no international market, limiting the incentive for firms to invest heavily in this area. Language has hindered the development of Japan's financial sector as well—but not manufacturing, he further argues. "In banking, you need language. In steel, you do not need language—you need product." Indeed, the United States let its manufacturing industry go too easily because U.S. firms could pursue opportunities in other industries, such as software and finance, says Itami. Japan, hindered by its language, cannot make a similar shift as easily.

Despite traumatic restructuring of the banking sector during the 1990s, Japanese firms maintained their competitive positions in many fields. Throughout the 1990s, spending on research and development by Japanese firms continued to rise, from ¥7.2 trillion in 1989 to ¥11.6 trillion 10 years later. Even as a percentage of sales, spending on R&D was up from 2.6% to 3.1% during the decade, suggesting that firms were putting an even higher priority on their R&D programs than earlier. The number of researchers in the corporate sector rose from 295,000 to 431,000 over the same period. Fujitsu alone has more than 1,000 professionals working in its laboratories. Now that problems with the financial sector are getting worked out, Japan's industrial strength is once again on the surface, Itami argues.

"Japan is becoming a sourcing country of many very important parts and materials," he notes. In application-oriented semiconductor chips, Japan is still leading the world. Meanwhile, Japanese production of high-performance steel and high-performance chemicals is continuing to rise, he adds.

JFE Steel Corp., the leading steel company in Japan in terms of operational earnings, focuses on high-performance steel to a much greater degree than its Asian competitors. Fully 20% of the company's production is not available from steel mills in China or South Korea. These "Only 1, Number 1 Products" include NANO Highten (a nanometer-level grain-controlled high-tensile steel developed by JFE), used in fuel efficient cars. The company also produces very high-grade electric steel, which has superior electromagnetic characteristics and is used in high-efficiency motors, such as those for hybrid autos. JFE also uses a thermomechanical control process to produce heavy plate steel for container ships.

Another 70% of JFE production is made up of high value-added steels such as hot-dip galvanized steel sheet for automotive outer panels, regular high-tensile steel sheet, tinplate steel for beverage cans, and regular electric steel used for electric transmitters and motors. Only 10% of JFE production is oriented to commodity-grade steel, such as hot-rolled steel for construction use (such as guard rails), a sector some Chinese firms focus on.

Japan's competitive advantages in technology appear to be in making continual refinements rather than break-through inventions. According to Thomson Scientific data, 43% of Japanese patents are filed in the telecommunications, information technology, and electronic sectors. Another 37% are filed in chemicals, materials, and instrumentation; 10% are in the automobile and transport industries. Energy and power, medical and pharmaceutical, and food and agriculture all take up less than 5% each.

Japanese firms have long been thought by some to lack creativity and be mere copiers and improvers of basic technology developed elsewhere. However, Itami argues that the orientation of Japanese firms toward invisible asset accumulation suggests that they will become better at conceptualizing new products and generating new ideas. Before, Japan had no base to form ideas, Itami notes, saying that creativity is like the tip of an iceberg. A huge body of experience and knowledge is necessary before creativity is possible, and Japan has been accumulating this little by little, he argues.

"Formation of ideas is a very stochastic phenomenon—you throw out many ideas, and one of them works," he observes. "Average people throwing out ideas have a very low probability of success," he notes. Corporate Japan now has the experience and knowledge to become much more innovative, he suggests.

Investors tend to view Japanese management in stark black-and-white terms, notes Thomas Roehl, associate professor in the MBA program at Western Washington University. Roehl collaborated with Itami in writing *Mobilizing Invisible Assets*. Market watchers either uncritically hail Japanese executives as brilliant and innovative gurus or mercilessly pan them like untalented, off-key contestants on *American Idol*.

Roehl refers to a pendulum swing with regards to investor perceptions of how well Japanese firms are run. When their book came out in 1987, Japanese management was all the rage with Japanese words such as *kaizen,* or "improvement," batted around by management consultants even in the United States.

The Japanese were thought by many to be unsurpassed in terms of making technology commercially viable at the time. When Yamazaki Machinery Works, Ltd., decided to automate its Minokamo plant, a visiting Ford manager learned that the firm's engineers were able to cut down the factory's 672 production tools to a barebones 45, reported *Fortune*. With only Bell Labs doing optoelectronics research in the United States, Japanese firms were feared to have carved out an insurmountable lead in the field by the mid 1980s. "The trouble is that the Japanese have ten Bell Labs," lamented one American researcher to the magazine.

With the crash of the bubble economy, the Japanese juggernaut became the sick man of Asia. "People in government circles talked about a 'Japan passing' ... as soon as [it became apparent] the economy was not going to come back," remembers Roehl. Admiration for Japanese management was replaced with derision, as lifetime employment systems and managers without specialized knowledge were blamed for dragging the corporate sector into a money-losing abyss.

"Investors overreact," says Roehl, and notes that many foreign observers remained dismissive of Japanese management styles until U.S. organizational failures, such as Enron, became apparent in the wake of the NASDAQ crash. "Only after 2000, when the U.S. side didn't look attractive, did people start to look for different models," he adds. Even today, few sing praises of Japanese organizational structure overseas, he observes.

Roehl stresses the need to avoid overgeneralizing about Japanese firms, noting that some manage invisible assets well and some do not. However, "a substantial number of Japanese firms have a competitive advantage," he notes. In particular, successful firms tend to be good at communicating across division and section lines.

He cites the example of a Japanese assembly line worker who stops production when he discovers a faulty part. Instead of just taking a cigarette break, in many Japanese firms, he is obligated to discuss how the part can be redesigned. The line engineer is also consulted. In short, workers from several different sections exchange information to improve the production process, he stresses.

Such ability to overcome the "silo effect," the tendency in organizations to limit horizontal communications, is especially useful in cross-firm tie-ups. Many firms are joining together to develop new technologies. Japanese managers easily talk across organizational lines, giving them an edge in such ventures, he notes. Sony Corp. and Samsung Electronics signed a cross-licensing agreement in 2004 regarding patents for some basic technologies, to avoid legal disputes and cut research and development costs. The two firms also inked a deal in 2006 to build a second plant to make LCD panels for flat-screen televisions for their joint venture S-LCD Corp. Both sides are learning and bringing back the joint knowledge to their internal and competitive ventures, observes Roehl. Sony's Bravia line flat-panel TVs are contributing to better-than-expected earnings for the firm in late 2005, reports the *Wall Street Journal*.

A distinction can be made between many cross-licensing agreements and efforts to jointly develop technology, he notes. Under a simple cross-licensing agreement, no new invisible assets are created. When two firms work together to develop products, they make invisible assets such as production expertise. The firms attempt to create value through a synergetic combination of the known-how of each firm.

However, investors face risks when placing bets on invisible asset management, Roehl notes, calling it a "market for lemons" problem. Just as a buyer of a used car does not know the vehicle's history or why the seller wants to unload it, investors in invisible assets face similar problems. They encounter enormous difficulties in assessing a company's strength in areas such as patented technology or organizational structure. Indeed, firms often join up in technology ventures to share risk because they *themselves* cannot value or accurately forecast the invisible assets that will accrue from their investments. Nagata and others offer to value intangible assets generated in such joint ventures. Investors who are not privy to insider information are seriously handicapped in assessing such business tie-ups.

The Japanese government has recognized that lack of transparency could limit the valuations the market is willing to put on such intangibles and has called for companies to provide more information. The Ministry of Economy, Trade, and Industry (METI) published its reference guidelines for intellectual property information disclosure in January 2004. It noted that firms need fair valuation in the capital markets to effectively exploit their intellectual property.

It is clear that if markets do not fairly value a firm's intellectual assets, they could well be at a disadvantage in terms of financing—this is a perennial problem for high-tech start ups. On the other hand, investors are hungry for more information. A survey by the Japan Academic Society of Investor Relations found that investors considered information on technology and intellectual property among the most important items *not* disclosed in financial statements. METI noted that the imbalance of information regarding IP resulted in companies being evaluated only at average values, with excellent companies undervalued and their cost of capital increased. This leads to stagnation of overall markets and the loss of a profit-generating opportunity for investors, the ministry warned.

The vast bulk of the corporate sector has not yet responded to such calls by the Koizumi administration to provide more information to investors and the media regarding their intellectual property management. The government points to Hitachi as being especially forward looking. The Japan Patent Office (JPO) notes that the firm "positions IP as an engine of their business activities and makes an effort to excavate and develop inventions and exploit patents strategically." The JPO adds that they have a clear strategy "to acquire the strategic patents which are inevitable and imperative to be used by other companies." To defend itself in patent litigation , Hitachi strives to get at least five patents in each product area and calls these its "five fighting patents."

In addition to using patents to defend product lines, Hitachi's strategy calls for using its patent portfolio to generate revenues. Its patent-exploitation strategy is divided into three major areas: royalty income, cross-licensing, and strategic exploitation. Hitachi plans to use its patents to cover specialized products in mature markets, thus contributing to high sales and profit growth. In markets for new products, the firm is striving to obtain the "best one" or "only one" patents to strengthen its overall patent portfolio. Meanwhile, if it withdraws from a product line, it strives to collect royalty income on its patents in the abandoned field.

Hitachi may be a well-heralded leader, but Kim, Ricciardi, and others are convinced that it is far from unique. Many world-class Japanese firms that weathered the decade-long economic storm have emerged leaner and meaner, with stronger balance sheets and heightened engineering prowess, Kim notes. As Japanese firms become more protective of their intellectual property, he expects many to carve out dominant positions in global markets and post higher earnings in the future. "We are excited about launching a research firm with an IP focus at such a time," Kim declares.

Investment Implications

Japan is back. Investors shunned the country for years following the collapse of the bubble economy, but many are now fundamentally rethinking their investment strategies in the country. To be sure, opportunities to pick up firms with deeply discounted tangible assets are much scarcer than a few years ago. However, with the banking sector largely recovered, and demand from China and the U.S. supporting growth (see Chapter 1, "From Ultimate Capital Destruction Machine to the Best Value in the World"), the country's competitive advantages in intangible asset cultivation are becoming increasingly conspicuous. Intangible assets are likely to account for the bulk of enterprise value of many firms in the current century. Japan could be on the verge of a major market revaluation of these largely off-balance sheet holdings.

Japanese firms are well positioned strategically to out race their overseas rivals in developing valuable intangible assets. First, Japanese firms invest heavily in research and development. Second, they are becoming more protective of their intellectual property and are finally beginning to attempt to extract financial value from such holdings. Third, superior Japanese firms strive to cultivate intangible assets in-house; many U.S. firms tend to rely on the market to procure them. Fourth, Japanese management, with its emphasis on workforce stability, encourages cultivation of such intangible assets by ensuring that employees also benefit from their creation.

As the economy normalizes and such strengths among Japanese firms become increasingly obvious, opportunities are bound to appear in the Tokyo equity market. Earnings growth will probably be surprisingly robust among many Japanese firms boasting enviable intangible asset portfolios. Retail investors are not well positioned to assess the strength of such holdings at individual Japanese firms, but they would probably do well to invest in Japan-specific mutual funds or exchange traded funds as part of a comprehensive effort to diversify internationally. Their investments overseas should not be limited to Europe, Latin America, or emerging market funds. Japan is the world's second-largest economy. Even the crudest attempts at building an internationally balanced diversified portfolio should include Japanese investments.

Institutional investors, on the other hand, have access to much more information and are often served by fully staffed research departments. If professional analysts are not already devoting much of their attention to assessing the hidden strengths of Japanese firms, they should probably rethink their country strategy. Are their funds' assessments of Japanese firms giving due weight to patent holdings, brand strength, licensing revenues, dominance of niche markets, management expertise, and control of vital technology? For years, it was safe to ignore Japan. No longer.

To date, despite the urgings of the government, few companies publish IP reports. Those that do include Toshiba Corp.; Olympus Corp.; Hitachi, Ltd.; Asahi Kasei Corp.; Hitachi Chemical Co., Ltd.; Bridgestone Corp.; Konica Minolta Holdings, Inc.; Ajinomoto Co., Inc.; Iseki & Co., Ltd.; Tokyo Electron Ltd.; Mitsui Engineering & Shipbuilding Co., Ltd.; and AnGes MG, Inc. Companies such as Asahi Kasei Corp.; NEC Corp.; Tokyo Electron, Ltd.; Mitsubishi Electric Corp.; JSR Corp.; Takeda Pharmaceutical Co., Ltd.; and Fujitsu Ltd. have sections addressing intellectual property strategy in their annual reports. Such information sources are, of course, the very tip of the iceberg. However, institutional investors who can most accurately assess Japan's intangible asset strengths and spot value-creating firms missed by other market participants will probably be the best performers in Tokyo in the years to come.

References

"Suruga Bank customers with Bio-Security Deposit …." Sasaki, Shigeru, Kawai, Hiroaki, and Akira Wakabayashi, *Fujitsu Scientific & Technical Journal (FSTJ)* 41, no. 3 (2005): 341–347.

"I think …." This quote and the following were taken from a conference call held on 16 March 2006.

"Ricciardi and Kim believe …." Light Year Research (Japan) K.K. Handout, 2006.

"He found empirical …." *Paper Quality, Cumulative Innovation, and Market Value: Evidence from Japanese Firm Level Panel Data.* Institute of Innovation Research Working Paper WP#05-06. Revised March 2005.

"Japanese companies spend a great deal …." Interview by the author in November 2005.

"The share of intangible assets in total …" Ministry of Economy, Trade, and Industry. *White Paper on International Economy and*

Trade 2004, See esp. Chapter Two — The "new value creation economy" and evolving modalities of competition, p. 5, which can be accessed at http://www.meti.go.jp/english/report/index.html.

"Another disparity ...." Deloitte Touche Tohmatsu, Nobuyuki Nagata. *IP Valuation—How to Value IP and Uses of Valuations.* Handout from Intellectual Property Management Seminar held by Deloitte and Foley & Lardner, LLP. February 9, 2006.

"This analysis is too primitive ...." Interview conducted by the author on 2 March 2006.

"For the most part ...." Interview conducted by the author on 7 February 2006.

"A government study ...." Ministry of Economy, Trade, and Industry. *Report on the Internationalization of Business Accounting in Japan.* June 2004. See esp. p. 13.

"The last 3 years ...." Interview conducted by the author on 2 March 2006.

"The Japanese government received about 3.71 million patent ...." World Intellectual Property Organization. www.wipo.int/ipstats/en/statistics/patents/pdf/patents_by_country.pdf.

"Kenjiro Takayanagi, a teacher at ...." Arai, Hisamitsu. *Intellectual Property Policies for the Twenty-First Century: The Japanese Experience in Wealth Creation.* Policy Advisory Commission of the World Intellectual Property Organization. December 1999. See esp. p. 39.

"Sakichi Toyoda ...." Arai, Hisamitsu. *Intellectual Property Policies for the Twenty-First Century: The Japanese Experience in Wealth Creation.* Policy Advisory Commission of the World Intellectual Property Organization. December 1999. See esp. p. 19.

"Following World War II, Japanese firms actively applied ...." U.S. Patent and Trademark Office. *Patent Counts by Country/State and Year, Utility Patents, January 1, 1963– December 31, 2004.* A Patent Technology Monitoring Division Report. April 2005.

"Some firms …." Arai, Hisamitsu. *Intellectual Property Policies for the Twenty-First Century: The Japanese Experience in Wealth Creation.* Policy Advisory Commission of the World Intellectual Property Organization. December 1999. See esp. p. 35.

"From 1963 through 2004, Japan had received fully 591,683 …." U.S. Patent and Trademark Office. *Patent Counts by Country/State and Year, Utility Patents, January 1, 1963– December 31, 2004.* A Patent Technology Monitoring Division Report. April 2005.

"In general Japan has a large number …." Fujitsu conference call, 16 March 2006.

"In a survey by *Fortune* …." *Fortune.* "The High Tech Race: Who's Ahead?" 13 October 1986. See esp. p. 26.

"In addition, the number of domestic patent registrations …." Japan Patent Office. *Japan Patent Office Annual Report* 2005. November 2005.http://www.deux.jpo.go.jp/cgi/search.cgi?query=annual+report+2005&lang=en&root=short.

"Perhaps worried about technological complacency, Prime Minister Junichiro Koizumi," policy speech to 154th session of the Diet, 4 February 2002, http://www.kantei.go.jp/foreign/koizumispeech/2002/02/04sisei_e.html.

Ichiro Nakayama …." Nakayama, Ichiro. "Intellectual Property Strategy in Japan." Slides from OECD, IPR, Innovation and Economic Performance Conference. 29 August 2003.

"The Tokyo High Court already …." Interview conducted by the author on 6 February 2006.

"The Japan Patent Office …" Takenaka, Toshiko and Ichiro Nakayama. "Will Intellectual Property Policy Save Japan from Recession? Japan's Basic Intellectual Property Law and Its Implementation Through the Strategic Program." *International Review of Intellectual Property and Competition Law* 35, no. 8 (2004): 877–1006.

"Although there has been limited progress …." Intellectual Property Policy Headquarters. Intellectual Property Strategic Program 2005.

10 June 2005. See esp. p. 40–41. http://www.kantei.go.jp/foreign/policy/titeki/kettei/050610_e.pdf.

"More than 3,800 patents were awarded to U.S. universities…" This and next three sentences from The Association of University Technology Managers™. *AUTM US Licensing Survey: FY 2004*, http://www.autm.net/surveys/dsp.surveyDetail.cfm?pid=28, See esp. A Message From the President.

"The Japanese government is doing …." Interview conducted by the author on 6 February 2006.

"As a result of government efforts …." *Japan Times.* "Intellectual Property must be managed like a valuable asset." 26 December 2005. p. 8–9.

"The Patent Office …." Yonetsu, Kiyoshi. *Activities of the JPO and the NCIPI.* Undated handout from the Japan Patent Office.

"Nonetheless, some, including …" Interview conducted by the author on 1 March 2006.

"More than 20 Japanese companies …." MIT Industrial Liaison Program member list at http://ilp-www.mit.edu/display_page.a4d?key=P2b.

"Spending on research and development was 3.2% …." OCED Science, Technology, and Industry Scoreboard 2005—Towards a Knowledge-based Economy. Chart A.5 Business R&D. http://puck.sourceoecd.org/vl=10125715/cl=15/nw=1/rpsv/scoreboard/index.htm.

"The industry has entered the era …." *Nikkei Net Interactive.* Nihon Keizai Shimbun, Inc. "Japanese Electronics Firms Using Patents to Keep Rivals in Check." 2 April 2005.

"President Tadashi Okamura, whose company has withdrawn …." *Nikkei Net Interactive.* Nihon Keizai Shimbun, Inc. "More Japanese Firms Resorting to Suits to Stem Technology Drain." 7 April 2004.

"Ten years ago, Japanese firms obtained patents …." Interview conducted by the author on 6 February 2006.

"We don't like to litigate …." Fujitsu conference call. 16 March 2006.

"Fujitsu filed suit in April 2004, charging Samsung SDI Co …." *Nikkei Net Interactive.* Nihon Keizai Shimbun, Inc. "Japan Firms Strengthen Resolve to Tackle Infringement." 8 April 2004.

"Fujitsu's joint venture with Hitachi, Fujitsu Hitachi Plasma Display, Ltd., was the world leader in PDPs …." *Nikkei Net Interactive.* Nihon Keizai Shimbun, Inc. "Fujitsu Sues Samsung SDI after Careful Study." 8 April 2004.

"… Samsung was coming up fast, boosting its …." *Nikkei Net Interactive.* Nihon Keizai Shimbun, Inc. "Japan Firms Strengthen Resolve to Tackle Infringement," 8 April 2004.

"The PDP market was expected to grow to ¥1 trillion …." *Nikkei Net Interactive.* Nihon Keizai Shimbun, Inc. "Fujitsu Sues Samsung SDI after Careful Study." 8 April 2004.

"Fujitsu apparently felt it could not afford …." *Nikkei Net Interactive*, Nihon Keizai Shimbun, Inc. "Fujitsu Chairman Believes in Defending Patents." 19 April 2004.

"Fujitsu started developing PDPs back in the 1960s …." *Nikkei Net Interactive.* Nihon Keizai Shimbun, Inc. "Fujitsu Sues Samsung over Plasma Panel Patents." 7 April 2004.

"Within a couple of weeks of the filing …." *Nikkei Net Interactive.* Nihon Keizai Shimbun, Inc. "Tokyo Customs Halts Samsung Plasma Display Imports." 21 April 2004.

"Tension escalated as the Minister of Commerce …." *Nikkei Net Interactive.* Nihon Keizai Shimbun, Inc. "S. Korea Government to Tokyo: Fujitsu-Samsung Row Is Corporate Issue." 22 April 2004.

"However, the decision by Tokyo Customs …." *Nikkei Net Interactive.* Nihon Keizai Shimbun, Inc. "Fujitsu, Samsung SDI Settle PDP Dispute." 14 June 2004.

"The patent revenue balance turned positive for the first time in 2003, and it grew to ¥316.3 billion by 2005." Ministry of Finance statistics. www.mof.go.jp/bpoffice/bpdata/es2bop.htm.

"However, the increased payments suggest …." *Nikkei Net Interactive.* Nihon Keizai Shimbun, Inc. "Patent Revenue to Turn Positive." 9 February 2004.

"The Development Bank of Japan has loaned …." *Nikkei Net Interactive.* Nihon Keizai Shimbun, Inc. "Banks Boosting Business Loans Backed by Intellectual Property." 28 February 2006.

"The second edition of his classic …." Itami, Hiroyuki and Thomas W. Roehl. *Mobilizing Invisible Assets.* Harvard University Press, 1987.

"My concept of invisible assets is broader …." This statement and the quotes that follow are from an interview conducted by the author on 1 March 2006.

"This firm [Canon] is investing …." *Nikkei Business.* "Looking to the Future after China's Yuan Revaluation," 1 April 2005.

"From April 2000, Hitachi, Ltd. …." Hitachi Ltd. *Kenkyu Kaihatsu oyobi Chitekizaisan Houkokusho.* 2005 (Research & Development and Intellectual Assets Report). June 2005. See esp. p. 15–16. http://www.hitachi.co.jp/about/activity/ip/index.html.

"Throughout the 1990s, spending on research and development …." Ministry of Internal Affairs and Communications, Statistics Bureau & Statistical Research and Training Institute. www.stat.go.jp/english/data/chouki/17.htm.

"According to Thomson Scientific data, 43% of …." FT Special Report Japan. "World Leader in Patents Concentrates on Incremental Innovations." *Financial Times.* 12 October 2005.

"Investors tend to view …." This statement and the quotes that follow are from an interview conducted by the author on 15 February 2006.

"When Yamazaki Machinery Works, Ltd. …." *Fortune.* "The High Tech Race: Who's Ahead?" 13 October 1986. See esp. p. 32.

"The trouble is that the Japanese have ten Bell Labs," *Fortune.* "The High Tech Race: Who's Ahead?" 13 October 1986. See esp. p. 37

"Sony Corp. and Samsung Electronics signed a cross-licensing …." *Nikkei Net Interactive.* Nihon Keizai Shimbun, Inc. "Sony, Samsung in Broad Pact on Electronics Technology." 20 December 2004.

"The two firms also inked in deal in 2006 to build …." *Nikkei Net Interactive.* Nihon Keizai Shimbun, Inc. "Sony-Samsung LCD Joint Venture to Build Second 8G Plant in South Korea." 10 April 2006.

"Sony's Bravia line flat-panel TVs are contributing …. Woods, Ginny Parker. "Sony's picture looks brighter, even if firm remains cautious." *The Wall Street Journal* (online). 6 February 2006.

"A survey by Japan Academic Society of Investor Relations …." METI. *Reference Guideline for Intellectual Property Disclosure.* January 2004. See esp. p. 4.

"METI noted that the imbalance …." METI. *Reference Guideline for Intellectual Property Disclosure.* January 2004. See esp. p. 4, footnote 3.

"The government points to Hitachi …." Sakuta, Yasuo. *IP Strategy of Hitachi.* Hitachi, Ltd., handout. See esp. p. 12. www.hitachi.com/IR-e/ev/040407-1/0404071.pdf.

"Its patent-exploitation strategy is …." Sakuta, Yasuo. *IP Strategy of Hitachi.* Hitachi, Ltd., handout. 7 April 2004. See esp. p. 8. www.hitachi.com/IR-e/ev/040407-1/0404071.pdf.

"Hitachi plans to use its patent portfolio …." Hitachi, Ltd. *Kenkyukaihatsu oyobi Chitekizaisan Houkokusho 2005.* June 2005. p. 13. www.hitachi.co.jp/about/strategy/ip/index.html.

"Those that do include Toshiba Corp …." Sumita, Takyuki. *Intellectual Assets & Management Reporting.* METI, handout. June 2005. See esp. p. 3.

3

CULTURAL ARBITRAGE

Foreign Hedge Funds Pursue Opportunities in Japan

From his office in an old villa, Guy Cihi (pronounced *see-he*) could just view the spires of Florence peeking above the green canopy of his olive trees, beyond the edges of his emerald swimming pool.

He spent much of 2000 at his desk, drafting documents to be reviewed by lawyers in Tokyo and the Cayman Islands. Even though he had never before managed a hedge fund, he was convinced that he and his partners could compete against the oldest, most prestigious names in global finance. All the conditions were in place, he believed, for Japanese investors to pour money into his new fund.

Although he was new to hedge fund management, Cihi had 15 years experience in Japan, and was described as a "genius" at using software to analyze and reach the country's target markets. He had already made a tidy fortune marketing U.S. intellectual property

57

throughout Asia. Not short on confidence, and lanky with high cheek-bones and salty brown hair, he sizes up people quickly with a disarm-ingly frank glance. He is quick to admit that he has a low tolerance for nonsense, and one pities unprepared brokers who call on him and try to bluster their way to a sale.

His previous company, Learning Technologies, used innovative marketing techniques to zero in on sources of demand with a sharp-shooter's precision. His acquaintance with them began in the mid-1980s, when he had just left school and was employed with a technology consulting firm.

Learning Technologies had recently emerged from bankruptcy and needed help exporting electronic devices and intellectual prop-erty to Japan. "All my other clients were scrambling to keep up with the onslaught of superior Japanese products, taking away their mar-ket share," Cihi remembers. "I was very intrigued by this particular client. It ran against the tide."

"I felt that I needed to get closer to their sources of demand in order to be able to propose workable solutions," Cihi adds thought-fully. "That seems to be one of the major themes of my life, seeking to understand what drives demand."

He ended up buying into Learning Technologies with money borrowed from his father and moved to Japan in 1985. From a tiny presence and $1.8 million in sales, Cihi and his partners eventually built it to over $300 million in revenues. The company sold subscrip-tions for research and other forms of intellectual property procured from top universities in the United States. This included academic research, software, and educational courseware.

Cihi's work led him to develop an understanding of how different products and services appealed to different demographic segments. He was surprised to find that demographic segments were not evenly distributed throughout the country, so he went about breaking down the relative scale of each targeted group. "We didn't go about it anecdotally. We implemented a strictly statistical approach and developed proprietary software systems to crunch the numbers," he says. To this day, he remains confident in his systematic approach for determining how different population segments react to new ideas.

He sold half his ownership in Learning Technologies in 1999, deciding that he wanted to explore new business opportunities offered by the Internet. Considering that profitability of his old firm was a striking 28% after taxes and that he still owned shares in the reliable cash cow, he adds wryly, "I didn't do half bad off that deal." Before the year's end, he left for Italy with his family for a break on his farm near Florence.

Having acquired substantial liquid assets from the sale of the firm, a parade of professional financial advisors from blue-chip investment houses soon began contacting him, offering help with managing his portfolio. He listened to their pitches but was not impressed. "The things they were saying didn't sound logical to me. I have a sensitive BS detector." The salesmen often fumbled for answers when Cihi pointedly asked for specifics of their asset-management strategies.

Battle-hardened professional traders opened his eyes. While attending venture capital conferences, he met two investment bank money managers—one from New York, the other from Tokyo. They confided in him how their business really worked, friendships developed, and a partnership formed. "I mean, think about it, why exactly would investment banks want to help smaller investors make money?" Cihi asks rhetorically. "It's the little guy's money they want to take. It's a zero sum game."

A big balance sheet to play with is a huge resource for trading desks, and the ultimate balance sheet in Japan is the cumulative savings of households. A classic example of the inherent potential for conflict in the industry is Big Project N, a Japanese fund launched by Nomura Asset Management Co. in February 2000. The fund raised

¥1 trillion from retail investors, investing it in securities at the same
time corporations, through their brokers, unloaded their cross-share
holdings. The fund's unit price began to fall sharply soon after its
launch, and, at one point in 2003, it had more than halved in value.
The fund has since recovered along with the general market upswing
in 2005, but those who sold out in disgust before 2005 got seriously
burned.

Cihi had been simultaneously searching for new Internet-based
business opportunities and a better way to manage his liquid assets.
Having befriended the two pros, it dawned on him that these ideas
could be merged. He envisioned a wealthy aging population in Japan
that would increasingly lean toward professional asset management.
He also saw a poor set of investment products and home-based
broadband access coming up fast.

"My partners agreed the timing was right. They quit their banks,
and we established AGS Capital in 2000. We were going to introduce
a fully transparent absolute return investment fund suitable for both
institutions and individuals," Cihi says. Armed with seed capital, an
absolute return strategy, extensive risk-management experience, and
marketing savvy, the sky seemed the limit for their new venture.

He spent the year 2000 flying back and forth between Italy and
Tokyo, working with his new partners. They turned to Keiji Matsumoto, now special counsel to the law firm of Mori, Hamada & Matsumoto, to help structure the fund.

They managed the whole operation frugally. To save money, Cihi
drafted the papers required to establish the firm—lawyers charge less
to review drafts than they do to write new documents. He had gained
plenty of experience with similar documentation from his years in
intellectual property licensing. About the same time, a friend started
a tech venture in the Shinjuku district of Tokyo. They secured a huge
space in one of the hot properties of the time, and they offered Cihi a
corner office—for free. Cihi confides, "I put the prop guys there

while I was off drafting contracts in Italy. It was a real guerilla start-up. We were totally independent and preparing ourselves to sell online to individual Japanese investors."

"The nail sticking out will be hammered down" is a common saying in Japan, and Cihi knew his exposed firm would be at risk of being flattened. He moved to Japan in 2001, before their fund's launch. For the next 6 months, he and his partners continued to work out of the cramped corner office loaned by a friend.

However, AGS Capital did not enjoy instant success. "We spent a lot of money discovering Japanese investors ...." His voice trails off when reflecting on those early days of his firm. "Well, we know what they think now." He admits that targeting institutions and individuals with the same fund was a mistake. "It's not only about risk and return; different investor expectations are a critical factor," he concludes.

Cihi himself made the cold calls to institutions. "The reception was always warm, and my Japanese improved real fast," he recalls. But the firm also targeted high-net-worth individuals. AGS advertised the existence of its fund through specialty financial journals. Online, customers could log in, add more money to their accounts, and sign up for seminars. He and his partners repeatedly appeared in a lifestyle glossy for wealthy Japanese and a more traditional stock traders' magazine. The approach was working; more than 1,000 investors soon contacted his firm.

After this promising start, the firm immediately ran into an insurmountable problem. Its primary investment strategy failed to make any money. "From day one, I explained to everyone this business only works if the fund makes money," says Cihi. "We can't go out and sell the same old garbage against the same old garbage. We didn't lose money, but we didn't make any, either." With mediocre returns, he was disinclined to ask investors to park their money in the fund. It ran counter to the reasons he had started the business in the first place.

"We had to go into pause mode," Cihi says. They stopped offering the fund to outside investors but continued to run it with their own capital. While one partner worked hard to fix his trading strategy, Cihi and his other partner continued to educate investors by holding seminars. However, they faced problems there as well. They found that their private clients needed extensive tutoring on hedge funds' advanced strategies and risk-management techniques. In the United States, brokerages have invested heavily in teaching the public about securities investments and strategies for decades. Japanese firms apparently had made less of an effort.

Cihi learned a hard truth about private investors' attitudes regarding stock investment. "Japan was still coming off the bubble," he remembers. The stock market was just a big casino in the minds of many.

He also found the lack of knowledge about basic risk-management strategies a daunting hurdle. Even so, they got capital commitments. With hard-won access to Japanese investors, the firm took the opportunity to raise money for other alternative investments—ones that Cihi believed in—but his own fund was not among them. Raising money for other ventures paid the bills, but it was definitely not what he and his partners had started AGS for. What Cihi needed to raise capital for his own fund was just one thing: a steady and strong annual return. "People line up for that," he says.

The firm's primary investment strategy, however, continued to disappoint. Cihi sought to understand the specific reasons the trading approach had stalled after 14 years of solid performance inside an investment bank, but he got nowhere. Despite the troubles, the manager was determined to protect the secret aspects of his strategy. Cihi was sympathetic—to a point. He realized that prop traders' careers, their livelihoods, depended on running strategies but not giving them to institutions. However, his partner's strategy was not working, and Cihi wanted to know why. He never did learn the details. Accepting responsibility for his failure to produce positive returns, the partner resigned, taking his precious algorithms with him. "That was a dark day for us all. He's a brilliant fellow, but it just wasn't meant to be," Cihi sighs.

"Strategies where the trade-selection process involves human decisions are at risk of human weaknesses," Cihi concludes. Confidence and emotional swings affect performance and increase risk. Cihi turned his attention to his other partner, Toru Tanaka, who had been steadily working on a different trading approach. A third-generation banker, Tanaka had previously set up options and derivatives trading systems for a Japanese bank in New York. The statistical arbitrage strategy he was working on at AGS all but eliminated humans from the trade-identification process.

Tanaka's prototype looked promising, but it would take more time to develop a robust statistical engine and risk-monitoring platform. In 2002, Cihi decided to put his marketing efforts on ice and concentrate, with his partner, on the development and calibration of this new trading system.

Three long years later, Cihi is finally confident in the new strategy. He notes, "Now we have a profitable statistical arbitrage strategy that identifies pair trade opportunities without human involvement." He is back to pounding the pavement, visiting financial institutions both in Japan and overseas. In his presentations, he shows that pro forma simulations suggest that his strategy would have earned 16% average annual returns over the last 5 years.

"We identify pair trade opportunities that are highly likely to profit from mean reversion," he explains. The key is identifying the right pair combinations, he notes. The system analyzes historical price data and identifies hundreds of two-stock combinations that are what Cihi calls "productively correlated." Cihi defines a productively correlated stock pair as one that has a recent history of signaling consistently profitable trade entry and exit points and offers minimal exposure to risk. Sometimes the pairs are in the same industry, but more often, they aren't even in the same sector.

"When the relative price of two productively correlated stocks moves away from its mean, the fund buys one stock and shorts an equal cash amount of the other—a classic cash-neutral pair trade," Cihi continues. Mean revision and profit occurs in about 65% of the cases, and it fails to occur in the rest. "That's the essence of statistical arbitrage—winning more than you lose," he sums up.

AGS manages portfolio risk by limiting each individual pair's gross exposure to 2% of fund assets and by implementing verified stop-loss techniques. "Conceptually, the strategy works well in any liquid market under normal price-volatility conditions," Cihi adds. Higher liquidity reduces risk and higher price volatility increases performance. To stack the deck in his investors' favor, the universe for Cihi's fund is limited to the largest 500 public corporations in Japan.

Most hedge fund strategies seem to be somewhat correlated to price volatility, which raises the question, what is price volatility related to? Cihi believes the answer somehow involves credit creation, but he voices this hypothesis without firm conviction. "Low price volatility would seem to indicate a sort of consensus [among market participants] on valuations," he muses.

Cihi is quick to draw a distinction between his strategy and others that claim a statistical arbitrage approach but are, in fact, quantifying fundamental data such as corporate income statements and balance sheets. He maintains that "financial statements are qualitative judgments, and digitizing them won't change the fact." AGS's new strategy operates solely on historical prices determined in the market.

His years of system design, statistical analysis, and, more recently, pair trading have clearly affected the way Cihi perceives things. "Two independent entities come together and form some kind of relationship with each other. They remain in that relationship for some set period, moving up and down. They'll hit highs, where they're incredibly close, and lows, where they drift apart. Sometimes a pair will break apart, but, more often than not, it manages to remain together." He expands the thought by adding, "This is very much how human relationships operate—a bond forms and the relationship waxes and wanes over time."

On a personal note he adds, "Now I approach my marriage with a completely different view. When things are really great between us, I realize that the next most likely thing is that we are going to drift apart. I no longer feel disappointment, though, because I know it's a necessary part of coming back together. We can't feel closer unless we've drifted. It's that simple."

Cihi and Tanaka entered the hedge fund business with a grand plan to develop a fully transparent absolute return fund for Japanese institutions and wealthy individuals. The firm now targets only institutional investors for its statistical arbitrage fund, and much else has changed, but Cihi continues to profess his love for the business. He smiles and says, "This work is a dream come true for me."

Cihi represents a new breed of hedge fund manager or advisor—Asia-based and focusing solely on markets in the region. Such managers and advisors are still relatively few compared with those in the United States or other developed markets. Whereas Asian equities make up 15% of global capitalization, Asian-strategy hedge funds account for only 6.5% of the industry's worldwide assets, according to Eurekahedge.

However, hedge fund investors are increasingly looking to the region for opportunities. More than 150 Asian hedge funds were launched in 2004, and another 100 were started in 2005, the research service reported. Total funds under management by the end of 2005 are expected to rise to about $105 billion, up from only $20 billion 3 years ago.

Japan is the big story for hedge funds in late 2005, says Rajeev Baddepudi, an analyst with Eurekahedge. About 170 hedge funds are managing up to $25 billion in the country. Investors poured $8.2 billion into Japanese hedge funds in 2004, attracted by returns of about 10%.

With the stock market rally in Japan, "Asia became the flavor of the day," notes Kirby Daley, Head of Capital Introduction Asia for the Fimat Division of Société Générale Securities in Tokyo. Hedge fund investors especially were very underweight in the region.

A former commodities trader with The Pillsbury Corp. in Kansas City, Daley left the U.S. in 1993 after the firm sold its flour mills. He eventually joined a Japanese commodity futures brokerage in Osaka, one of the few Americans doing Japanese commodity futures broking at the time. Later he moved to Daiwa Futures in Tokyo, which opened a foreign exchange desk after the law changed in 1998 to allow individuals to trade on margin.

In 2001, he was hired by a former client, Fimat, and expanded its commodities trading in Tokyo in a high-profile effort chronicled by the *Asian Wall Street Journal.* Fimat was originally a group of SocGen brokers on the floor of the Paris-based Marché à Terme International de France (MATIF), the French Futures and Options Exchange, which has since grown into a global brokerage house. He joined the firm's prime brokerage arm the following year.

Prime brokers handle all the trading and financing needs of a hedge fund. Hedge funds trade many different asset classes, and they want to compare prices across markets constantly for their trading. Stock loan services, enabling funds to short the market, are among the most important services that prime brokers offer. When hedge funds short equity shares, they borrow the securities, for a fee, from their prime broker, hoping to be able to buy them from the market at a cheaper price before the stock loan due date.

Offering such services requires intensive risk monitoring. If a hedge fund takes very risky positions and the market moves against it in a big way quickly, before financing levels can be adjusted or margin calls can be made, the hedge fund could blow up, forcing the prime broker to suffer losses, Daley adds.

Prime brokers also introduce their hedge fund customers to institutional investors, reasoning that if their clients have more money, they will trade more and generate more commissions. Daley was knocking on doors in Tokyo for overseas hedge funds before the overseas surge of interest in Japan in 2003. "Our European- and U.S.-based customers wanted to source Asian money, especially Japanese money, so it was my job to get to know all the investors out here," he says.

Japanese institutions have been aggressively piling into hedge funds in recent years. With Japanese long-term interest rates among the lowest in the world, and stock market rallies repeatedly fizzling out in recent years, many domestic insurance firms and pension funds are desperate for yield. Almost 60% of Japanese institutional investors allocated funds to hedge funds in 2004, up sharply from 2001, when only 30% took the plunge, according to a Russell Investment Group survey. However, that does not mean they are satisfied with this alternative asset class.

"I just had lunch with a life insurer analyst lamenting that the global fund-of-funds he invests in invests in mediocre Japanese funds because they invest in the ones that market overseas and are easy to reach," recounts Daley. Global fund-of-funds apparently do not always search out better-performing, harder-to-find Japanese funds that do not market aggressively at hedge fund conferences held abroad. "I don't like that," the analyst told him.

Even without the high rates of return, Japan is becoming increasingly attractive to global hedge managers because of its idiosyncratic and independent nature. Such uniqueness is a long-sought-after trait by global asset allocators when contemplating investing alternatives.

This thinking dates back to Harry Markowitz, observes Robert Webb, finance professor at the University of Virginia and author of the book *Macroeconomic Information and Financial Trading*. Markowitz, in his classic treatise *Portfolio Selection*, introduced a new

way of looking at risk—focusing not on the risk of an individual security, but on the risk of a security in a portfolio, Webb notes. "The rel-
evant measure of security risk is not the variance or standard
deviation of a security, but how a security fluctuates relative to the
portfolio as a whole—that is, the covariance of the security's return
with the portfolio."

The argument for investing then shifts. "A person could be interested in a security for its expected return or because of its impact on
reducing risk," Webb says. Many believe Japan is just the sort of market that provides opportunities for finding securities that move inde-
pendently of the other holdings of international investors.

Japanese markets may behave much differently from the rest of
the world even when under the influence of similar factors, says Ricciardi. "In particular, if inflation unexpectedly reared its head in the
U.S., it's likely stock and other asset prices would get hit very hard,"
he observes. Markets around the world could tumble as U.S. rates
headed higher. "Ironically, that is just the type of scenario that would
work best in Japan," he adds. With the country struggling under
deflation for 15 years, increased pricing power is just what many
banks and firms need to support their earnings.

If global funds are trying to reduce the volatility of their returns
by increasing their exposure to Japan, they have to look elsewhere
than blue-chip players such as Toyota Motor Corp. or Sony Corp.,
warns Ricciardi. Such firms provide limited diversification benefits
because both their markets and their investor bases are global, he
notes. Ideally, investors should hunt down firms with a local orientation, which do well when global cycles turn down, and are not held by
foreigners. As a tongue-in-cheek example, Ricciardi suggests
"*okonomiyaki* makers in Hiroshima," referring to purveyors of a piz-
zalike Kansai specialty.

Such companies may be hard to locate, but they are true diamonds for global hedge funds. Even if the returns of such firms are
relatively low, they can reduce the expected volatility of the returns of

the global fund. In addition, by combining such investments with added leverage, these players can increase their expected returns while keeping risk constant, Ricciardi stresses.

The flood of institutional money, both from overseas and from domestic institutions, is changing the shape of the hedge fund industry in Japan. Demands for risk reporting and substantial infrastructures have increased dramatically over the last 2 years.

"We used to call it the Alfred E. Neuman Syndrome," says Gareth Phillips, one of the founding partners of Triloka Capital Management, referring to the "What, me worry?" stance of many investors in the past. That is changing now.

"The type of people coming in are much more institutionalized and sophisticated …. In order to attract larger pools of money, the level of infrastructure that a fund now needs is quite daunting." He rattles off the positions required by his investors—compliance officer, operational professionals, CFO, financial controller.

Rising costs are likely to force consolidation in the industry. Demand will always exist for the one guy or two guys with three or four staff, concedes Phillips. However, global asset allocators cannot invest in such small businesses because they are unlikely to have the required risk-management safeguards and compliance controls.

Specialist funds that have not done well have sought out partners, Phillips notes. If fund managers focus on a single area that does not produce opportunities, their performance is hurt. Convertible bond price volatility was quite low in the first half of 2005. Because hedge fund managers need price changes to trade, such market stability damaged the performance of firms specializing in these securities, he notes.

To try to avoid such problems, Phillips and his partners pursue a multistrategy approach across the whole Asian region. They have a thick playbook and are staffed with experts in fundamental long-short, quantitative arbitrage, event-driven, macro, and volatility trading.

The fund is somewhat unique; few are able to launch with such a diversified desk. "Multistrategies are not that common in Asia … to get five or six really good managers is hard," he notes. Previously having worked at the trading desk of Lehman Brothers, Phillips and his fellow partners had friends at Fidelity and other institutions. "I've been in Japan for more than 10 years now, others a similar time frame, and with the foreign community being close-knit, we all knew each other, to some extent."

Events such as corporate restructuring, secondary offerings, and exchanges adding or dropping members of stock indices provide opportunities for traders to anticipate market moves and thus make money. The investment partners and their traders know what strategies have or have not worked in the past. Implementing several strategies at once in reaction to a market event can increase profits. "I think a multistrategy approach does have the potential to increase the trading edge," Phillips observes. He summarizes his firm's approach to trading Japanese markets as "cultural arbitrage"—anticipating how Japanese markets will move as their behavior increasingly approaches that of their Western counterparts.

Japan has trading advantages over other Asian markets, Phillips observes. Its markets are extremely liquid. Getting hundreds of millions of dollars of exposure within, say, 10 minutes, is no problem for many positions. "Tens of millions of dollars would move some Southeast Asian markets, like the Philippines, whereas in Japan, you could multiply this fiftyfold without too much of a ripple," he notes. Many Japanese firms are active in China as well, giving traders additional opportunities relating to the mainland. Commission-type strategies are fairly cheap (no stamp or transaction taxes) and stock lending is readily available—shorting is harder in Southeast Asian markets, he adds.

Traders tend to be agnostic regarding market themes. However, Phillips saw a number of potential money-making stories in Japan in 2005—the Japan reflation story, banks recovering, mergers and acquisitions driving corporate restructuring, to name a few. However, the main reason to be here is demographic, he concludes, noting that Asia has much of the world's population.

Even though the Japanese markets have advantages, setting up in Tokyo can be frustrating. "Japan is probably the most difficult place to run a hedge fund, from a viewpoint of the regulatory environment," he notes. "They do not make it easy, particularly for foreign firms."

Discretionary licenses in Japan grant fund managers full freedom in allocating their fund's investments, whereas those financial managers with advisory licenses cannot invest on behalf of their clients—they can only provide recommendations. The Financial Services Authority hands out discretionary-type licenses. "It can often end up being potluck, depending upon the individual at the regulator and his discretion as to whether he adopts a green light or red light with respect to [discretionary] licensing." Established asset managers often get the necessary approvals easily, but new companies can find it particularly tortuous. "They are nervous about your ability to manage Japanese public and pension money," says Phillips. "It's not an unreasonable concern, but it's not transparent.

"In the United States and the United Kingdom, the rules are usually statute- and code-based—you can, in theory, challenge the regulator's decision." Ultimately, such bureaucratic hurdles will hinder the development of the economy. It will change, but at a cautious and slow pace, he adds.

Faced with such regulatory hurdles, some hedge fund managers and advisors are setting up shop overseas, even when they focus their attention on Japan.

During the dreary commute from Narita Airport, travelers often get stuck in traffic jams beside the endless warehouses that line the murky waters of Tokyo Bay. Arrivals to Singapore, in contrast, usually zip along in the umbrage of *angsana,* flame of the forest, and cassia trees, arriving downtown in minutes. With lower costs, first-class offices, and, in many cases, better infrastructure, Singapore wins lifestyle points as well. The tropical city has excellent schools, and English is widely spoken, easing the plight of foreign wives on extended stays. The resort paradise of Phuket, Thailand, is only a 1 hour and 45-minute plane ride away.

Indeed, the glowing reputation of the city among expatriates is largely unchanged from the time of Sir Stamford Raffles, who established a British trading station here in the early 19th century. He wrote the Duchess of Somerset in 1822, "Here is life and activity; and it would be difficult to name a place on the face of the globe with brighter prospects or more pleasant satisfaction."

Previously, the government attempted to attract Asian headquarters of multinational corporations. Now the city-state faces increasing competition from mainland centers such as Shanghai, as international firms relocate manufacturing operations to the mainland. Always nimble, Singapore planners have shifted gears and are re-creating their town as an offshore asset-management center.

"I think Singapore wants to play a Boston role," notes Richard Lemmerman, one of three founders of the hedge fund adviser Creo Capital (Asia) Pte., Ltd. In the United States, many asset managers have converged on this New England city, while investment banks cluster in Manhattan. Lemmerman sees Singapore targeting the asset managers, while global investment banks will continue to set up branches in Hong Kong and Tokyo.

Lemmerman appreciates the town's bureaucratic efficiency. A busy long-short manager who deals in very liquid securities throughout Asia, he has no time to waste. One way the government is striving to attract funds such as his is easing the start-up process. In the 2005 budget, the government approved a 12-month window period for approved start-up managers to meet general rules relating to tax exemptions of offshore domiciled funds, reported Eurekahedge.

Singapore has a very conducive regulatory environment for hedge funds, acknowledges Lemmerman. "We've been very quick in terms of getting approved and set up. We know people in Hong Kong who haven't been able set up for up to 9 months." With license-exempt status, funds can begin operations in a matter of weeks, he adds.

He is upbeat about his firm's prospects as capital floods into the industry and more hedge funds move to the region. "We have a lot of local knowledge, and we feel we are a more organically grown fund [than many competitors]," he notes. An old Japan hand, Lemmerman went to Tokyo in the early 1980s to study Japanese and work as a stock analyst at Yamaichi Research Institute. After getting his MBA at the Wharton School, he returned to Japan to work at Salomon Brothers in 1987 and then ran the equity and derivative trading operations at Lehman Brothers in Tokyo. Later he headed Bloomberg Tradebook, which is an Asian electronic trading business.

He and his other two partners, Ed Strover, the fund's portfolio manager, and Chief Operating Officer Paul Cuthbert-Brown, have more than 50 years combined experience in Asia. Lemmerman notes that technical expertise is not enough to make it in the region because Asian markets are different from those in the West. Some learn program trading in the United States and head out to Asia, but awareness of local and customization issues may be more important than technical knowledge from the home market. "You may have the general skill set, but do you have the people who know how to do things in the local market or not?

"These are tremendously exciting times," adds Lemmerman, who generally devotes much of his trading book to Japan. "Markets will go up and will go down, but some of the things that are happening in Japan now, such as reform of the post office, are pretty significant issues. The situation will be more open, less opaque."

He notes that the current changes in Japan are different from those occurring elsewhere in the region. The breakdown of *keiretsu* ties (traditional cross-shareholding relationships) in Japan and introduction of Anglo-Saxon corporate governance standards tend to make a more equal playing ground for all market participants, including foreigners, he believes.

Other issues prevail elsewhere. Many smaller economies are dominated by powerful families, so investors are forced to deal with minority shareholder issues. In South Korea, Samsung chairman Kun-Hee Lee's family remains a force to be reckoned with. Meanwhile, some governments force local firms to implement policies that are uneconomic. Many regional oil companies were not able to pass on price increases to final consumers. "This is quite an issue in places like India, Indonesia, and Thailand," he observes.

Despite such differences, many countries besides Japan are moving closer to market pricing, he observes. "For the fund that goes both long and short, these changes allow for many opportunities in the market," he notes. "The dynamic exists for trading the speed of liberalization."

So many funds are setting up in Asia that there are even worries of a dearth of skilled professionals to manage all the money. Tudor, Citadel, Ramius, Drake Capital, Highbridge, and Ivy have all set up shop in the region in recent years, notes Baddepudi at Eurekahedge. Headhunters are prowling around industry seminars, scoping out talent. At this stage in the game, they may be facing slim pickings.

Because training people to work on a trading floor is so time consuming and costly, competition for experienced individuals has always been fierce. The pool of seasoned traders and insightful analysts in Asia is even smaller. Money managers at hedge funds have their fingers on hair triggers, and they speculate with their bosses' funds. Global funds are eager to scoop up those individuals with a proven track record of making money in Asian markets. However, only a relative handful have surmounted daunting linguistic hurdles and acquired the technical and industry knowledge to be able to successfully run a trading operation.

Simon A. Ross, who was hired to work in Tokyo with a multibillion-dollar hedge fund in late 2005, considers himself lucky to have survived a 15-year bear market. With broad shoulders and clipped blond hair, Ross, who is in his late 30s, still looks like he would be as comfortable on a rugby field as a trading floor. Indeed, he discusses his years in fund management with the palpable excitement of a sportsman recounting a recent big-game safari on the Serengeti. After hundreds of visits to Japanese firms, he knows the ground like few jungle guides in the city. His empathy for the country and its people, which is by no means universally shared among expat financiers, has undoubtedly played a role in his amazingly fruitful fund raising and often stellar performance. However, the market has also been bruising at times, and he takes nothing for granted.

"I have been fortunate always to have good people around to give me a hand up when I have stumbled," he reflects gratefully. "Managing money is an ongoing experiment in an effort to achieve the right formula."

When the clanging of the pile drivers on the Hanoi downtown street came to an abrupt halt, Ross pondered his future. His career in Vietnam was at a standstill in spring 1994. After graduating from Georgetown University's School of Foreign Service 2 years earlier, he had headed to the fast-growing country with $2,000 in his pocket to sniff out opportunities. Within a week of arriving in Hanoi, he was a site administrator on a construction site for the first international standard office block in the city. "I wanted to be a real estate developer, like my old man," says Ross.

Working with Vietnamese subcontractors, he did demolition for a foreign firm. He was known as Alex because to the Vietnamese he looked like the Russian sailors in town, who they call "Olech." Unfortunately, the project's architect had decided to cut costs by neglecting to install sheet piling around the construction site to protect neighboring buildings. Vibrations from the load pilings, used to drill holes to the bedrock into which concrete is poured to form building supports, also cracked the foundation of a hotel next door. Work at the site was suspended for 6 months.

Ross then decided to try to get the exclusive rights to distribute cosmetics in Vietnam for a multinational company. He selected a unique partner in his business plan—the communist Women's Union. On paper, the partnership made sense; the group had educational programs in every town in the country, and they could export hard currency because they ran a tourist operation. However, after politely listening to his business plan in Singapore, company officials brushed him off. "I was only 23," remembers Ross. "They said, 'That's very nice, thank you for your ideas,' and that was it."

With his options in Vietnam apparently exhausted, he turned his eyes back to Japan. He had studied Japanese and international politics at the School of Foreign Service and had even won a Rotary Scholarship to spend 2 years at Keio University to study industrial engineering. When he graduated, however, the Japanese stock market was imploding, and asset prices were plummeting. The outlook for the country appeared grim, so he headed to Vietnam. Now out of work, he decided to call on some contacts he had made during a stint at a British investment manager during his years in Tokyo. He ended up on the equity sales desk of Schroder Securities in Tokyo, later to be acquired by Credit Suisse First Boston.

Ross made daily calls to clients and tried to drum up business. He competed with larger American and Japanese investment banks, which were often staffed with dozens of company analysts, strategists, and economists. Ross decided to do his own research into Japanese companies. He visited hundreds, looking for anything that would excite investors and make money. He did a lot of commission his first year. It was all from one client—Soros Funds Management.

The hedge fund lifted him out 6 months later. He was one of only two people working in Tokyo for the legendary financier, and Ross became a one-man research department. He studied various subsectors, picking stocks. "One month it was paperboard, the next month it was lithium-ion batteries and condominium developers." He had to write sector reports and produce pro forma financial statements on the companies he researched.

His education on investing really began at Soros. "Everything I know, I learned from my bosses at Soros," he says. "They taught me how to look to make money."

He became familiar with the dynamics of stock price movements. "When retail sales were down 20% for a 6-month period, and then all of a sudden they went from negative 20 to negative 10, I have learned to be a buyer in the shift ... as opposed to wait[ing] until they were up 5 and the stock had already gone up 30%," he explains. Ross spent almost 2 years there.

In 1998, Ross went to AIG Global Investment Corp. to set up a Japanese equity effort. At the time, the Japanese banking system was crumbling, and Japanese investors were desperately shoveling their money offshore. AIG was enjoying great success marketing their foreign bond funds, but the business was one-sided. AIG management saw the risk of being wholly dependent on the yen carry-trade, Ross remembers. Indeed, the dangers of depending on offshore-bound flows of capital were highlighted by the LTCM crisis that set in place a chain of events that reversed capital flows, and the yen appreciated sharply toward the end of the year.

"I came in to build a Japanese equity effort with a slush fund out of Dublin," he explains. "My bosses said, 'Why don't you come up with an investment trust product to compete with Fidelity and Nomura?'"

Ross spent 1999 through 2000 building two funds, worth together about half a billion U.S. dollars. His funds were high risk, focused on what he perceived to be good ideas, with limited diversification. All his investors were domestic. Two second-line Japanese securities firms and a Japanese trust bank marketed the funds.

He had to convince the domestic brokers to peddle his funds to their clients. For this purpose, he made a presentation in the auditorium of the head office at one of the brokers. Two hundred salesmen attended, all sharks looking for the 3% front-load commission the firm would earn. He spoke in Japanese for about an hour and a half.

Return on equity would head upward in Japan, he argued. The country had been shifting away from a collateral culture to a credit culture and would ultimately become equity-focused. Cross-shareholders and the government weren't going to be providing capital to companies, but they would get their money from return-focused investors, so naturally management would do what was in the best interest of their shareholders.

His fund was called Shihonka. *Shihon* means "capital" in Japanese. *Ka* can be written with two different Chinese characters—one means "specialist," the other means "change." When the first character is used in conjunction with *shihon*, the word "capitalist" is formed. Ross used the second Chinese character, meaning a "change to equitization."

The fate of the fund rested on his performance that afternoon. If he fell flat with the sales force, few would bother to mention his fund to potential investors. Luckily, he impressed one person who wandered into the auditorium halfway through his talk. The chairman of the firm had come in to hear what he had to say. At the end of his speech, the chairman stood up and applauded, triggering a standing ovation by all in the room.

"I later learned that [the chairman] had told the sales team to fill me with a $100 million quota because he liked the way I bowed," Ross remembers. "Regardless of whether or not I made sense, what was important was how I bowed."

His fund was a spectacular success that first year. "The first 6 months of that fund, I made 100%, taking massive sector risk in all the areas that went up the most in 1999. I had no banks. I had all tech stocks. I paid a 30% dividend out after the first 5 months. Two weeks later, the fund was up another 35%. At the end of 1999, with all the Y2K liquidity, my mutual fund was up 3 days consecutively more than

10% each day; it was one of those rare times only some get to experience in their careers."

With such a performance, the media started beating a path to his door. Headlines about his pouring money into "wealth-creating firms" appeared in the stock newspapers. His fund became one of the top performers in Japan, ranked no. 6 among all actively managed domestic funds in January 2000. His position had improved to no. 3 by April of that year.

In addition to managing his fund, Ross marketed it to domestic investors. "I would run around Japan giving speeches," he explains. Local brokers would drag him to small cities to encourage people to invest. Many foreign analysts regularly make presentations to professional money managers in Tokyo, but Ross was one of the few who were called on to convince housewives and retirees in the countryside to commit their money to the market.

In the basement of a Niigata Prefecture branch office, a securities salesman introduced him to a rice farmer's wife. Surrounded by gray desks in the cramped room, Ross patiently explained his fund's philosophy for an hour to the sweet but shabbily dressed woman. She asked him only three questions: Where he was from? How many brothers and sisters did he have? Did he like Japan? After the meeting, she invested $5 million in his fund.

He had to figure out how to appeal to each audience, how to win over each group of potential investors. He was asked to go to Noda City out in Chiba Prefecture, where Kikkoman Corp., the soy sauce maker, is headquartered. He spoke in the city ward office to about 150 middle-age women. After he complimented them on their soy sauce and thanked them for making his *sashimi* tastier, they tittered. In Fukuoka on the southern island of Kyushu, investors greeted him with a standing ovation as soon as he walked into the room. His charisma, and the amazing 280% annualized return registered in 1999, kept the money rolling in.

NASDAQ plummeted from the spring of 2000, dragging down Japanese stocks with it. Ross's fund suffered major losses. That year, he was down about 35%. "It was a horror story—all the tech stocks got killed, I blew it," he remembers. To reduce his business exposure to large export firms, he spun out a midcap value focus fund, which was a top performer in 2001. However, by 2002, he felt things were slowing to a halt, and he wanted to short stock again.

He decided to form a hedge fund with a proprietary trader friend, who would manage the risk on his ideas. "I would decide what; he would decide when and how much."

A leading prime broker introduced them to the major players investing in hedge funds, taking them on a global road show. "We met a Chicago investor first. It was our first meeting off the plane from Tokyo. Our pitch was, 'We are going to make 30% gross annually with 15% volatility,'" he remembers.

They were laughed out of the room. "We were told it wasn't possible in the current world environment and would never be possible again," he said. That stuck in his head for the rest of the trip, as they plugged on to New York, London, and Switzerland.

He was surprised by the caution of the investors. "It was all about taking the right risk at the right time," he explains of the strategy pursued by the old-school hedge funds. "It was never about hedging out all your risk, minimizing any risk you take whatsoever, or about generating small linear monthly returns."

They managed to raise only $6 million. Nonetheless, they launched in October 2002. They were up 50% the first year in 2003, off of 16% volatility, defying their skeptics. "We got the credit cycle right, and, of course, then everyone came in and we raised it to $300 million," he says of his fund.

The following year, volatility in big-cap stocks, the lifeblood of his strategy, went to nothing. "We make the big fundamental trend calls across industries; we aren't small-cap men," says Ross. Their firm recorded a 7% decline, all from costs attributable to index options for disaster insurance, which they spent 12% on when the fund was up 50% in 2003. They started getting asset redemptions in 2005 to such a degree that they couldn't invest. If hedge funds cannot lock up their funds for specified periods, they cannot take extended bets. "We gave our last $65 million back at the end of July, after writing in June in our monthly report that the best way to make money was to double up on the [Nikkei 225°] index and concentrate on the best long ideas." He adds that they did just that with their own money left in the fund in August and were up 30% for the month. "We took on capital that didn't share our own risk outlook, so other limited partners that did were suffering as a consequence; returning capital was the right thing to do."

Ross is philosophical about his experience as an independent hedge fund manager. "The hedge fund business has gone from a get-rich business to a stay-rich business," he observes. "Hedge funds have become hedged funds, with increased layers of fiduciary responsibility that have changed the relationship between risk and return." Benchmarking has promoted mediocrity as well, he notes.

Investor Implications

Foreign hedge funds are proliferating in Japan. To be sure, the country offers enticing opportunities. High rates of return have boosted fund performance in recent years. Because securities prices in Japan often react much differently to similar stimuli, such as inflationary fears, than overseas markets, the country offers global funds a unique diversification opportunity. Tokyo markets enjoy deep liquidity, and trading costs are often relatively low. In short, the country offers hedge funds ample choice in pursuing trading strategies designed to capitalize on the growth of the heavily populated Asian region.

°© Nihon Keizai Shimbun, Inc.

Nonetheless, the industry is suffering from growing pains. Barriers to setting up a fund can be onerous. Raising capital locally from high-net-worth individuals, a traditional financing source, can pose a challenge for foreign hedge funds. Meanwhile, institutional investors are demanding increasingly high levels of risk management and relatively quick access to their funds, which boosts the costs and limits the flexibility of hedge funds. The rapid growth of the industry is also squeezing the talent pool of experienced, talented managers available to oversee the flow of money into the country. *Caveat emptor* is the rule for investors considering hedge fund investments in Japan.

References

"From his office in an old villa ...." Interview conducted by the author on 10 November 2005.

"... was Big Project N, a Japanese fund launched ...." *Nikkei Net Interactive.* The Nihon Keizai Shimbun, Inc. "Trusts That Lost Out in IT Bubble Returning," and graphic called "Signs of Recovery," 7 November 2005.

"Whereas Asian equities make up 15% of global capitalization ...." *Key Trends in Asian Hedge Funds 2004.* See www.eurekahedge.com, p. 3.

"More than 150 Asian hedge funds were launched in 2004 ...." This and following four sentences are from an interview conducted by the author in November 2005.

"With the stock market rally in Japan ...." Interview conducted by the author on 4 July 2005.

"Almost 60% of such investors ...." Russell Investment Group, *The 2005-2006 Russell Survey on Alternative Investing,* p. 72.

"This thinking dates back to ...." Interview conducted by the author on 4 December 2005.

"Japanese markets may behave much differently ...." Interview conducted by the author on 29 November 2005.

"We used to call it ...." Interview conducted by the author on 5 July 2005. At the time of printing, Gareth Phillips had left Triloka Capital Management.

"Indeed, the glowing reputation of the city ...." Wurtzburg, C. E. *Raffles of the Eastern Isles.* Edited by Clifford Witting. Oxford University Press: 1990. See esp. p. 606.

"I think Singapore wants to play ...." This statement and following quotes are from an interview conducted by the author on 21 October 2005.

"In the 2005 budget ...." Eurekahedge. *Key Trends in Asian Hedge Funds 2004.* See www.eurekahedge.com, p. 4.

"Tudor, Citadel, Ramius ...." Interview with Rajeev Baddepudi conducted by the author in November 2005.

"I have always been fortunate ...." Interview conducted by the author on 28 February 2006.

"When the clanging of the pile drivers ...." This statement and following quotes are from an interview conducted by the author on 7 November 2005.

"His position had improved to no. 3 ...." His fund was ranked no. 3 among actively managed funds in a survey published 12 April 2000 by *Kabushiki Shimbun.*

4

THE FUTURE OF JAPANESE MANAGEMENT

Private Equity Firms Lead Japanese Restructuring Efforts

A fierce typhoon struck the Izu Peninsula, to the southwest of Tokyo, at night during late August 2005. Torrential rain fell on the lush cedar forests that blanket the mountains in the region, while towering waves crashed along the shoreline. Airlines cancelled flights, and passenger ferry service between Tokyo and the Izu Islands was also suspended. The major highway leading to Hakone, a resort town nestled deep in the mountains, was closed for 3 days.

Since the days of the shoguns, the wealthy of Tokyo have flocked to Hakone. Located on the shores of Lake Ashi, the town hosted the feudal lord processions that passed through along the Tokaido Road on their way to Edo. Some of the inns that then catered to both nobility and the imperial family continue to host visitors today. Local hot springs have drawn tourists from time immemorial, while Hiroshige both carved the local views of Mt. Fuji into his *ukiyoe* blocks and helped shape the artistic sensibilities of the nation. From the Meiji Period on, Westerners fled to the area to escape the oppressive heat in the capital city, and embassies built summer residences around the lake. During the bubble period of the late 1980s, luxurious mountain retreats multiplied like *shiitake* mushrooms among the pines.

The morning following Typhoon Mawar, thousands of visitors headed to Hakone from Tokyo were at risk of being stranded in their cars for hours on flooded roads. Take Hashimoto, manager of the first infrastructure fund in Japan—Japan Infrastructure Group (JIG)—hurried to the scene.

JIG had bought a toll road in the area for ¥1.2 billion in November 2003. Having heard reports of the typhoon, he worried about any human cost as well as damage to his highway. When he arrived at the entrance gate, he was relieved to find that the road was open and no one had been hurt on it. It ran along the top of a mountain range and had escaped the flooding that blocked traffic in the low-lying valleys and on the coast. Route 1, a major highway that ran alongside JIG's turnpike, was shut.

Hashimoto and five of his staff then jumped into action. They brought signs to the turn-off to the toll road, telling stalled drivers on the clogged highway that there was an alternative route. They even banged on car windows and gave people directions. About 500 cars followed their suggestion and turned off the highway, heading to the turnpike on the ridge.

Hashimoto and the workers on his toll road were inspired. They were not just collecting coins from drivers. "We have a greater dream—to change Japan itself, not just to run a toll road," he enthuses.

Gone are the heady days when toll road operators could count on steadily rising traffic as Japan's population increased. Car traffic has fallen to half of peak levels 15 years ago on the turnpike. Payrolls steadily increased under the previous operator, and by the time JIG had acquired the strip of asphalt, many bored employees were just killing time, trying to look busy. Hashimoto started letting people go and eventually cut personnel costs by more than 50%.

Hashimoto trained and motivated the workers who remained, telling them that this highway was a pilot case. If they were successful there, they could go on to head Japan Highway Corporation, he encouraged. JIG was the only specialized private toll road operator in the country. Most private toll roads are owned and run by big corporations that regard them as noncore businesses and usually ignore them.

Hakone Turnpike, run by Tokyu Corp., one of the country's largest railroad conglomerates, was in a similar neglected state in 2003. From the time the firm was established more than 80 years ago, it had acquired as much land as possible along its trunk lines. Because the railway business is regulated in Japan, its return is relatively low. Tokyu looked to make money by developing real estate along its train tracks for both residential and commercial use.

Keita Goto, Tokyu's ambitious founder, also dreamed of building a highway from Tokyo to Hakone. However, when he initially applied for a license for its construction, the government refused to issue one. At the time, just following World War II, the government was planning to create a highway corporation to build a network of expressways. Because the main part of the Tokyo-Hakone road that Goto was envisioning was along a planned major thoroughfare from Tokyo to Osaka, the government was not about to award a license for the whole length of his road. However, Goto did eventually receive permission to build part of his planned highway, the Hakone Turnpike, which did not interfere with the government's own highway project.

Tokyu jumped at the chance. The company was in a long-running battle with Seibu to develop the resort town, and Tokyu managers thought the road would give them the necessary leverage to embark on huge construction projects. After the bubble burst in the early 1990s, Tokyu abandoned its grandiose schemes, and the road led to nowhere in its plans.

Hashimoto was familiar with the turnpike, having taken it for 25 years to avoid congestion on other highways. With sharp curves and sweeping vistas, it was fun to drive. He had grand plans for it and initially looked into staging a Grand Prix auto race there. After some research, however, he was surprised to find that the typical user of the road was not a young sports car driver out for a weekend whirl with his date, but a strictly speed limit–obeying retiree accompanied by his wife. Such drivers were not enamored with checkered flags and thunderous eight-cylinder engines. He realized that if race cars zoomed through the mountains, in the following days, his road would be probably be deserted.

Considering potential attractions for elderly roadsters, he decided that they would probably appreciate a place where they could relax and enjoy views of the surrounding mountains and forests. The turnpike already had a restaurant, but it catered to traffic of a different era—tour buses, which disgorged ravenous hordes of people for short stops. They would eat quickly, buy some knick-knacks or sweets from piles stacked in a gift shop, and leave. However, few buses came now. Most visitors drove their own cars, so the kitchen rarely ran at full capacity.

Hashimoto decided to completely refurbish the restaurant and change its operations. "What I meant to achieve ... was to use the restaurant operation as a leverage to increase traffic," he notes. He spread out the tables and offered snacks at counters along the wall, so the downstairs came to resemble a food court. However, the centerpiece of newly named Turnpike Lounge was the second floor, which came to resemble a coffee shop in an airy downtown hotel lobby. Carpeting and comfortable chairs were installed, with low tables for drinks. He envisioned a clubby, exclusive atmosphere—a destination for people using the road, not a pit stop. A glass wall faced the west and the long, graceful slopes of Mt. Fuji, which towered in the distance. Even stalls in the upstairs bathrooms boasted spectacular views.

The Turnpike Lounge charged ¥600 for admission to the second floor when it opened in 2005, with free coffee available to guests and discounts to people who used the toll road. To his immense satisfaction, when he sat in the lounge for a day, he saw that most visitors were couples around age 60, and they stayed for at least 30 minutes. Drivers flocked to the lounge in the fall to view the bright colorful seasonal foliage. "November is a big, big month," Hashimoto notes.

Before JIG took over the turnpike, it was unprofitable for a number of years. Within 2 years of the purchase, however, the turnpike recorded a satisfactory operating profit margin, in double digits, despite a further decline in revenues. Hashimoto did not expect immediate growth in revenues—but he recorded profits, despite boosting spending on TV and radio advertising, upgrading the toll road's website, and increasing signage giving directions to the highway. He expects to boost revenues with other means this year, such as selling the rights to name the road.

He finds that few Japanese understand what he does. He thinks that even his colleagues at Macquarie, an Australian specialist investment firm and the road's co-investor, weren't sure that such deals could work in Japan. "I was a test case," he notes. He started with a relatively small investment when compared to the firm's other toll road investments worldwide. With Hashimoto pioneering the fund's efforts in Japan, he had his three children, the youngest only 8, sitting on the side of the turnpike, counting cars 2 years before the deal. The financing of the purchase of the toll road also broke new ground. The Bank of Tokyo-Mitsubishi, Sumitomo Trust and Banking Co. Ltd., and the Development Bank of Japan awarded his fund a nonrecourse loan, the first such financing for a toll road in Japan.

With a staff of seven now, he can give his kids a break. JIG under Hashimoto is exploring other old infrastructure facilities to purchase. He is looking at other toll roads, as well as railways, airlines, trams, and monorails—older and less economically efficient facilities, with strong cash flows, that can be run better.

Private equity deals are reshaping the face of corporate Japan. Foreign buyout firms are credited with introducing strategic purchases to the country. Much of the increase in buyouts is stemming not from a rising number of firms struggling to meet their obligations, but rather increased confidence among corporate managers. More have decided they are better able to run their firms if they sell off noncore operations and focus their attention on their primary businesses.

The number of purchases by private equity firms has increased steadily from the late 1990s, according to Thompson Financial. Such firms acquired only 30 companies in 1999. In 2004, they bought out more than 130 firms doing deals worth $7.4 billion. The number of funds has risen steadily as well. In 1997, there was only one private equity group in Japan—Advantage Partners, LLP. By July 2005, 92 more new private equity funds had been raised in Japan. Even with the surge in growth, many believe that there is considerable room for further gains. In the United States, $63 is raised in private equity funds for every $1,000 of gross domestic product. Funds in the United Kingdom are even more active; they raise $71 for every $1,000 of GDP. In a similar comparison, Japanese funds have tapped only $3. Even if the Japanese funds are relatively restrained in their activity compared to the wheelers and dealers overseas, there is clearly ample room to grow—by the same measure, private equity penetration in Japan also lags France, Germany, Taiwan, and South Korea.

A huge potential market also exists for investors in such funds; just 14% of Japanese institutional investors allocated funds to private equity firms in 2004, according to a survey by Russell International

Group. Interest is rising rapidly in such funds, however; allocations more than doubled from the previous year in 2005, from ¥43 billion to almost ¥100 billion. Private equity can be an amazingly profitable business, with managers of funds doubling or tripling their money in a few short years in the case of successful turnarounds. Japanese financial institutions, hungry for yield, are likely to continue to pour money into private equity. Respondents to the Russell survey, based on an admittedly small sample size, expected to boost the share of private equity in 2007 to 4.5%, up from the 2.4% targeted in 2005.

The tremendous impact these funds are having on the culture of Japanese capitalism far outweighs their size. Of course, the landmark deals such as the Ripplewood purchases of Long-Term Credit Bank of Japan and Japan Telecom grabbed headlines in the financial press for weeks. However, their influence is felt far beyond either the banking or telecommunications sectors alone. Private equity firms are providing a mechanism for pricing assets where none existed a decade ago, accelerating the restructuring of the entire corporate sector. For example, Seibu Railway was delisted from the Tokyo Stock Exchange in December 2004 after it was discovered that the firm had under-reported shares held by top shareholders. Yoshiaki Tsutsumi, reported to be the world's richest man by *Forbes* in 1990 with a reputed wealth of $16 billion, apparently exerted effective control over the railway conglomerate by owning a large stake in Kokudo, its parent firm. He eventually received a suspended prison term for insider trading and falsifying documents. The former president of Seibu Railway, Terumasa Koyanagi, killed himself in February 2005 after being grilled by investigators about his role in the scandal.

With its shares no longer actively traded, Seibu Railway stockholders could no longer easily evaluate the value of their holdings. However, reorganization progressed as the railway group was approached by a number of groups interested in the properties and assets of the firm. M&A Consulting, headed by Yoshiaki Murakami,

offered to buy Seibu Railway in February 2005. When shareholders
turned him down, Goldman Sachs put an offer on a table. Finally, in
November, Cerberus Group and Nikko Principal Investment
announced an offer worth about $1.4 billion for control of a new
holding company, Seibu Group Holdings.

In this way, private equity groups have helped break apart fossilized industries, enabling firms to unload nonperforming assets and
shift investments into more profitable areas. They are infusing a new
dynamism and energy to previously moribund companies that were
shackled by debt and saddled with loss-making subsidiaries. In addition, well-run firms can easily shed divisions that are profitable but
unrelated to their core business, to the funds, further streamlining
industries. Despite their leading role in the revitalization of Japan,
private equity firms were unheard of 10 years ago. In fact, there was
only one in the entire country, Advantage Partners, and it was largely
quiet until the government accelerated deregulation of the financial
sector in the mid-1990s.

The deregulation of financial holding companies was just what
Advantage Partners founder Richard Folsom, and his partner,
Taisuke Sasanuma, were waiting for. As clean-cut, good-looking, and
mild-mannered as a sheriff in a 1950s Hollywood Western, Folsom
downplayed his firm's striking success in a meeting in November
2005. He frankly discussed the nuts and bolts of recent deals, display-
ing his long-time interest in the mechanics of building successful
companies.

Folsom had first come to Japan as a Mormon missionary in 1980
and spent 2 years on the northern island of Hokkaido. After majoring
in Japanese and economics in college, he looked for a job that would
take him back to the country. Bain and Company hired him and
brought him to Tokyo in 1985. There he met Sasanuma, a graduate of
Keio University who had previously worked at Sekisui Chemical

Corp. While at Bain, they met with the managers at Bain Capital, one of the most successful private equity groups in the U.S.

"Their approach was actually very new back then," he says. "In the mid- to late 1980s, buyouts were basically done by bankers and investment bankers, focusing on the financial side, balance sheet restructuring and divesture, and what not." Bain created deal structures but also strove to improve operational profitability.

"We saw that and thought that was a great idea," he adds. In the early 1990s, they started thinking that they could do private equity in Japan as well.

After graduating from Wharton Business School, Folsom returned to Tokyo. Although it was still too early to start a fund, he and Sasanuma wanted to get one step closer to running their own private equity firm. They started several venture capital businesses—a value-added tax-reclaim service for large corporations as well as a specialized insurance brokerage business.

Finally, in 1996, the announcement that they were waiting for occurred. The government said it was planning to repeal the law banning financial holding companies from holding majority shares in a company. "That got us in the business," Folsom observes. They raised their first private equity fund the following year.

"In general, we look for opportunities where we see companies with some basic strength," explains Folsom. "Ideal" means something that gives a firm a competitive advantage but, under current management or constraints, is not fully utilized.

Daiei was a classic example. With their loyal customer base and convenient store locations, Daiei experienced roaring success through the 1970s and '80s. "It was a pioneer in the retail business," Folsom recounts. Known as *shufu no tomo* (translated as "friend of the housewife"), Daiei was her one-stop store that satisfied all her shopping needs. Daiei successfully led the move away from small vegetable, meat, and fish stores to a new industry format: consolidated, large supermarkets. Isao Nakauchi, the firm's founder, closely held the company for decades.

However, like so many other firms during the heady days of easy money of the late 1980s, it spread itself into unrelated businesses, such as theme parks, golf courses, hotel resorts, and even a baseball team. That left Daiei's core business—grocers and supermarkets—uncared for and not properly managed, Folsom observes.

Meanwhile, with the burst of the bubble, Daiei's real estate investments collapsed in value. Burdened with heavy debts, the firm's balance sheet became precarious, and they were forced to restructure with the involvement of the Industrial Revitalization Corporation of Japan (IRCJ). All the while, Daiei was hemorrhaging cash—the firm announced in February 2005 that it expected to lose a staggering ¥510 billion in the fiscal period ending that month.

"They [the IRCJ] did a lot of initial heavy lifting to get the balance sheet back in shape," Folsom says. After negotiations, Daiei's banks agreed to forgive about half of Daiei's ¥3 trillion. Then the public corporation sold off Daiei's noncore assets, such as the baseball team and theme parks, paid off more debt, converted some to equity, and received even more debt forgiveness. That combination brought total obligations down to about ¥600 billion. Daiei started looking "much more attractive," Folsom notes. IRCJ selected Advantage Partners and the trading firm Marubeni Corp. to turn around the struggling firm in March 2005. Advantage Partners invested ¥43.4 billion for a 23.4% share, Marubeni added ¥18.6 billion to raise its stake to 10.9%, and the IRCJ held a one-third share as well. Daiei dropped its few remaining noncore assets, going through a divestment process, after Folsom's fund bought the firm.

Assessing the value of a retail or manufacturing firm is in some ways easier than coming to grips with a financial firm, Folsom notes. Bad debts, which can be highly opaque, are not the issue—debt obligations are. "You can make an informed decision on how much debt obligation you can afford to pay based on your understanding of their operating conditions—the cash flow," he says, adding that is just basic due diligence.

Folsom notes that the core businesses of Daiei, which included discount retailers, department stores, ¥100 stores, and the general merchandise Daiei stores themselves, remained strong. He initially focused on the 250 Daiei brand-name stores, which were basic grocery supermarkets. Shoppers could also buy apparel, home appliances, and household goods—many of which were developed and made specifically for Daiei—at booths in the stores. One of his fund's first steps was to bring in outside tenants, who could offer more sophisticated category-killer type products for these spaces.

Newly hired COO Yasuyuki Higuchi also tackled distribution problems. Previously CEO with Hewlett-Packard in Japan and before that with Compaq, he oversaw the merger between these two companies and so had experience restructuring large corporations. To be sure, he saw much that he liked with Daiei distribution methods. Daiei had previously broken new ground in Japan, implementing a completely centralized distribution system—all merchandise passed through the main center before being shipped to each store. However, such a system, which increased overall efficiency, was a drawback for fresh produce. Fruits and vegetables lost about a day in transit, and shoppers were not impressed with the results.

"You walk into a grocery store in Japan, and the first thing you go through is the produce section," points out Folsom. Without crispy heads of lettuce, hard and juicy apples, and firm, sweet tomatoes, Daiei would lose extremely picky housewives to the competition. By September first, only 3 months after taking charge, Higuchi announced a Freshness Declaration, promising to provide more locally grown fruits and vegetables.

Following the takeover, Higuchi's group also decided to close 54 out of 263 core stores, tightening the firm's network to focus on the urban belt stretching from Tokyo to Osaka. Stores in northern and western Honshu and on Shikoku Island were spun off. Even if the more distant stores were profitable, they were a drain on the firm's distribution system, Folsom notes. Meanwhile, the firm is planning to roll out 100 new stores over the next 3 years, and it is sprucing up and renovating existing stores as well.

Folsom and his team realized that the Daiei staff needed to be on board with the changes for them to work. "One of the things this company needed was to set a very clear vision and communicate that internally to employees," Folsom says, noting that Daiei employed more than 50,000 people, including part-timers. To guide the troops, they brought in Fumiko Hayashi, previously head of BMW Tokyo, as CEO. An iconic businesswoman in Japan, Hayashi is one of the few who has broken through to the executive suites. She was ranked among the 10 most powerful business women in the world in *Fortune*'s 2005 survey, and Folsom enthuses that she is "very energetic, a very powerful motivator."

With Hayashi's leadership and communication skills, and Higuchi's restructuring and operational expertise, the new top leadership is working well together, Folsom notes. In addition, Daiei seems to have solved the always nettlesome issue of corporate board independence in Japan, leading to improved corporate governance. Fully half of the eight-member managing board is independent, with a partner from Advantage Partners and a representative of Marubeni serving terms currently with two officials from the IRCJ. In addition to Hayashi and Higuchi, two other Daiei managers were promoted to serve on the board as insiders.

Expectations are running high that Folsom and his team will be able to turn around the previously ailing grocer. "A lot of things have happened that need to translate into results," he cautions, but adds that the flurry of announcements of changes at Daiei has led the market to look ahead to improved performance. At the time of our interview, the share price of the firm had tripled from the level at which they made their investment. Advantage Partners was not in a position to sell yet; IRCJ has options to exit first, and the private equity group still had obligations to refinance and pay Daiei's debt. However, their timeframe is longer. "Generally, it takes 3 or 4 years to make the restructuring, to lead to momentum to impact earnings," Folsom says. Still, things are looking good for their investment.

Folsom's experience points to Japanese employees adapting to the brave new world of corporate restructuring as well. Private equity deals were unheard of 10 years ago and, even today, the word *layoff* rarely is seen in newspaper headlines, but Japanese workers appear to be acknowledging the need for changes in workforce practices.

For example, Folsom's group bought two companies, Shinnihon Salt and Ako Kaisui, from Asahi Kasei in November 2003. Employees of the parent company were seconded to the subsidiary Shinnihon Salt, so they had to resign from the parent company to join the now-severed firm to continue to work there.

"Over a 2½-day period, we met with 15 groups of dozens of employees at a time," remembers Folsom. He and his team spent 40 minutes with each group, just sitting around a table explaining the situation, trying to convince them to resign and join the new company. Asahi Kasei held out jobs for all who wanted to stay with the parent, so they had a choice. However, only a handful of the 300 workers chose not to join the new firm

Some of Advantage Partners' turnaround techniques appear to have distinctive Japanese flavor. Many Japanese firms have long practiced *nemawashi* (consensus building) and *ringi* (circulating drafts for group approval) before implementing major strategic changes. Folsom's group appears to behave similarly: "We spend a lot of time communicating with employees," he says. His group took the famous beverage and soup company Pokka private in late September 2005 with a public tender offer by a management buyout team. Following the buyout, his group gathered the firm's employees in five major meetings in Tokyo, Osaka, and Nagoya. "We talked about the state of the company, [where there was] room for improvement," says Folsom. His management team involves employees in a range of task forces and project teams. These report directly to the board and issue recommendations to implement changes.

Other market watchers are impressed with Advantage Partners' track record. Investment advisor James Fiorillo Ortega points to the initial signs that Richard Folsom's team has succeeded in turning around Daiei as indicative of a new era in Japanese corporate management. Indeed, new practices at Daiei suggest a possible evolution in corporate governance in Japan by increasing board independence but maintaining significant employee input into management decision making.

Arguments that Japanese managers should strive to achieve Western standards in corporate governance fall flat when the recent demise of Enron Corp. is considered. To be sure, warnings regarding the conflict of interests between company owners and management date back to Adam Smith, who stressed that corporate directors, overlooking other people's money, were not likely to be as careful as when watching over their own. However, shareholders in Japan face different problems with regard to stakeholder rights than those in the United States, where corporate board malfeasance often runs along the line of executive enrichment through outrageous payouts, resulting in stock dilution and incentives to falsify financial statements. In Japan, bounty giving is less dramatic, while corporations coddling workers, maintaining money-losing operations, or extending loans to failing firms tends to be more problematic. Increasingly, investors in Japan are expressing a desire for higher priority placed on shareholder interests relative to other stakeholders. The Japanese corporate sector appears to be moving in this direction but remains cognizant that other stakeholders cannot be ignored.

The Japanese market for private equity is in many ways much more attractive than those of other Asian economies. Many of Japan's older, larger firms with established market positions and proven track records are perceived to be good buyout opportunities. Such firms have reliable cash flows, the lifeblood of private equity investment. In addition, smaller family-run firms can be left with nobody at the helm if founders retire without setting up a replacement management team. Such firms facing succession problems are in need of management expertise and provide potential private equity targets as well. Possibly as a result of worries about the vulnerability of local companies, as far back as 1997, the Osaka Chamber of Commerce launched a system to promote match-ups of firms in the city.

In addition, ownership rights in Japan have been stress-tested— despite the public outcry over the tax-free gains reaped by Ripplewood in the Shinsei Bank deal, the government honored the contract. Folsom says that there is a big difference between Japan and China. In Japan, "you can get your money out," he says, while there are no such guarantees on the mainland.

"China is going to be interesting, nobody denies that," he concedes. However, he notes that investing in Chinese private equity is just too risky for mainstream institutional investors. "If you own a company, you own a company in Japan," he pithily declares. In China, you don't know if your ownership is going to be guaranteed, he adds.

Many foreign private equity funds are finding Japan increasingly open to foreign investment. Much has changed since Roy Kuan, a CVC Asia Pacific managing director, moved from Hong Kong to Tokyo in 2003 to hang out his firm's shingle and to pursue management buyout opportunities. CVC is the largest private equity group in Europe. When his firm arrived, deals were generally small, no larger that $80 million or so. In addition, most firms weren't interested in selling unless their backs were against the wall.

In some ways, the business was similar to private equity in South Korea, a market Kuan and his colleagues knew well. CVC Asia Pacific had previously acquired several Korean entities, including Winia-Mando, an air-conditioner maker; CJ CGV, the country's leading movie theater chain; and Magnachip Semiconductor, a nonmemory semiconductor business sold off by Hynix Semiconductor. Kuan's firm, CVC, had to search out such opportunities, which were well-run companies unwanted by their parent firms because they were marginal to their core businesses. Most headline-grabbing deals in Korea involved *chaebol,* such as Daewoo or Halla, which faced liquidations and were forced to sell off divisions. The Korea Asset Management Company, Kamco, acquired distressed loans and converted them into controlling positions in companies, and auctioned off those business stakes to private investors. Often such firms were in dire need of restructuring. CVC Asia Pacific, on the other hand, prefers to acquire more mature firms and participate actively on the board but allow management to run day-to-day operations.

When Kuan arrived in Japan, the ground seemed vaguely familiar. He found the IRCJ also holding auctions, which were well run and transparent, but with rigid rules, in some regards similar to those of Kamco, but vastly different from those privately held sales in the West. Once again, other than those firms on the government auction block, few firms were up for sale.

However, Kuan and his colleagues found that Japanese companies gradually came to develop an interest in selling off noncore businesses. His fund was eventually able to purchase Showa Yakuin Kako, a niche dental products and generic pharmaceuticals maker, from Ajinomoto Co. Ltd., the food and beverage giant. Showa Yakuin was well run but did not fit into the corporate strategy of its parent, he notes.

"Three years ago, [Ajinomoto] would not have thought of divesting in such a subsidiary," he observes.

He notes that pharmaceutical makers, which have been doing quite well, are also focusing on their core businesses. Yamanouchi

Pharmaceutical Co. recently sold off Shaklee Japan KK, a nutritional product company, he says.

Deals are getting bigger as well, he adds. The multibillion-dollar purchases by Ripplewood of Japan Telecom Co. Ltd. and Carlyle Group's buyout of DDI Pocket dwarfed previous buyouts, he points out. Competition is also heating up. Local firms such as Richard Folsom's Advantage Partners, as well as fund spin-offs by financial giants such as Nomura and Mizuho, are looking for deals along with foreign players such as his CVC and Carlyle, he noted. Local players often can go toe to toe against their foreign rivals, he notes, and such foreign firms' sole advantage is often only more experience in overseas markets. Apparently, investor interest is also on the rise. In May 2005, CVC Capital Partners announced the closing of the largest private equity fund ever raised in the Asia Pacific region, totaling almost $2 billion.

Despite some similarities with its East Asian neighbor, the market for Japanese private equity is vastly different in several respects, Kuan stresses. Fewer managers at Japanese firms are motivated to buy out their companies, he notes. Japanese managers still often dominate corporate boards in Japan and can run their companies as they see fit. In such cases, there is little need for them to buy shares to take control of their firm's operations, he notes. In South Korea and elsewhere in Asia, managers are forced to pay more attention to shareholder wishes because they are often beholden to truly independent managing boards.

With the dominance of management of corporate boards in Japan, "even after you own the business, you may not be in as a controlling position as you should be," Kuan notes. Although firing executives is always an option, "it's not something you do lightly." Many funds, such as CVC Asia Pacific, prefer not to actively manage the companies they invest in and indeed do not have the resources to do so.

Kuan doubts that the firms will be traded as fluidly in Japan as in the United States any time soon because the concept of company, or *kaisha*, is so different. In Japanese corporate culture, attachment to employees and subsidiaries is often much stronger than in the West. Still, Kuan sees ample opportunities for his company's fund.

The Japanese government's grudging tolerance of foreign-run private equity funds is reminiscent of the policy pursued by Meiji Era bureaucrats to hire foreign experts to help the nation catch up with its Western counterparts. In both cases, the Japanese government was willing to pay top dollar for foreign expertise, something it deemed necessary to ensure the competitiveness of the nation. During the initial wave of modernization in the second half of the nineteenth century, the government hired hundreds of foreign experts to transfer technology and nation-building skills to the Japanese. Such luminaries as Erwin Baelz, the personal physician of the imperial family and the Meiji Era elites, and Gustave Boissonade, a French jurist who helped draft Japan's civil and criminal code, made contributions as the country made the leap from a feudal society to a modern nation-state. Although some stayed for decades, for many of the *o-yatoi gaikokujin* (translated as "hired foreigners"), the average length of service was 5 years.

Indeed, the government did not intend their positions to be permanent, hoping they would bring their local replacements up to speed quickly. However, the bureaucrats recognized the value of the foreigners' expertise and were willing to pay handsomely for it. In 1874, the national government employed 520 *o-yatoi gaikokujin*. The Ministry of Public Works' payroll for such foreign workers was ¥2.3 million, fully one-third of the annual budget the same year.

Given such a precedent, even the lavish profits made by Ripplewood and other foreign funds in recent years in buyout deals could be considered a bargain. While historical comparisons must be made cautiously, the billions that Ripplewood earned in the Shinsei deal was a very small percentage of the approximately $73 billion budgeted for public works spending for FY04. The country is paying for expertise in one of finance's most profitable fields—one that *New York Times* columnist Ben Stein called "the best business in America—by far—and it is run by very brilliant men and women." Private equity is highly secretive in the United States and dominated by a handful of firms that often have close connections with the highest levels of government. The network of deal makers on Wall Street is exclusive, and entry fees are expensive. However, in a few short years, Japan has made inroads even into this *terra incognita*. Japanese are setting up private equity groups as well; at least one former executive from the IRCJ has already established his own fund.

When the next downturn occurs overseas and U.S. firms find themselves increasingly vulnerable, it would be naïve to think that Japanese private equity funds will ignore opportunities to expand their operations to foreign countries. At that time, foreign investors will be thinking less about opportunities in Japan and more about what opportunities will be left over after well-capitalized, yield-hungry Japanese funds have scoured markets worldwide looking for deals.

Investment Implications

Private equity firms have found Japan to be a lucrative market. Buyout targets, boasting stable market shares and secure cash flows, are plentiful. Ownership rights are stronger than some other Asian markets, notably China. Conversely, private equity firms have been able to revitalize troubled firms by strategically focusing their operations through unloading loss-producing businesses, cutting overhead, and taking other measures. Playing a major role in the restructuring of the corporate sector, they are providing a ready market for often difficult-to-price distressed assets and parts of corporate groups that parent firms no longer want. The presence of private equity representatives on corporate boards often boosts independence and improves governance. The Japanese concept of corporation, with its traditional emphasis on the interests of nonshareholding stakeholders, remains much different from views in other countries, but corporate governance ideals are beginning to edge more toward a greater priority on shareholder rights. With such a shift, shareholder interests are likely to be more jealously guarded, and the equity market will ultimately benefit from such improved oversight.

Even as competition heats up among private equity firms for buyout candidates, the penetration of such funds into Japanese markets remains far below that of many other countries. This suggests ample room for growth in the industry remains, and professional investors can continue to expect outsized returns from well-managed funds. Such funds will likely be discriminating on price and will eschew targets with outsized debt burdens or other liabilities that could bleed cash flows.

References

"A fierce typhoon ...." *Nikkei Net Interactive*. Nihon Keizai Shimbun, Inc. "Typhoon Strikes Chiba, Traffic Disrupted." 26 August 2005.

"Take Hashimoto, manager of the first ...." Interview conducted by the author on 8 November 2005.

"Number of purchases ...." Thompson Financial data provided by Robert Babbish.

"In 1997, there was only ...." Folsom, Richard L. *An Overview of Private Equity in Japan*. Advantage Partners, LLP. April 2006. See esp. p. 6.

"In the United States, $63 is raised in private equity funds ...." Folsom, Richard L. An Overview of Private Equity in Japan. Advantage Partners, LLP. April 2006. See esp. p. 6.

"There is also a huge potential market ...." Russell Investment Group. *The 2005-2006 Russell Survey on Alternative Investing*. See esp. p. 67.

"For example, Seibu Railways ...." *Nikkei Net Interactive*, Nihon Keizai Shimbun Inc. "Chronology of Events Involving Seibu Railway Ownership Fraud." 3 March 2005.

"Yoshiaki Tsutsumi, reported to be the richest ...." *International Herald Tribune*. "Tsutsumis Plan Bid for Seibu Railway." 31 October 1990.

Nikkei Net Interactive. Nihon Keizai Shimbun, Inc. "Reform of the Seibu Group Enters Critical Phase." 13 January 2005.

"He eventually received a suspended ...." *International Herald Tribune*. "Tsutsumis Plan Bid for Seibu Railway." 31 October 1990.

"The former president of Seibu ...." *Nikkei Net Interactive*. Nihon Keizai Shimbun, Inc. "Ex-Seibu Railway President Koyanagi Hangs Himself." 19 February 2005.

"M&A Consulting, headed by ...." *Nikkei Net Interactive*. Nihon Keizai Shimbun, Inc. "Seibu Group Rejecting Sharehold Activist's Buyout Plan." 5 February 2005.

"When shareholders turned him down ...." *Nikkei Net Interactive*. Nihon Keizai Shimbun, Inc. "Morgan Stanley to Join Seibu Bids." 9 May 2005.

"Finally, in November ...." Morse, Andrew. "Seibu Battle Set to End with $1.4 Billion Deal." *The Wall Street Journal*. 10 November 2005. p. 3.

"The deregulation of financial holding companies ...." This statement and following quotes are from an interview conducted by the author on 9 November 2005.

"The firm was still hemoraging money." *Nikkei Net Interactive*, Nihon Keizai Shimbun, Inc. "Daiei projects 510 billion yen net loss." 7 February 2005.

"Investment advisor James Fiorillo Ortega points ...." Interview conducted by the author on 3 July 2005.

"To be sure, warnings regarding the conflict of interests ...." Smith, Adam. *Wealth of Nations*. Penguin Classics edition. Penguin, 1999. See esp. vol. 2, p. 330, 331.

"As far back as 1997 ...." Economic Planning Agency. *Economic Survey of Japan (1996–1997)*. p. 132, footnote 17.

"Much has changed ...." Interview conducted by the author in December 2005.

"Such luminaries as ...." Jones, H. J. *Live Machines, Hired Foreigners, and Meiji Japan*. Vancouver: University of British Columbia Press, 1980. See esp. p. 18, 104.

"While some stayed for decades ...." Jones, H. J. *Live Machines, Hired Foreigners, and Meiji Japan*. Vancouver: University of British Columbia Press, 1980. See e. p. 70.

"In 1874, the national government employed...." The Dentsu Advertising Museum website, www.dentsu.com/MUSEUM/meiji/index1.html and Jones, H. J. *Live Machines, Hired Foreigners, and Meiji Japan*. Vancouver: University of British Columbia Press, 1980. See esp. p. 13.

"While historical comparisons must be made..." Ministry of Finance, *Outline of the FY2004 Budget*, http://www.mof.go.jp/english/budget/brief/2004/2004d_01.htm.

"... the best business in America ...." Stein, Ben, "Three Cheers (and a Big Question) for Yale." *The New York Times*. 23 October 2005.

"Japanese themselves are setting up" *Nikkei Net Interactive*, Nihon Keizai Shimbun, Inc. "Ex-IRCJ Official Sets up Regional Corporate Rehab Fund." 7 December 2005.

5

BARBARIANS AT THE *Genkan**

Japan's Fledgling M&A Market Yet to Internationalize

Steven Thomas, co-head of mergers and acquisitions (M&A) at UBS in Tokyo, was surprised by the request from his human resources department in spring 2005. UBS had stood at, or very near, the top of Thomson Financial's league tables for cross-border M&A activity in Japan for much of the last 5 years.

Precious little could catch this unflappable English banker off guard after the turmoil of Asian crises of the late 1990s. With graying brown temples and wearing a dark, tailored suit in an expansive wood-paneled conference room, he looks every inch the investment bank veteran, having earned his stripes in the swift, large-scale restructuring of the South Korean economy and the flurry of inward

Genkan is translated as the entry-way to a Japanese house.

107

investment into troubled Japanese companies several years earlier. His descriptions of the recent turf battles in Japanese corporate finance have the refined air of a British infantry captain downplaying his experiences in the trenches.

The HR request for a lecture to its own department on his hitherto esoteric business—the buying and selling of corporations—raised his eyebrows. Why the new interest? When people in Tokyo found out he was an investment banker, usually they asked him for stock picks, not explanations of corporate tender offers and legal defenses. Japanese M&A activity had yet to recover to 1999 levels in dollar terms, when about 1,200 deals, totaling approximately $199 billion, had been chalked up, according Thomson Financial. Indeed, many foreign investment bankers were becoming frustrated as the promise of money-making opportunities in M&A in the new millennium had not yet been fulfilled. However, Thomas and other bankers were about to find their arcane calling thrust into media circus spotlights.

It turned out that the human resources department members were being bombarded by questions from their friends, who were watching the takeover battle between Livedoor Co., Ltd., and Fuji Television Network, Inc., on the morning news shows. "What is going on?" their friends wanted to know.

The saga between Livedoor and Fuji TV was probably the highest-profile hostile takeover attempt ever to occur in Japan. Involving a maverick businessman challenging a media giant, the spectacle of a brash outsider taking on the system had the public enthralled. Fuji TV had launched a tender offer for Nippon Broadcasting System, Inc., in January with the goal of acquiring half of the outstanding shares of the radio broadcaster by early March. However, Livedoor, an Internet portal company owned by Takafumi Horie, stunned the business community by suddenly announcing that it had acquired 35% of the outstanding shares of Nippon Broadcasting and was aiming for a majority stake as well. Livedoor had acquired much of these shares in off-hour trading financed by issuing convertible bonds to

Lehman Brothers. Such a move allowed the firm to skate past a Securities and Exchange Law banning firms from acquiring a controlling third or larger stake in a firm by any means other than a takeover bid.

Nippon Broadcasting defiantly tried to block Livedoor's bid by issuing share warrants to Fuji TV convertible into 47.2 million shares, more than Nippon Broadcasting's outstanding share amount of 32.8 million. That would have drastically reduced Livedoor's percentage stake in the radio broadcaster. However, Livedoor asked the Tokyo District Court to bar the share warrant issuance, and the court complied, issuing a preliminary injunction. Nippon Broadcasting appealed to both the Tokyo district and high courts but lost both times.

Livedoor and Fuji TV finally worked out a deal in May under which the television firm acquired a majority stake in the radio broadcaster, and the Internet firm entered an alliance with Fuji TV. Livedoor earned ¥150 billion on a ¥100 billion investment, or a cool $1.3 billion, according to Nihon Keizai Shimbun, Inc.

"It happened very suddenly," remembers Thomas. From the day Horie announced his hostile takeover attempt, the TV morning news shows carried all the twists and turns of the players in the complex corporate drama. "All this was discussed in the finest detail and, happily, correct detail," Thomas remembers.

Unhappily for Horie, rough times were ahead. The iconoclast was still riding high in September. He filed his candidacy for a Diet seat that month, saying, "Why am I running in the election? Because there is a chance I could become prime minister," reported the Nihon Keizai Shimbun, Inc. He lost the vote count. A few months later, rumors regarding his firm sparked panic selling, roiling the Tokyo Stock Exchange and forcing it to halt trading. On January 23, 2006, he was arrested on suspicion of disclosing false information regarding his company's activities. His firm was delisted about 3 months later.

A year after his bid for Nippon Broadcasting, Livedoor's leader languished in a detention house. However, his impact on decisions in corporate boardrooms and executives offices should not be overlooked. Horie's unorthodox takeover attempt of Nippon Broadcasting was a wakeup call to corporate managers across the nation.

"That [Livedoor's bid] created a new understanding," Thomas notes, adding that it put fear into a huge number of Japanese executives, who thought, "Well, maybe I'm next." Overnight, everybody in town was talking about M&A deals.

This was unprecedented. In the 1990s, many investment bankers thought that Japanese companies would start opening up for sale as they struggled in the depressed economy. However, initially that did not happen. Although Thomas was living in Tokyo, he spent much of the mid-1990s working either back in London or in South Korea. "The rest of Asia totally opened up for M&A in what is, in a way, the most unfortunate circumstances, which is absolute distress and no alternatives." He was kept busy elsewhere; the Japanese market was slow.

Finally, late in the decade, the Financial Services Agency pushed local banks to the wall, and they started cutting support to their borrowers. The Industrial Bank of Japan notified Nissan Motor Co., Ltd. that it was unwilling to support the company any longer, and eventually the automaker was acquired by Renault SA group. In addition, second-tier insurance companies were getting into trouble because of their guaranteed returns saving style contracts. That created an opening for foreign firms, which quickly moved in. AXA Life Insurance Co. bought Nippon Life Insurance Co. in 1999, while later GE acquired Toho Mutual Life Insurance Co. Prudential Insurance Co. purchased Kyoei Life Insurance Co. as well.

M&A deals in Japan were traditionally organized by the main banks or regulators, or were considered something very shady and were conducted by corporate raiders. Then in 1999, Thomas worked on an unsolicited bid by the U.K.'s Cable & Wireless for International Digital Communications (IDC). IDC shareholders accepted Cable & Wireless's bid, which was more generous than a competing offer by Nippon Telegraph and Communications Corp. "Suddenly M&A was on the map," he notes. "It was no longer dirty and dangerous, but it was not mainstream."

Japanese firms have recovered slowly over the past 5 years. In addition to a long period of organic restructuring, they have benefited from better global conditions—China has been a big boost, says Thomas. "Against the original theory that distress would create M&A opportunities, a healthy environment has actually caused Japanese companies to have the confidence in some cases to get real and start to do M&A," he notes.

Firms have looked overseas for partners, but they also now have the confidence to identify what is core and noncore among their businesses and to sell off their nonessential lines. "We are starting to see organized auctions," Thomas notes. Firms are hiring banks, distributing confidential information memoranda, and going through a business process. Before, firms were much shyer when approaching potential buyers.

"Now, it's 'Here's the book, here's the bidding schedule. Let's get on with it,'" Thomas says. "Japan has normalized," he sums up. "It has not internationalized; it is more of a normal country regarding M&A."

Foreigners have had a major impact on the M&A market. In particular, private equity firms have introduced the model of strategic purchases. "In the early '90s, the business model of a fund buying a weak company, improving it, and selling it off did not exist," Thomas notes. Leveraged buyout funds are now active in Japan and "very much accepted," he notes.

Ripplewood's takeover of Long-Term Credit Bank of Japan was the highest profile of any private equity fund purchase. Assured of the willingness of the government to buy back any of the bank's loans that had fallen in value by 20% or more within 3 years, Ripplewood Holdings, LLC, paid about $1.2 billion for the bank in 2000. It sold 35% of the bank's total shares for $2.4 billion in 2004. This caused a backlash among the public because the group's investors paid no

Japanese tax on their earnings from the deal. "They were called vulture funds and were seriously misunderstood," says Thomas, referring to the private equity groups. "We as bankers were quite nervous to suggest that [Japanese firms] might want to sell to a private equity company," remembers Thomas.

However, perceptions regarding such groups have completely changed, he notes, crediting, in part, the success of the Vodafone deal, which he had advised. Vodafone started buying shares of Japan Telecom in late 2000, eventually taking a controlling stake in September 2001. Because Vodafone was not interested in the fixed-line operations of the Japanese company, it sold that business to Ripplewood in August 2003 for about $2.3 billion. It was the biggest leveraged buyout (LBO) ever in Japan. "From that time on—that deal, plus a lot more private equity activity—[private equity groups] were no longer vulture funds," notes Thomas.

After Ripplewood bought Japan Telecom, it wasn't just firing people and asset stripping, he stresses. As part of newly hired Japan Telecom president Hideki Kurashige's strategy, the firm entered the IT consulting and Internet protocol services. This necessitated aggressive recruitment of midcareer employees, especially systems engineers, *Nikkei Business* reported. When Japan Telecom started hiring people, Ripplewood's approach was increasingly accepted, notes Thomas.

"I think it's the old story—people are afraid of the unknown," says Thomas. LBOs were unheard of in Japan, and the outcome of such deals was uncertain. Following the restructuring of Japan Telecom, Ripplewood sold the firm to broadband operator Softbank Corp. for $3.1 billion. "As they started exiting investments and these businesses were passed on to the next owner, and they were in good shape, the story got out that it's actually a rather healthy process after all," Thomas explains.

He stresses that not only foreigners are running private equity funds. Japanese firms such as M&A Consulting and MKS Partners are also doing deals he notes.

"Every day, every hour" people are discussing deals, Thomas observes. "Everybody is talking M&A. The private equity guys are constantly out there, taking proposals to the bigger companies— 'How about this division? How about that division?' The smaller companies follow the discussion—'Will the entire company be available for sale?' 'Today you are listed on the stock market, how about taking the company private again?' All these conversations are mainstream, as in any normal capitalistic economy."

Prime Minister Koizumi announced in January 2003 that the government would strive to double cumulative foreign direct investment (FDI) in Japan within 5 years. "Foreign direct investment in Japan will bring new technology and innovative management methods, and will also lead to greater employment opportunities," the prime minister told the assembled law-makers.

The government acknowledged that the flow of FDI into Japan was a mere trickle compared with that in other countries. FDI in Japan in 2000 accounted for only a tiny 1% of GDP, compared with 28% in the United States and 32% in the United Kingdom.

Most FDI flows between developed economies consists of M&A activity because capital stock already exists in these countries. Therefore, to boost FDI, the government must facilitate cross-border M&As. Such deals in Japan have hovered between 100 and 200 transactions a year in recent years versus more than 1,300 in the United States in 2005 alone, according to Thomson Financial. In terms of size of deals, the disparity is even more striking—only $4 billion dollars was announced in Japan in 2005, versus more than $157 billion in the United States, still citing Thomson Financial figures.

"We really appreciate the prime minister setting the stake in the soil …. That was music to our ears," says Nicholas Benes, who is governor and chair of the Foreign Direct Investment Committee at the American Chamber of Commerce in Japan (ACCJ). Japan does not need money; what it needs are new business models and methods to boost productivity, he adds.

Japanese companies, often small fish in the global sea, see the sharks circling. Some are becoming more open to mergers with foreign companies because of concerns about size, notes Peter Espig, vice president at Olympus Capital Holdings Asia. Sectors such as chemicals and pharmaceuticals have consolidated tremendously in America and Europe. "If you look at, let's say, the pharmaceutical sector 10 years ago and list the top 10 countries in the world, the landscape would have been much different from now …. At that time, you would have seen Japanese companies on top, or very close," Espig notes. Takeda Pharmaceutical Co., Ltd., Japan's largest drug company, did not even make the *Fortune* Global 500 top 12 ranking in the industry in 2005.

Overseas companies have grown through M&A whereas Japanese firms have not, and now their small size is a dangerous disadvantage in many fields. Pharmaceutical firms must develop new medicines to remain competitive, so research and development expenses are huge—the number of hits and misses are quite big, Espig adds. "That is the driver for increased M&A," he points out.

Indeed, some in the Japanese government worry that many foreign firms dwarf their Japanese competitors. Pfizer Inc.'s total market capitalization was $300 billion in August 2004, whereas Takeda was worth only $40 billion, pointed out the Ministry of Economy, Trade, and Industry in March 2005. Microsoft Corp. was more than six times larger than Canon, Inc., and Wal-Mart Stores, Inc. was eight times larger than Seven Eleven Japan Co., Ltd. Japanese firms are looking and feeling increasingly vulnerable.

Citing a dramatic dissolution of cross-share holdings leading to a rising threat of hostile takeovers, the ministry formed the Corporate Value Study Group in September 2004. Its discussions focused on four basic principles—enhancement of corporate value, equal footing with global standards, no discrimination between foreign and domestic companies, and increased options for shareholders and management. METI and the Ministry of Justice based their report, *The Guidelines for Protection of Corporate Value*, which was released in May 2005, on the findings of this group.

The Guidelines surprised some market watchers. Far from pandering to managers at Japanese firms, some of whom traditionally brooked no interference from shareholders in their business decisions, *The Guidelines* explicitly stipulated that use of defensive measures must meet certain conditions to be deemed "reasonable." To use defense measures, *The Guidelines* said, takeover attempts must threaten corporate value. For example, if the bidder is a green mailer or shareholders do not have enough information to value underpriced offers, the potential for the company to achieve its long-term potential would be lost. Defense measures should also not be excessive—that is, they should not eliminate the shareholders' right to choose between differing plans by boards and bidders. Finally, the decision to adopt defensive measures must be taken in an "independent" manner by the board. *The Guidelines* noted that outside parties, such as financial advisors or lawyers, should be involved in both analysis of the offer and the defensive measures.

Some legal scholars are struck by how much *The Guidelines* resemble U.S. commercial laws pertaining to hostile takeover activity. Columbia Law School professor Curtis J. Milhaupt wrote in the *Columbia Law Review* that "the report represents a major endorsement of Delaware takeover jurisprudence in the formulation of public policy." For example, he notes that the case of Unocal Corp. vs. Mesa Petroleum Co. "authorizes defensive measures in response to a threat to corporate policy and effectiveness, provided the response is proportionate to the threat." This decision resembles the conclusions of *The Guidelines*.

Many market watchers welcomed *The Guidelines* as a step forward in ushering in a new era of deal making, resulting in more streamlined and profitable firms and increased shareholder value.

The ACCJ called the principles of *The Guidelines* "excellent" and pushed for them to become binding in nature. However, the ACCJ warned as well that it was "dangerous to selectively import the complete menu of U.S.-style takeover defenses" without strengthening corporate governance, by having independent outside directors.

The ACCJ is not alone in worrying about the lack of independence of Japanese corporate boards. The biggest problem with Japanese corporate governance is insufficient independent oversight, Marc Goldstein notes. He works for Institutional Shareholder Services, which provides analysis and vote recommendations of shareholder meeting agendas of 2,800 listed firms across Japan to their clients.

"There are too few independent directors," he flatly says.

Many aspects of corporate governance in Japan are governed by the Commercial Code, to a greater degree than in the United States or the United Kingdom, he explains. The Commercial Code has a definition of outside director but no definition of independent director. Even when companies have outside directors, they tend to lack independence because they are from a parent company, a main bank, or from some other business partner, Goldstein observes.

He is not sure whether the answer is government or stock exchange action. "In a lot of countries, it's the stock exchange that takes the lead and comes up with a code of best practice," he observes, pointing to the United Kingdom as an example. "Listed companies have to either agree to comply with each of the recommendations in the code or explain to shareholders why they choose not to comply." The market decides whether to accept those reasons.

"I was on an advisory committee to the Tokyo Stock Exchange. We concluded our work in early 2004. Several of us on the committee, myself included, favored that sort of approach for Japan. It was a nonstarter due to resistance from the business community."

Since then, the Tokyo Exchange has struggled with governance issues. In November 2005, the exchange issued a draft proposal prohibiting listed firms from issuing "gold shares" with special veto rights, although it backed down later, deciding to allow such golden shares as long as shareholder interests would not suffer.

Goldstein argues that the lack of independent oversight and quality of corporate governance will remain long-term problems for foreign investors. The rigid labor market limits possible improvements, he notes. "Lifetime employment is certainly weakening, but it is still considered the ideal, even if companies are honoring it in the breech. At top executive levels, it is still the norm," he adds.

Top managers have typically been with their firm their entire lives, and they don't have much experience in other corporations, he elaborates. That limits their ability to act as outside directors with other companies.

"At the top levels, people do not retire, either," he points out. When someone steps down as CEO, he does not go home and spend time with his grandchildren; he becomes chairman, honorary chairman, or advisor. Such people just hang around, interfering with their successors who are trying to make necessary changes, he complains.

Compensation, historically tied to seniority, is yet another problem. Although that is changing at the margins, most companies still abide by this system, he adds. "The labor market is changing, and people's expectations are changing, but the change is slow."

"I wouldn't expect Japanese boardrooms or Japanese executive suites to mirror in those in the U.K. or U.S. any time over the next decade," he concludes.

Seismic tremors have shaken the foundation of corporate Japan in recent years. While causing no cracks in the edifices of most large firms and leaving management teams largely unscathed, hostile takeover attempts are becoming increasingly frequent attacks on the way managers run their firms. Most skirmishes have been among the

Japanese themselves, belying efforts by both the government and corporate leaders to paint hostile takeovers as a foreign threat.

Hostile takeovers have a negative connotation for many market observers and lack the decorum and predictability so beloved of entrenched management. However, these certainly have their role in the restructuring of Japan. Espig worked on the financing structure of a white-knight rescue proposal of a firm from a hostile takeover by another company; both were Japanese. Hostile takeovers, he acknowledges, sound terrible. "When you think of the concept of a hostile takeover, of somebody buying a company, ripping out all its cash, and selling the assets, it sounds really awful."

Then he mentioned Sotoh Co., Ltd. The second-section firm is a dyer of woolen fabrics. "The company had a market capitalization of $130 million, sitting on $220 million in liquid assets. Then you look at the shareholder breakdown, and the CEO owned less than 1%. Now is that correct?"

Hostile takeover attempts are becoming more frequent in Japan. Even when hostile firms cannot wrestle management of a target firm from their existing board, they have dramatically impacted business policies. In December 2003, Steel Partners launched hostile takeover bids for Sotoh, and Yushiro Chemical Industry Co., a first-section producer of metalworking oil. In response, Sotoh first came up with a management buyout plan and then decided to raise its dividend from ¥13 a share to ¥200, bolstering its share price, After watching the company's share price double, Steel Partners decided to take profits. Yushiro dramatically raised its dividend to raise its share price to fend off the takeover attempt as well.

In the well-publicized UFJ Group-Sumitomo Trust & Banking Co., Ltd. battle, two elephantine banks clumsily bashed heads for months. The dogged persistence of the rejected, unwanted suitor Sumitomo Trust & Banking reflected a loss of decorum rarely seen in the blue-suited, white-shirted world of Japanese banking. The UFJ Group, which Nihon Keizai Shimbun, Inc. noted was struggling to

meet the minimum capital ratio necessary to maintain overseas operations in spring 2004, agreed to sell its trust bank to Sumitomo Trust
& Banking in May. Negotiations between two firms were rough, and
Sumitomo reduced its offered price for UFJ Trust Bank assets as
well, according to the newspaper. On July 14, the UFJ Group rocked
the financial world by backing out of its agreement with Sumitomo
Trust & Banking and announced that it had decided instead to merge
with Mitsubishi Tokyo Financial Group, Inc. UFJ Trust Bank would
be included in the new deal.

Sumitomo Trust & Banking fought for the right to acquire UFJ
Trust Bank in the courts, but to no avail. The Tokyo District Court initially ordered a halt to the merger negotiations between the UFJ and
Mitsubishi Tokyo Financial groups. However, the Tokyo High Court
reversed this decision. Finally, Sumitomo Trust & Banking appealed
to the Supreme Court, which turned down the plea in August. The
lack of a breach-of-contract penalty in the agreement was a pivotal
factor in the decision, according to Nihon Keizai Shimbun, Inc. The
UFJ and Mitsubishi Tokyo Financial groups went on to form Mitsubishi UFJ Financial Group in October. In February 2006, the Tokyo
District Court also dismissed a ¥100 billion damage suit filed by Sumitomo Trust and Banking against the former UFJ Holdings.

Yusuke Nishi is one of a new generation of dealmakers who are
reshaping corporate Japan. Nishi, along with another partner,
founded Steel Partner Japan K.K. in 2001.

Nishi joined Nikko Securities in 1988 after graduating from college. After spending 1 year in Jakarta directing a joint venture
between Nikko Securities and the Salim Group, an Indonesian con-
glomerate, he returned to Tokyo to join Nikko's M&A advisory practice. Business at that time, he remembers, was "very quiet." After the
bubble burst, many Japanese firms were retrenching from their overseas investments. Things started to pick up in 1999, when he moved
to Jardine Fleming, which participated in one of the landmark M&A

cases in the early 2000, the alliance between the German company Boehringer Ingelheim and the Japanese firm SS Pharmaceutical (SSP), which was eventually realized through the first successful unsolicited tender offer for a publicly traded company.

Boehringer Ingelheim owned 10% of SSP and wanted to acquire more shares and develop a closer working relationship. After offering to buy shares at a 30% premium in January 2000, the German firm acquired more than one-third of the firm and eventually took a majority stake.

By slowly buying into firms and negotiating with management, strategic buyers such as Boehringer Ingelheim found that they could overcome the traditional reluctance of cross shareholders toward selling. Initially, such shareholders might have had doubts about the motivations of the purchaser. However, after realizing that they have a valuable strategic buyer, one that is working with management to improve operations, they might gradually change their mind and finally sell their stake.

Shareholder attitudes are changing as well, Nishi notes. Five years ago, pension fund managers were friendly to the companies they owned. Now they have become increasingly neutral, he observes, and some have become proshareholder value. "They have to care about their own fiduciary duty," he notes, and now they tend to evaluate offers on a "case-by-case basis."

Indeed, there are signs that the Pension Fund Association is beginning to flex its muscles. The association has largely taken a hands-off approach to management of companies that it owns. However, because it holds about ¥3 trillion of shares, its potential clout is considerable. The association voted against changes to company charters only 1% of the time in 2004. The following year, as firms tried to implement measures to thwart takeover attempts, the association voted against company charter amendments 30% of the time, Nihon Keizai Shimbun, Inc., reported. Of 154 proposals by firms to increase their authorized stock to bolster the amount of share to block unwanted takeover attempts, the association rejected those by 146 firms.

Economic turbulence, caused by technological change, government deregulation, and trade liberalization, often generates waves of merger and acquisition activity, says Robert Bruner, dean of the Darden Business School at the University of Virginia. "The way to understand M&A is as a mechanism by which companies and industries adjust to new conditions," summarizes Bruner.

A great wave of mergers and acquisitions, marked by large deals and more hostile takeovers than previous restructuring periods, swept the United States from 1981 to 1987, notes Bruner in *Applied Mergers and Acquisitions*. He points to a number of factors causing economic turbulence in the United States during this period.

This decade was marked by tremendous political and economic changes he observes. President Ronald Reagan ushered in an era of less obtrusive government. Oil prices dropped dramatically, triggering bankruptcies and real estate collapses, and straining financial institutions. Advances in personal computing liberated companies from the need for large data-processing facilities, he adds. Meanwhile, Toyota Corp. and other foreign manufacturers were making high-quality products at a lower cost than U.S. firms, putting pressure on margins.

A buoyant stock market, coupled with falling interest rates, led private equity investors, such as Kohlberg Kravis Roberts & Co. (KKR) and Forstmann Little & Co., to scout out companies for leveraged buyouts. William E. Simon, a former Secretary of the Treasury, put such debt-financed takeovers on the map. His firm, Wesray Corp. , purchased Gibson Greeting Cards in 1982 and sold it the following year, making $200 million. Simon himself pocketed $70 million dollars on an initial investment of less than $1 million.

Activist investors, such as Carl Icahn and Saul Steinburg, also demonstrated that old-line manufacturing firms could be turned around and made to perform at a high rate of efficiency, boosting their value, Bruner observes. Their success also brought more attention to the opportunities that merger and acquisition activity presented. Meanwhile, standing behind some of the private equity and hostile investors were Michael Milken and Drexel Burnham Lambert. Junk bonds are less than investment grade and sometimes difficult to place, but this firm developed an ability to analyze these bonds, equity-based securities, and other assets, and find investors who had an appetite for them, notes Bruner. Milken was actively backing private equity and hostile investors to build his book of business.

"Of course, the astonishing growth of high-yield debt financing brought other firms into the market [and] led to increased competition," Bruner noted. "This always happens in capital markets. Extraordinary growth and buoyancy leads to optimism and manic behavior that leads to excess," says Bruner. Milken pleaded guilty to six counts of securities fraud in 1990, served almost 2 years in prison, and handed over more than $1 billion in fines and related payments. The U.S. economy slipped into recession in 1991.

The U.S. in the early 1980s is a useful reference when considering the potential development of the Japanese merger and acquisition market. Certainly, Japanese policymakers, who have painstakingly analyzed U.S. laws pertaining to M&A activity, intend to learn from the U.S. experience. Private equity funds in Tokyo today, as they were in the United States in the 1980s, are the vanguard of corporate restructuring efforts. Meanwhile, signs of Bruner's economic turbulence are everywhere. Financial stress is apparent as banks wrestle with their onerous burden of bad debt. In politics, the "market fundamentalists" are in ascendancy, shaking up the old way of doing things. The government is deregulating many industries. Foreign competition, especially from low-cost Chinese producers, is threatening Japan's grip on some markets. Commodity prices are extremely volatile. Bruner notes in Japan that the turbulence caused by technological change, in the form of the expansion of Internet businesses, is striking. In addition to Livedoor's attempted takeover of Nippon Broadcasting System, Rakuten, Inc., a virtual mall operator, also launched a failed attempt to acquire Tokyo Broadcasting System, Inc., later in 2005.

Although both bids were unsuccessful, that does not suggest that the wave of mergers and acquisitions in Japan has run its course. Hostile transactions are rare, even in the United States. Bruner notes that successful hostile takeovers account for only a tenth of 1% of merger and acquisition activity. "We shouldn't be surprised, therefore, to see relatively small, very small incidence of hostile deals in the Japan, if Japan's experience is to be anything like the United States'."

Some foreigners looking to expand in Japan continue to be frustrated. It remains unclear whether Koizumi will achieve his goal of doubling the cumulative domestic FDI from about ¥6.6 trillion in 2001 to about ¥13.2 trillion by the end of 2006. Inward FDI flows totaled ¥733 billion in 2003 and ¥845 billion in 2004, when the cumulative total reached ¥10.1 trillion, according to a report by the United Nations Conference of Trade and Development. Nonetheless, in March 2006, the government set a new goal of 5% of GDP, or about ¥28 trillion, more than twice the cumulative total in 2004, to be achieved by 2010.

Hurdles to further FDI growth remain. "The tax differential between some European countries, like England, and Japan is quite large," observes Tom O'Sullivan, Chief Operating Officer of Gartmore Investment Japan, Ltd. The top statutory corporate tax rate in Japan is 40.9%, the highest of any OECD country, according to a study by the U.S. Congressional Budget Office. The U.K. tax rate was substantially lower, at 30%. Tax rates are thought to impact capital flows; when tax rates are cut, the after-tax return on investment goes up relative to other countries, increasing the attractiveness of that market. The corporate tax cuts in 1999 in Japan were cited as a factor in the subsequent strengthening of the yen as capital flowed into the country chasing the higher returns.

Some believe the government has done just about all it can to boost investment from overseas. "To give the regulators their due, they have done all we can reasonably ask, in terms of changing the corporate law ... changing M&A-specific regulations," observes Steven Thomas at UBS. "It is now much easier to spin off divisions. There are very few foreign investment approval requirements ... it's just rubber-stamped if there are any anyway."

Recent deregulation does not necessarily point to more opportunities for foreigners, Thomas warns, adding that there has been a significant reduction in cross-border M&A activity by normal corporations. While private equity firms are actively pursuing strategic buyout opportunities, most multinationals are not "beating down the doors to do deals in Japan." Such firms simply cannot buy Japanese industry leaders in a friendly way, he notes. The top Japanese firms are not interested in selling. Whereas many foreign multinationals would like to buy the no. 1 player in their industry, or the even the no. 2, they do not really want to buy the no. 12, he explains. Unfortunately, only the weaker, smaller players are for sale.

"If you buy no. 12, you just get into the same mess that no. 12 was in already," he notes. Such a purchase would probably dilute global earnings and would also create a management headache because the newly purchased firm is a long way from corporate headquarters in the United States or Europe, he adds.

"You approach the no. 1 player, they go, 'No, thank you,' and that's it .... If you buy something in a hostile process, it's a far more difficult integration process." As a result, foreign firms looking at Japan are easily diverted to other Asian markets, he notes.

"Most foreign companies don't want to do anything hostile," echoes Benes. "It will damn you into not having any other deals …. Foreigners need friendly deals."

Investment bankers dissatisfied with the current number of cross-board deals might be encouraged if they review the U.S. experience from previous decades. Despite the surge in M&A activity in the U.S. from the early 1980s, relatively few deals involved foreign partners until the latter half of the decade. The number of foreign purchases of U.S. companies did not surpass 300 until 1986 and did not surpass 1,000 until 1996, according to Thomson Financial data. Clearly, international deal-making took some time to take off in the United States as well.

Cross-border deals are a much different animal than domestic mergers and acquisitions. Indeed, they are often pursued for fundamentally different reasons than domestic transactions, notes Bruner. Crucially, some researchers speculate that companies wanting to extend the reach of their intangible assets, or those of a target firm, are motivated to cement cross-border deals. Japanese firms are becoming increasingly focused on intangible asset management as we saw in Chapter 2, "Intellectual Property Wars". As they attempt to extract more financial value from their brands and intellectual property, interest in tie-ups with foreign firms is likely to rise. The Japanese merger and acquisition market is unlikely to remain inward-looking for long.

References

"Steven Thomas …." This statement and following quotes are from an interview conducted by the author on 11 November 2005.

"Fuji TV had launched a tender offer …." *Nikkei Net Interactive*. Nihon Keizai Shimbun, Inc. "Chronology of Events Related to Fuji

TV–Livedoor Battle." 23 March 2005. and *Nikkei Net Interactive*. Nihon Keizai Shimbun, Inc., "Livedoor, Fuji TV Step Up Bids for Nippon Broadcasting Control, 22 February, 2005.

"However, Livedoor, an Internet portal company…" *Nikkei Net Interactive*. Nihon Keizai Shimbun, Inc. "Chronology of Events Related to Fuji TV-Livedoor Battle." 23 March 2005.

"Livedoor had acquired the shares in off-hour trading …." *Nikkei Net Interactive*. Nihon Keizai Shimbun, Inc. "Tug of War over Nippon Broadcasting Moves into Court." 24 February 2005.

"Such a move allowed the firm …." *Nikkei Net Interactive*. Nihon Keizai Shimbun, Inc. "Livedoor–Fuji TV Battle Reveals M&A Loopholes," 23 February 2005.

"Nippon Broadcasting defiantly tried to block …." *Nikkei Net Interactive*. Nihon Keizai Shimbun, Inc. "Nippon Broadcast to Issue ¥15.8 Billion Share Warrant to Fuji TV," 23 February 2005.

"However, Livedoor asked …." *Nikkei Net Interactive*. Nihon Keizai Shimbun, Inc. "Chronology of Events Related to Fuji TV–Livedoor Battle." 23 March 2005.

"Nippon Broadcasting appealed to both the district and high courts but lost …." *Nikkei Net Interactive*. Nihon Keizai Shimbun, Inc. "High Court Slams Nippon Broadcasting Anti-Takeover Tactics." 24 March, 2005.

"Livedoor and Fuji TV worked out a deal …." *Nikkei Net Interactive*. Nihon Keizai Shimbun, Inc. "Fuji TV, Livedoor Complete Deals to End Battle for NBS." 23 May 2005.

"Livedoor earned ¥150 billion …." *Nikkei Net Interactive*. Nihon Keizai Shimbun, Inc. "Livedoor–Fuji TV Battle Leaves Mixed Legacy." 19 April 2005.

"He filed his candidacy for a Diet seat in September …." *Nikkei Net Interactive*. Nihon Keizai Shimbun, Inc. "Remarks of Livedoor President Horie." 23 January 2006.

"A few months later, rumors regarding his firm sparked panic selling …." *Nikkei Net Interactive*. Nihon Keizai Shimbun, Inc. "Livedoor Shock: Individuals' Panic Selling Sparked TSE Trade Halt." 19 January 2006.

"On January 23, 2006, he was arrested …." *Nikkei Net Interactive*. Nihon Keizai Shimbun, Inc. "Livedoor's Horie Arrested for Alleged False Disclosure." 23 January 2006.

"His firm was delisted …." *Nikkei Net Interactive*. Nihon Keizai Shimbun, Inc. "Curtain to Fall on Livedoor's Six-Year Listing; Individuals in a Bind." 13 April 2006.

"A year after his bid for Nippon Broadcasting …." *Nikkei Net Interactive*. Nihon Keizai Shimbun, Inc. "Court Rejects Horie's Bid for Release on Bail." 16 March 2006.

"AXA Life Insurance Co. bought Nippon Life Insurance Co. in 1999…" *Nikkei Net Interactive*. Nihon Keizai Shimbun, Inc. "Rolling Stones Energizing M&A Field." 18 April 2005.

"…GE acquired Toho Mutual Life Insurance Co. in 2000 …." Wan, Allen and Sachi Izumi, "AIG to buy GE's Japan insurance unit," Marketwatch.com, 26 June 2003.

"Prudential Insurance Co. purchased Kyoei Life Insurance Co. as well." *Nikkei Net Interactive*. Nihon Keizai Shimbun, Inc. "AIG's GE Edison Acquisition Starts Fight for Survival," 30 June 2003.

"IDC shareholders accepted …." BBC News. "Business: The Company File Cable and Wireless Trumps in Japan." 9 June 1999.

"Ripplewood Holdings …." Fujii, Yoshihiro. "Shinsei's Relisting Sparks Cheers, Criticism." *Nikkei Net Interactive*. Nihon Keizai Shimbun, Inc. 8 March 2004.

FT Special Report Japan: Investment Banking. "Tax Bureau Charged with Derailing Growth in Investment." *Financial Times*. 27 June 2005. p. 3.

"Vodafone started buying shares of Japan Telecom…" CNN Money, "Vodafone seeking JT?" 10 December 2000 and CNN.com Europe, "Vodafone to buy J-Phone Stake", 20 September, 2001

"As part of newly hired Japan Telecom president …." *Nikkei Business*. "Japan to Offer IT Consulting Services." 29 March 2004.

Collins, Timothy, "Special Report—Stars of Asia—Financiers." *Business Week* online. 12 July 2004.

"Following the restructuring of Japan Telecom …." Collins, Timothy. "Special Report—Stars of Asia—Financiers." Business Week online. 12 July 2004.

"Prime Minister Koizumi announced in …." Japan Investment Council Expert Committee. *Japan: An Attractive Destination for International Investment*, 19 May 2003, See esp. p. 1. http://www.investment-japan.go.jp/bn_news.htm.

"The government acknowledged that FDI …." Japan Investment Council Expert Committee. *Japan: An Attractive Destination for International Investment*, 19 May 2003, See esp. p. 2, http://www.investment-japan.go.jp/bn_news. htm.

"We really appreciate …." Interview conducted by the author on 12 August 2005.

"Some are becoming more open …." Interview conducted by the author in July 2005. At the time of printing, Peter Espig had left Olympus Capital.

"Takeda Pharmaceutical Co., Ltd., Japan's largest …." See http://money.cnn.com/magazines/fortune/global500/2005/ for list.

"… total market capitalization was …." Summary Outline of Discussion Points Corporate Value Study Group. www.meti.go.jp/english/information/downloadfiles/Corporate%20Value.pdf., See esp. p. 3

"Its discussions focused …." Discussion Points Corporate Value Study Group. www.meti.go.jp/english/information/downloadfiles/Corporate%20Value.pdf., See esp. p. 2.

"Columbia Law School professor Curtis J. Milhaupt ...." Milhaupt, Curtis, J. "In the Shadow of Delaware? The Rise of Hostile Takeovers in Japan." *Columbia Law Review* 105 (November 2005): 2171–2216. See esp. p. 2197.

"For example, he notes that the case of Unocal ...." Milhaupt, Curtis, J. "In the Shadow of Delaware? The Rise of Hostile Takeovers in Japan." *Columbia Law Review* 105 (November 2005): 2171–2216. See esp. p. 2196.

"The ACCJ called the principles ...." Kyodo News. "ACCJ Seeks Legal Anti-hostile Takeover Measures." 16 May 2005.

"The biggest problem ...." Interview conducted by the author on 21 September 2005.

"Since then, the Tokyo Exchange has cautiously ...." *Nikkei Net Interactive*. Nihon Keizai Shimbun, Inc. "TSE to Allow Golden Share Issuance under Certain Conditions." 17 December 2005.

"Espig worked on the financing structure ...." Interview conducted by the author in July 2005.

"In December 2003, Steel Partners launched ...." *Nikkei Net Interactive*. Nihon Keizai Shimbun, Inc. "Steel Partners Sells 40% of Its Sotoh Shareholdings." 19 March 2004.

Nikkei Net Interactive. Nihon Keizai Shimbun, Inc. "Yushiro, Sotoh to Fight Takeover Bids by US Fund." 16 January 2004.

"The UFJ group, which Nikkei Keizai Shimbun, Inc., noted was struggling ...." *Nikkei Net Interactive*. Nihon Keizai Shimbun, Inc. "UFJ to Sell Trust Unit to Sumitomo." 24 May 2004.

"Negotiations between two firms were rough ...." Nikkei Net Interactive. Nihon Keizai Shimbun, Inc. "Megamerger (4): UFJ-Sumitomo Trust Talks Faced Many Difficulties." 18 August 2004.

"The Tokyo District Court initially ordered ...." *Nikkei Net Interactive*. Nihon Keizai Shimbun, Inc. "Tokyo Court Orders Halt to MTFG-UFJ Merger Talks." 27 July 2004.

Nikkei Net Interactive. Nihon Keizai Shimbun, Inc. "High Court Allows UFJ, MTFG to Resume Merger Talks." 11 August 2004.

"Finally, Sumitomo appealed to the Tokyo High Court ...." *Nikkei Net Interactive.* Nihon Keizai Shimbun, Inc. "Legal Battle over MTFG-UFJ Merger May Spur U.S.-Style M&As." 31 August 2004.

"In February 2006, the Tokyo District Court ...." *Nikkei Net Interactive.* Nihon Keizai Shimbun, Inc. "Tokyo Court Rejects Sumitomo Trust Damage Suit Against UFJ." 13 February 2006.

"Nishi, along with another partner ...." Interview conducted by the author on 8 November 2005.

"The association voted against changes ...." *Nikkei Net Interactive.* Nihon Keizai Shimbun, Inc. "Pension Fund Association Voted Against 90% of Anti-Takeover Measure." 27 June 2005.

"Economic turbulence can often ...." Interview conducted by the author on 23 January 2006.

"A great wave of ...." Bruner, Robert F. *Applied Mergers and Acquisitions.* John Wiley & Sons, Inc., 2004. See esp. p. 74.

"His firm, Wesray Corp., purchased ...." Arenson, Karen. "How Wall Street Bred an Ivan Boesky." *The New York Times.* 23 November 1986.

"Milken pleaded guilty to six counts of securities fraud in 1990 ...." *The New York Times.* "Prosecutors and Regulators Urge Clinton Not to Pardon Milken." 15 January 2001.

"In addition to Livedoor's attempted takeover of Nippon Broadcast ..." *Nikkei Net Interactive.* Nihon Keizai Shimbun, Inc. *ANALYSIS: Rakuten's Bid for TBS Fizzles.* 1 December 2005.

"It remains unclear whether Koizumi will be ...." US-Japan Economic Partnership for Growth. *United States-Japan Investment Initiative 2005 Report.* July 2005. See esp. p. 2.

"Inward FDI flows totaled ¥733 billion ...." United Nations Conference of Trade and Development Foreign Direct Investment database. World Investment Directory online.

"Nonetheless, in March 2006 ...." *Nikkei Net Interactive*. Nihon Keizai Shimbun, Inc. "Japan Aims to Boost Foreign Investment Balance to 5% of GDP in '10." 9 March 2006.

"The tax differential between some European countries ...." Interview conducted by the author on 12 August 2005.

"The top statutory corporate tax rate ...." United States Congress. Congressional Budget Office. *Corporate Income Tax Rates: International Comparisons*. November 2005. See esp. p. 22.

"To give the regulators their due ...." Interview conducted by the author on 11 November 2005.

"Most foreign companies don't want to do anything hostile ...." Interview conducted by the author on 12 August 2005.

"Cross-border deals are often fueled ...." Bruner, Robert F. *Applied Mergers and Acquisitions*. John Wiley & Sons, Inc., 2004. See esp. p. 98.

"Crucially, companies wanting to extend ...." Bruner, Robert F. *Applied Mergers and Acquisitions*. John Wiley & Sons, Inc., 2004. See esp. p. 103.

6

THE MANHATTAN OF ASIA

Tokyo Experiences Stunning Urban Renaissance

Beyond the leafy red canna stalks lining his swimming pool, Koichi Mera looks out over the grounds of the Getty Villa from the back patio of his home in Malibu, California, in December 2005. Mera and his wife, who is an artist, looked forward to the January 2006 reopening of the museum, which is modeled after a first-century Roman house, the Villa dei Papiri, and home to a staggering 44,000 works of art.

They had been waiting a long time. Closed for renovations in 1997, the Getty Villa expansion had been mired in litigation for years—it was originally scheduled to be completed in 2002. Nearby homeowner associations had been able to delay the $275 million project, despite the Los Angeles City Council approving an extension to the villa's original conditional use permit back in 1999.

Such delays to construction projects are extremely rare in Japan, notes Mera, who is an adjunct professor at the Marshall School of Business at the University of Southern California. A prolific scholar, he co-wrote *The Asian Financial Crisis and the Role of Real Estate* and also contributed a chapter to *Unlocking Bureaucrat's Kingdom: Deregulation and the Japanese Economy.* Even in the relaxed setting of his Malibu home, his square jaw is set rigidly as he gazes intently at his questioner. Such focused attention is undoubtedly a legacy of spending decades discussing complex land policies across the globe. Only briefly, when noting the stubborn resistance of his neighbors to even small changes to his property, does he chuckle and allow a faint, tolerant smile to appear on his lips.

Mera wrote an influential paper that was widely circulated at the World Bank in the early 1970s and changed how international development theorists there viewed big cities. Before his analysis, Mera noticed a general perception among urban planners that big cities were inefficient and undesirable. Now most in policy-making circles agree with him and other experts who have concluded that large urban areas are engines of growth. He has taught urban economics at both Harvard and Tokyo University.

Land regulation is vastly different in Japan and the United States, and these differences partly explain the recent explosion of real estate investment in Tokyo, Mera points out. Developers in the United States must comply with both state and city regulations, as well as demands from the local community. The U.S. system is based on the assumption that contractors cannot be trusted. City inspectors come in at every stage and check their work.

"By comparison, the Japanese system is fairly simple," Mera explains. Japan has a national building code, but that is about it. Rules are largely the same for builders, from the southern island of Okinawa to the northern tip of Hokkaido. Municipal regulations are quite limited, he notes, and there are much less stringent inspections.

The Japanese approach does have some risks, of course. The lax regulatory code has been abused in the past. The Ministry of Land, Infrastructure, and Transport announced in November 2005 that 16 buildings were at risk of collapse in an earthquake because a privately run inspection firm authorized by the government did not detect false structural assessments. Large sections of Kobe were reduced to rubble during the Great Hanshin Earthquake of 1995. Some of the damages could have been avoided if the builders had strictly adhered to construction laws, observes Mera.

Recently, building codes in Japan have been liberalized to allow greater freedom in land use. This has been made possible by expanding the discretion of individual bureaucrats in approving proposed projects, but Mera notes that the system's previous virtue of treating all developers and builders equally has been sacrificed. Big developers, such as Mitsubishi or Mitsui, can now proceed more quickly with their plans. Smaller players, without connections in the ministries, may not be so lucky, he warns.

Despite such unfairness, the relatively permissive regulatory environment gives developers in Tokyo much more freedom to reshape the urban landscape than, say, the Getty Villa board of trustees have in Malibu. And it's not just major developments that must overcome obstacles in the United States that are largely unknown in Japan. U.S. homeowners as well face high hurdles even when remodeling their houses, Mera has discovered. An architectural review committee must approve any changes to homes in his neighborhood. Neighbors' comments have a great impact on the committee's decisions, he notes. "I think neighbors say no to any kind of change," he wryly observes.

In Seijogakuen-mae, a prestigious Tokyo suburb, his neighbors had no say on any changes he wanted to make on his house. Residential homes faced some city height and size regulations, but if houses complied with those, no one had the right to complain.

Use rules for land in Tokyo are also much less restrictive than in the United States, Mera points out. Real estate in the United States is classified by use into residential, commercial, and industrial zones. In Tokyo, as in many other Asian cities, such strict categories are not etched in stone. Owners of the small buildings that line many downtown Tokyo streets use their downstairs for stores or workshops and live upstairs. With exclusive use zoning designations relatively rare, it is easier for a developer to work in the Asian system, Mera says.

To be sure, a lenient regulatory code is just one factor supporting the current construction boom in Tokyo, albeit one that is often overlooked. Accelerating economic growth, rock-bottom prices, financial innovation, a flood of money from private and foreign funds, and a burgeoning real estate investment trust (REIT) market are supporting growth as well. Developers are radically transforming the Tokyo landscape at a pace that is shocking even to the most jaundiced observers.

The Renaissance of Tokyo's Business District

A snowman in the downtown Marunouchi district of Tokyo is as rare as it would be in Malibu, but one stood guard, white and rotund, in a blanket of snow outside the Tokyo Building in November 2005. Hundreds of people milled outside, some touching the snow in disbelief, to see if it was real. It was—shipped in for the skyscraper's grand opening.

A choral group sang "Amazing Grace" as dozens of photographers fiddled with their cameras. Judging by their shouts when Natsumi Abe appeared, many were there to take pictures of the star, a former member of the girl pop group "Morning *Musume*," rather than the 32-story building. Staid-looking Mitsubishi Estate Co., Ltd. president Keiji Kimura received a much less enthusiastic response when he appeared. However, he did not seem to mind the clear favoritism of the crowd as he pushed a button, along with the celebrities Abe and Noriko Kato, lighting up the newest addition to the city's skyline.

If there is such a thing as a nerve center to corporate Japan, it is located in the Marunouchi District of Tokyo. About 240,000 people work in the 4,000 offices in the Marunouchi, Otemachi, and Yuraku-cho districts. During the Tokugawa Period, feudal lords made their homes in the Marunouchi District, just outside the fortifications of the imperial palace. After the Meiji Restoration, their estates were razed and much of the neighborhood was made into a military parade ground. When the government offered it for sale in 1890, there were few bidders, and Yanosuke Iwasaki, founder of the Mitsubishi trading house, was able to buy up much of the area. It was a far-sighted investment. Tokyo Station, the hub of the nation's transportation network, was within walking distance, so Marunouchi became the first business district in Japan. Red-brick buildings soon lined the streets, and the district became known as Londontown. The area retained its dominance through both the Great Kanto Earthquake of 1923 and the bombings of the city during World War II.

However, by the 1990s, the district suffered from several problems. With height restrictions of only 31 meters up through 1963, office ceilings were low because architects attempted to squeeze as many floors as possible in the squat buildings. That year new regulations limiting building size based on floor area ratios were introduced, but the rigid system still limited construction of new office buildings. Modern firms often need high ceilings to accommodate the cables and wiring strung beneath raised floors for their computer systems. By the age of the Internet, many offices in the Marunouchi area were hopelessly anachronistic. In addition, inspections following the Kobe earthquake of 1995 revealed that many needed renovations for earthquake protection. As a result, Mitsubishi Estate, the local landlord, decided many buildings should be demolished.

Deregulation assisted in the redevelopment of the region. Although city building codes were lenient, municipal authorities strictly controlled the volume size of local buildings. In principle, firms were allowed to have a total area 1000% of underlining floor space for offices. However, the government gave firms opportunities to increase the total area of newly constructed buildings from 2002. For example, if firms created common-use areas accessible to the public, such as retail shopping areas or hotels, a further 300% increase of the floor area ratio was allowed. In addition, such space in buildings was permitted to be exchanged—one building could have even more than 1000% of floor area devoted to office space if retail area replaced it in another Marunouchi building. For example, office space was increased in the Tokyo Building because the planned Peninsula Hotel took up more than 300% of the floor space in another building.

In addition, the government also permitted the exchange of air rights from the same year. In a system similar to some U.S. cities, air rights from historical buildings could be transferred to other buildings in the neighborhood, allowing taller buildings than before. Once again, buildings were no longer limited by the 1300% ceiling on floor area ratios. JR East, owner of Tokyo Station, is a part owner of Tokyo Building as well because it contributed its air rights to the new structure.

Mitsubishi, which owned and managed 31 of 98 buildings in the Marunouchi/Otemachi/Yurakucho area, took advantage of such deregulation by launching a massive two-stage reconstruction of the entire business district. Tokyo Building was the fourth building to open in a decade-long, ¥500 billion effort to create a new cityscape in front of Tokyo Station. Another seven or eight buildings will be built in a planned second stage, which is slated to cost another ¥450 billion.

Those investors who have watched Japan struggle through its "lost decade" may be scratching their heads and wondering, "Where will tenants come from to fill up these buildings?" Indeed, the Marunouchi Redevelopment Project comes in the wake of two other major construction schemes, both close by.

They are clearly visible from the thirty-first floor of the Marunouchi Building, completed in 2002 and a very short walk from Tokyo Station. From the windows facing west, the city appears to stretch endlessly into the gray mists of evening. Far below, the flat roofs of older buildings abruptly end in a chasm of glittering neon— the Ginza shopping district. A cluster of buildings just beyond appears to crowd the ribbon of railways cutting through the city. In 2003, the Shiodome area, which boasts 3.23 million square feet of office space, opened for business. Firms such as Dentsu, Inc.; Kyodo News; and Nippon Television Network Corp. have moved offices there, resulting in wags calling the area a "media *jokamachi,*" or media castle town. Even farther on, a tall metallic tower, its shape resembling a gun barrel, threatens the sky—the Roppongi Hills complex, which houses another 4 million square feet for offices and opened the same year. This deluge of office space hitting the market all at once was called the "2003 problem." Many worried that the long downward trend in Tokyo real estate prices would be further extended.

However, the Shiodome and Roppongi Hills developments are full and demand for office space is continuing to increase, notes Masahiro Kobayashi, Deputy General Manager at Mitsubishi Estate. In addition to economic growth, Kobayashi cites structural changes in the corporate sector as underpinning demand for high-quality offices. Companies are getting larger because of increasing M&A transactions, so they need more office space. For example, one of the main tenants of the newly built Marunouchi Building is Mitsubishi UFJ Securities Co., Ltd. This was formed in 2005 through a merger of Mitsubishi Securities Co., Ltd. and UFJ Tsubasa Securities Co., Ltd., members of the Mitsubishi and UFJ banking groups whose merger was discussed in the last chapter.

Meanwhile, Mitsubishi Securities was created in 2002 from a merger of Kokusai Securities Co., Ltd.; Tokyo-Mitsubishi Securities Co., Ltd.; Tokyo-Mitsubishi Personal Securities Co., Ltd.; and Isse Securities Co., Ltd. UFJ Tsubasa Securities Co., Ltd. was formed in 2000 from a merger of four firms … well, let's stop there. It is clear that as companies take over related business, they will need constantly bigger offices in which to house the newly created firms.

Second, the M&A boom is also fueling consolidation among professional firms, which are demanding bigger and better offices as well. Traditionally, law offices in Japan have been small, with firms having only a couple of senior partners. They are now exploding in size, boosting capacity to handle the complex M&A transactions that are now a big business. "We have little choice but to rely on the services of large law firms in handling cases that require vast expertise," Kazuhiko Toyama, COO of the Industrial Revitalization Corp. of Japan, told Nihon Keizai Shimbun, Inc. Mori, Hamada & Matsumoto, one of the most prestigious law firms in Japan, has 199 lawyers and now requires six floors in the Marunouchi Kitaguchi Building, which is part of the OAZO complex, which opened in September 2004.

As demand for high-quality office space heats up throughout the city, the Marunouchi area is in a commanding position to reassert its dominance as a financial center because of its advanced telecommunications network. From a low-tech holdout, the district is rocketing to the forefront of the information age through a fluke of industrial design.

The air in Marunouchi was not always as clean as it is today; clouds of toxic gases engulfed Tokyo in the 1970s. Buildings sent plumes of smoke into the sky, threatening even the rows of elegant, neatly pruned pine trees in the Outer Garden of the Imperial Palace. Local authorities decided drastic measures were needed and ordered the extensive drilling of tunnels throughout the Marunouchi area to create a massive district heating and cooling (DHC) system.

More than 3 decades later, Syuichi Nomura of Marunouchi Heating Supply Co. climbed down a ladder leading to Marubeni Dai-ichi tunnel. We had entered the company's underground Otemachi center via stairs next to Karugamo Pond, across the street from the Imperial Palace. After putting on hard hats, we walked through a cavernous room housing massive freezers that chilled water for circulation in nearby buildings. The headquarters of firms such as Mizuho Bank, The Japan Development Bank, and the financial newspaper, *Nihon Keizai Shimbun*, were all cooled in the summer by these machines. Ducking and crawling through some tunnels, we then edged down a catwalk to a ladder. At the bottom was the tunnel that Nomura now peered down.

We were about 75 feet underground. When engineers built the tunnel in 1996, they had to contend with a maze of underground infrastructure, including five subway tunnels as well as all the gas, electricity, water, and sewer lines that served the business district. However, the builders of the first ducts decades ago did not even anticipate one of the tunnels' most valuable uses.

In the space between yellow steam pipes on the left side of the tunnel, two fiber optic lines were tightly wedged, part of a 14,000-kilometer network of single-mode cables that linked the whole business district.

These dark fibers, or fiber optic cables, were installed by Marunouchi Direct Access, Ltd. "By chance, Marunouchi Heating had all these ducts," says Toru Okusa, director of the joint venture between Mitsubishi Estate Co., Ltd., and Marubeni Corp.

However, the tunnel system alone was not enough. If Mitsubishi did not own 30 buildings in the area, there would be no incentive to invest in an extensive fiber optic network. Most buildings in the

Marunouchi area, which spans more than 100 hectares, have access to the network. The system of fiber optic cables is also linked to the Marunouchi Data Center, where building tenants or telecommunications firms can lease space to install equipment or servers.

"In a new building, if you have to put your own servers in; then it takes up space and requires expensive generators and air-conditioning," Okusa notes, adding that servers can be provided to new tenants in as quickly as 2 weeks. Numerous telecommunication firms, such as KDDI and Cable & Wireless, use Marunouchi Direct Access optical fibers, meaning competition between such companies is fierce, driving down telecommunication costs. Even Roppongi Hills has tried to cut network costs to compete with this area, says Okusa. The Marunouchi Direct Access network can also link users to Internet exchange points directly, which reduces costs for tenants as well.

Such a network, located in the heart of the nation's business district, could have major implications. Because most buildings in the area are included in the same network, tenants in various buildings can be linked in local area networks (LANs) with little effort. This could reduce costs associated with mergers and acquisitions; if one firm bought out or merged with another in the same area, their individual networks could be linked rapidly, speeding integration of operations. The Marunouchi Direct Access system is better, more secure, and cheaper than the virtual private networks (VPNs) that companies often use to link LAN systems between buildings, says the company. Because hundreds of firms are headquartered in Marunouchi, such business tie-ups are likely to become increasingly frequent. The existence of such a network may help ease such activity.

With so many corporate headquarters located in the area, investment banks and funds are likely to increasingly concentrate in the district—rather than spend valuable minutes in long transits between potential investment targets and fund managers, analysts and bankers can jump in a taxi for a short ride or even walk. JP Morgan has seven floors in newly opened Tokyo Building. Law firms, consulting businesses, and auditors will likely find it convenient to set up shop near their clients as well.

Although it has always been the business center of Tokyo, its spacious streets have seemed somehow lacking in vitality in the past—only depressingly dark coffee shops, bookstores lined with monotonous texts, or dull bank branches greeted pedestrians who had the temerity to go for a stroll in the neighborhood. Although one of the most glamorous department store streets in the world, Ginza-dori, was only a short stroll from nearby Yurakucho Station, few shoppers wandered under the tracks into the dreary maze of financial company headquarters on the other side. On weekends, much of the district was a ghost town.

Now the Otemachi region has taken on new life. Swank shops such as Kate Spade and Tiffany & Co. line Nakadori, a broad, tree-lined avenue that lures shoppers to a further 140 stores in the Marunouchi Building. The juxtaposition of trendy retailers and other residents in the previously staid neighborhood can be jarring; Brooks Brothers shares a building with the Ministry of Education, Culture, Sports, Science, and Technology. Still, it appears that planners here have taken to heart some of the admonishments of Jane Jacobs, author of *The Death and Life of Great American Cities*, and are trying to revitalize the area by encouraging various uses.

Real Estate Investors Zero In on Hot Neighborhoods

Not all of Tokyo looks as good as Marunouchi. Indeed, vast swaths of the city remain low-rise older buildings. Akira Mori, one of the largest landlords in Tokyo, says that much of the city's building stock is outdated. Indeed, widespread demolitions triggered alarms during summer 2005 about a possible increase in asbestos-related deaths in the city. The razing of aging buildings with high concentrations of the cancer-causing material is rapidly spreading.

However, health worries about the demolition of older buildings are not stemming the rush of businesses and residents to newly developed areas. Many are flocking to areas such as Shiodome and Roppongi Hills, where residences, offices, and entertainment facilities are integrated into the same complexes, Mori points out.

Akira Mori is the third son of the late Taikichiro Mori, a real estate investor who was the richest man in the world in the early 1990s, according to *Forbes* magazine. Akira Mori and his brother, Minoru, both inherited fortunes from their father. Minoru Mori took over Mori Building, and Akira Mori presides over Mori Trust, which expects record sales and profits in the fiscal period ending March 2006.

Population has increased in the three central wards of Tokyo because of the attractiveness of the new developments. With more young people moving into the city, "Schools are in short supply," says Mori, sitting behind a sprawling wooden conference table at his firm's headquarters in Toranomon in March 2006. Mori, who is in his sixties with ruffled gray hair, carries himself with the quiet, understated dignity of a medical doctor with a thriving practice, and is graciously attentive to his visitor. Despite overseeing a multibillion-dollar empire, he patiently answers questions, never conspicuously checking his watch.

"Overall demographic trends are irrelevant [to the Tokyo market]," Mori observes. "As long as business activities are centered in Tokyo, the property market will continue to develop."

In fact, real estate prices are being supported by unprecedented factors, Mori notes. "Usually when the economy gets better, interest rates rise, and then rents go up. Now the opposite is occurring, and rents are rising even though interest rates remain low."

Money is also coming in from overseas, as foreign institutions buy up shares in real estate investment trusts (REITs). "It's an extremely benign environment for real estate investing," Mori adds.

Although upward pressure on long-term interest rates is limited, they are unlikely to stay at current levels forever, Mori says. As interest rates rise over the long term, REITs will face rising cost of capital, and margins will be squeezed. "If interest rates rise by 100 basis points, that could have a dramatic impact on the market," Mori notes.

Good and bad locations will become more differentiated, and REITs that do not own attractive properties likely will face problems, Mori warns. Mori Trust is concentrating its holdings on high-growth areas. It owns Marunouchi Trust Tower North near Tokyo Station, Tokyo Shiodome Building, and Shiroyama Trust Tower near Roppongi. Such locations, where demand for office space is intensifying, will not be hurt by interest-rate increases, he argues.

In addition, funds heavily dependent on rents from residential properties, which are extremely sensitive to changes in the economy, will be exposed if interest rates rise, Mori warns. In addition to extensive office holdings, Mori Trust has diversified into hotel operations to avoid such dependency; Conrad Tokyo opened in the upper levels of Tokyo Shiodome Building in summer 2005.

Ultimately, the emergence of new city centers will tax the city's existing infrastructure, Mori warns. "As activity concentrates in the heart of Tokyo, more work on the city's arteries and veins are necessary," Mori observes. Desire to increase such investment may be behind Tokyo Mayor Shintaro Ishihara's call for future Olympic games, Mori adds.

The background of John Tofflemire, an Italian American from Detroit, could hardly be more different from the regal past of Akira Mori. Tofflemire spent a year as a young man driving a cab through dangerous New York City neighborhoods, much like Robert De

Niro's character Travis Bickle in the movie Taxi Driver. Though he, too, dodged muggings and shady characters, Tofflemire found the metropolis fascinating, and his passion for urban landscapes ultimately led him to acquire a Ph.D. in urban and regional economics at the University of Pennsylvania. His enthusiasm, coupled with aging matinee-idol looks and a light-gray pompadour, previously made him a popular commenter for financial TV news channels. He rarely appears on TV nowadays; he is too busy providing confidential investment advice to heavy-hitters in the Tokyo market.

Tofflemire wholeheartedly agrees with the real estate mogul that only parts of Tokyo are growing. He has long been convinced that communications and communication technology are the nervous systems of urban environments—the reasons that people come together. Now running Sapient Real Estate Consulting in Tokyo, he believes the convergence of transportation and communication linkages in Tokyo will lead to the building of a new high-rise corridor stretching from the Imperial Place, through Otemachi and Kasumigaseki, to Shinagawa. Central Tokyo, he gushes, will become the new Manhattan of Asia.

"People mistakenly believe that telecommunications causes cities to disperse," he observes. "That's completely wrong. What [it does] is cause people with certain skills to come together and market those skills to a larger market and in greater depth." He notes that George J. Stigler's 1951 paper *The Division of Labor is Limited by the Extent of the Market* showed that the extent of markets is determined by the ability to have control through good communications. Stigler won the Nobel Prize in Economics in 1982.

Fascinated by the wealth and power that urban areas represent, Tofflemire continues to study the old imperial capitals of Europe. Venice is one of his favorites. His wife attended university in nearby Padova, and he first saw the city when they visited her friend's parents, who lived near the Rialto Bridge in an old villa—so old, in fact, that the house appears in a sixteenth-century painting. He was completely floored by the city's grandeur. "The thing that struck me was, 'My God, this was one of the greatest empires that ever existed in history,'" he remembers.

"Cities are places where people make money. They make money for two reasons—one, because of greed, and two, because of fear." Tofflemire says. The fear that drove Venetians was the fear of being subjugated. Indeed, the brutal struggle of medieval Italian principalities for survival inspired Machiavelli to write his famous amoral treatise on the exercise of power.

Japan, like Venice, is probably more motivated by fear than greed, reflects Tofflemire. Japan's industrialization during the late nineteenth century was motivated by a fear of domination by the West, while the restructuring of Japan in the late twentieth and early twenty-first centuries is, to a significant extent, driven by fears of being eclipsed, both politically and economically, by China, he says.

Tofflemire arrived in Japan in June 1992, near the peak of the Tokyo real estate bubble, to develop an econometric model for China's Fujian province for Mitsubishi Research Institute (MRI). After working on a number of international consulting projects at MRI, he left to join Richard Ellis, the British real estate brokerage firm, in 1996. The firm became CB Richard Ellis in 1998 and then merged with Ikoma Shoji, a Japanese real estate brokerage firm, in 1999.

Tofflemire, seeing opportunities in the Tokyo commercial real estate market finally emerging after a decade of stagnation, decided to strike out on his own in 2004. Land prices in Tokyo are starting to go up, he notes, while acknowledging that widespread declines continue outside city centers. Commercial land prices in Tokyo rose 0.6% in the year that ended July 2005, the first such increase since 1990, according to the Ministry of Land, Infrastructure, and Transport. After years of being off the radar screen, Tokyo is once again

attracting the attention of global real estate investors. Tokyo was cited
in a 2004 survey by the Association of Foreign Investors in Real
Estate as one of the top three cities for real estate investment, the
first time the city made the cut since the survey started asking the
question in 2001.

Some market watchers attribute the price increases to purchases
by REITs , flush with funds, and worry about the sustainability of the
recovery. The first two Japanese REITs, Nippon Building Fund, Inc.,
and Japan Real Estate Investment, were launched in September
2001. Twenty-six such trusts were listed on the Tokyo Stock Exchange
by December 2005 with a combined capitalization of ¥1.8 trillion.
The Tokyo Stock Exchange REIT Index, launched at the end of
March 2003, climbed from 1,000 to 1,768.87 by May 8, 2006, according to the exchange.

Tofflemire sees no cause for alarm. "I don't think it's a bubble; it's
rational," he reflects. "If it was, no intelligent investor could do deals.
And I know they are doing deals. There are arbitrage plays out there
where you can make money."

The spread between lending and capitalization rates in Tokyo was
one of the world's largest in 2005. Capitalization rates, or cap rates,
are calculated by dividing the net income generated by a property
over its purchase price and are a standard measure of return used in
real estate investment. Although cap rates have fallen in recent years,
they remain higher than lending rates. "You can invest, buy buildings,
and sell them into the REIT market," Tofflemire observes.

A very active mezzanine debt market is another new development helping to support commercial real estate prices, Tofflemire
says. Debt on buildings can be sliced into various tranches based on
risk. Loans amounting to the first 70% or so of a building's value are
deemed relatively low risk—and termed vanilla. Such loans are
exposed to only low-probability dangers such as earthquakes and terrorist attacks—otherwise, borrowers are almost certain to get their

money back. Japanese lenders will do vanilla lending at very competitive rates, Tofflemire says.

Mezzanine debt is that which is typically above the amount vanilla lenders will comfortably extend. As debt approaches 100% of the value of the building, lenders must get more sophisticated at assessing risks to the building's cash flow and their ability to get repaid. Mezzanine debt, as a result, is much more expensive.

Tofflemire notes that the mezzanine debt market is becoming much broader and deeper; most foreign investment banks are very sophisticated lenders in this segment. Domestic banks are coming up to speed as well. With banks slicing the various levels of debt according to risk levels more closely and pricing them accordingly, the loan market has ballooned, Tofflemire adds. The explosion of the REIT market, which started in 2001, has increased market transparency and helped the banks make such strides. Meanwhile, as lending rates have fallen, borrowers can bid on more properties

That is not to say the market is without risk. Because cap rates can be a function of debt, investors boost their exposure through leverage. If an investor buys and cap rates fall, the property's price goes down, potentially wiping out the initial equity. Falling rents are bad news.

A law establishing fixed-term leases in 2000 also modestly increased the attractiveness of securitized property in the city. Previously, business leases lasted only 2 years. Traditional 2-year leases in Japan are more secure than they appear because relocation costs are high and this increases inertia of Japanese firms, notes Tofflemire. As a result, the risk on such cash flows is considerably less than it appears to Western minds unfamiliar with Japan, he argues. Nonetheless, fixed-term leases now last up to 20 years, formally locking in returns for a much longer period. Although this is still a small percentage of the market, many new buildings offer only such leases.

These new leases have created some uncertainty regarding condominium units. "One of the dirty secrets of the market is whether
these fixed-term leases … would, in fact, stand a legal challenge,"
Tofflemire warns. Market players are uncertain whether the new law
regarding fixed-term leases or an old law safeguarding tenant rights,
The Landlord and Tenant Act, will prove dominant in condominium
rental developments. The old act makes it easy for tenants to leave.
"At some point, if somebody wants to get out of a long-term lease and
the landlord says, 'No,' if they take them to court to test the law, then
we'll find out." However, the sophisticated lenders in the mezzanine
debt market are fully aware of this ambiguity.

Aside from the continued spread between cap rates and borrowing costs, which ensures positive cash flow for real estate investors,
they can also book gains on properties by selling them into the REIT
market. A huge spread still exists between lower- and higher-grade
property in the city. With the new liquidity in the land market, people
can now arbitrage between the two classes. Such opportunities are
attracting some of the largest real estate funds in the world.

One such investor is Morgan Stanley Real Estate Fund (MSREF) . It
is one of the biggest players in the real estate market, with more than
$10 billion under management in Japan. Sonny Kalsi, a managing
director at Morgan Stanley who came to Japan in 1997 expecting to
stay only 2 or 3 years, says the fund has vastly exceeded expectations.
Kalsi cut his teeth in the distressed debt market buying properties put
up for sale during the savings and loan crises in the United States.
MSREF saw an opportunity in Japan during the banking sector crisis
in the late 1990s; it acquired its first property in 1998.

Eight years later, Morgan Stanley has a staff of 200 accountants,
lawyers, leasing specialists, and architects in the property asset-
management business. All major aspects of a real estate deal can be
handled in-house. The fund looks for good properties with clear inefficiency in management, which can be addressed by this team. Kalsi

points to the redevelopment of the Ebisu Prime property as an example of how his firm operates. They acquired the property from failed Chiyoda Mutual Life Insurance in 2001. The property's image had been tarnished by its owner, who did not invest or maintain it properly. Morgan Stanley brought in new retail tenants, installed an ATM in the lobby, and renovated the building's common areas. In addition, it ran ads on FM radio and posted posters at the nearest JR station. After sprucing up the property and improving its reputation in the market, Morgan Stanley sold it for a substantial profit to an insurance company in 2005.

Kalsi is upbeat regarding the prospects for further growth of Japanese real estate. Although acknowledging that an economic slowdown could hurt business, he points to a number of factors that suggest that demand for grade-A office space will continue to rise. As long as the economy grows, Japanese firms will grow with it, demanding more office space to house their operations. Japanese companies are also increasing their office space per worker, from 10 to 15 square meters a decade or so ago to 25 square meters today. Office workers get 35 square meters in the United States, so there is still room for growth, he adds.

Kalsi also points to fair and transparent zoning, empowering developers and giving them more freedom to do what they want with properties. Morgan Stanley headquarters in Tokyo is basically in a residential district, he notes. Its Yebisu Garden Place offices were formerly the site of a Sapporo brewery. Liberal zoning laws enabled the property to be developed commercially.

Tokyo Mid-town:
A New Gateway for the Nation

Cities are not merely locations; they often act as incubators for new ideas and ways of seeing the world. As nexuses for gatherings of creative and ambitious people, as well as sources of wealth for financing architectural and artistic endeavors, urban areas have often acted as fertile breeding grounds for new intellectual movements. Encircled with the resplendent Ringstrasse, *fin de siècle* Vienna was home to many innovators in architecture, psychology, art, and music. The central European capital "with its acutely felt tremors of social and political disintegration, proved one of the most fertile breeding grounds of our century's a-historical culture," wrote Carl E. Schorske in the twentieth century. Perhaps *commencement du siècle* Tokyo will be viewed as a similarly fecund period by later historians.

Property developers, no less than high-tech firms, are focusing on how to develop their holdings of the intellectual assets discussed in Chapter 2, "Intellectual Property Wars." Not merely content to construct buildings, they are engaged in an intensive cultural introspection, attempting to ascertain how Tokyo can best compete with cosmopolitan centers across the globe. Indeed, when developers brainstormed about how to develop the former site of the Self-Defense Forces Building in the Roppongi district in Tokyo, they compared the city with New York, London, and Paris, remembers Takashi Nakayama, project manager of the planning group for the Tokyo Mid-town Development Department at Mitsui Fudosan Co., Ltd . He and others on his team strove to look beyond the after-effects of the collapse of the bubble economy and debated how the city should evolve into the twenty-first century. The development is scheduled to open in spring 2007.

Nakayama, echoing Tofflemire, observes that all cities are places where people come together, collect information, and create new things. His group envisioned making Tokyo Mid-town a base for such activity. To be sure, the Roppongi neighborhood is much different from the central business district. It is farther west on the Shuto Expressway No. 3, away from Tokyo Station and the amazing transportation links that bind Marunouchi with the rest of the country.

Roppongi has always been primarily a residential community. In addition, the area is home to many embassies and foreigners. Up to 1 out of every 6 of the 10,000 people living within a mile from Roppongi crossing is from overseas, notes Nakayama. Foreign brokers and financial journalists hang out in the many bars on the strip.

Reporters gazed down on the district from a conference hall in Roppongi Hills, where Mitsui held a press conference in November 2005. The skeleton of the Tokyo Mid-town Tower, which was already almost fully leased, loomed over Roppongi crossing. Fuji Photo Film. Co., Ltd.; Fuji Xerox Co., Ltd.; and Yahoo Japan Corp. had signed contracts. Four TV cameras rolled and about a hundred journalists listened intently as Koichi Omuro, the executive vice president for Mitsui Fudosan, introduced the participants in the project. Ritz-Carlton will run a five-star hotel in the top floors of the skyscraper. Oakwood Worldwide will manage luxury-service apartments for executives visiting the city, while John Hopkins will operate a clinic for such residents, along with the Japanese firm High Technology. Slides showed a park where pampered residents could stroll. Ensconced in such surroundings, whiny expats would have to relinquish their complaint, dating back to the *o-yatoi-gaijin*, that Japan was a "hardship post."

However, Nakayama is anticipating that Tokyo Mid-town will not just be a collection of office and apartment buildings that provide a steady stream of rents to project investors, (including the National Mutual Insurance Federation of Agricultural Cooperatives; Yasuda Mutual Life Insurance Company; Sekisui House, Ltd.; Fukoku Mutual Life Insurance Company; and Daido Life Insurance Company). In their internal discussions, the developers commented on the shift of factories to the low-cost Chinese mainland and acknowledged that Japan had to move away from its reliance on manufacturing to prosper in the new century. They hit upon the concept of "Japan Value" as a focus of the Tokyo Mid-town project. "Japan

Value" would be the added value that Japan creates and transmits to the rest of the world in the future. Reflecting on the success Japan has had with industrial and product design in the past, the developers decided to create a base for design and art activities in the city.

Art from across the city is converging on the Roppongi district. The National Art Center will open here in 2007. Meanwhile, the Mori Art Museum opened in summer 2003 in Roppongi Hills. The complex, Japan's answer to the radiant cities envisioned by architect Le Corbusier, also boosts nine movie screens and more than 2,000 seats, and is now home to the Tokyo International Film Festival, which was previously held in Shibuya.

In the nearby Tokyo Mid-town Tower, the Japan Industrial Design Association has already signed a lease on the fifth floor, along with the Nihon Graphic Kyokai. Suntory Museum of Art, with its collection of rare lacquer ware, will also move to the complex. Meanwhile, a sleek building with slanting roofs suggestive of *origami* folds will be built to house 21/21 Design Site, a think tank devoted to disseminate Japanese design concepts to the rest of the world. The center will house the offices of the Japan Industrial Design Promotion Organization.

In Japanese homes, the *genkan,* or front entryway, often welcomes visitors with an alcove for pottery, *ikebana,* or art displays. Mitsui Fudosan appears to be building a new *genkan* for the entire nation.

Tokyo as a Cultural Beacon in Asia

Motohisa Furukawa, a lawmaker in the Diet, says Tokyo could become the Manhattan of Asia, much like Tofflemire is forecasting. However, Furukawa is not talking about just a dramatic new skyline. He envisions Tokyo becoming a cultural beacon and center for business activity for the entire region.

"New York City is not typical America," observes Furukawa, who studied at Columbia University on the Upper West Side of Manhattan. The still-youthful-looking Diet man, in his early forties, frequently grins while discussing his views about the Japanese capital. "Average America is more like ... Texas," he jokingly speculates. "However, if you want to understand America, you must understand New York. If foreigners go to America, they want to see the city. People visit from all over the world. So finance, fashion, entertainment thrive."

Japan is part of Asia, of that there is no doubt. Every spring, paddies in the countryside turn emerald green with rice shoots, as they have for centuries. Some of first irrigation channels in the country's flat agricultural plains were initially carved out by Korean engineers using Chinese technology more than 1,000 years ago. Elegant Chinese characters grace even mundane signs along city streets in Tokyo, as they do in Beijing, Hong Kong, Singapore, and Taipei.

However, Japan is also different from the rest of the region, maintains Furukawa. Having adopted Western technology and institutions much faster than the rest of the region, Japan has separated itself from its neighbors. He points to the parallel situation across the Pacific Ocean.

Japan in Asia could take the same role as New York City in the United States, he argues. "Asian young people like Japanese pop culture," he notes, and adds that designers such as Louis Vuitton display their goods in Japan because they know if they are popular in Tokyo, then they will succeed in other Asia markets. This is similar to how New York leads the U.S. fashion industry, he observes.

"Japan should encourage other Asians to visit, as well as Westerners who want to understand this region. If many people come, that could stimulate activity," he proposes.

Hurdles remain to such plans, not the least of which is a daunting linguistic barrier for foreigners. Nonetheless, Tokyo does have one advantage that may prove decisive: financial clout. Its vitality is also impressive—any visitor to the city can feel its energy, which stems from the excitement of ambitious people working hard and believing their efforts will be rewarded. Meanwhile, internationalization efforts are proceeding. The Tokyo Stock Exchange plans to open an office in Beijing in 2006 to recruit candidates for listing. Hong Kong–based Zinhua Finance listed on TSE's Mothers market in 2004, while South Korean steelmaker POSCO joined the TSE First Section in 2005.

Nonetheless, discussions of Tokyo's future are always clouded by worries about Japan's dwindling population. In the next chapter, some suggest that concern about dwindling numbers of Japanese is over-wrought. Others even see signs that some demographic trends bode well for certain investment strategies.

Investment Implications

Skeptics of the recovery in the Tokyo real estate market often point out that land price gains have not spread out evenly throughout the entire Japanese archipelago. Such a cavalier dismissal of the city's urban renaissance, conspicuously visible to anyone walking the streets of Marunouchi or Roppongi, reveals a disregard of the first rule of real estate investment: Location largely dictates price. To be sure, real estate market gains have been centered in areas with strong transportation and communication links to the rest of the nation, and central Tokyo is a prime beneficiary of the recent boom. Indeed, many towns in the distant countryside could well continue their descent into relative penury. Even in the capital, some properties that are badly located, poorly designed, or backed with ill-conceived financing plans, could lose money in the years ahead. However, just because the whole country is not sharing equally in the recovery of real estate values does not mean that rebounding areas are being mispriced. Indeed, as the effects of deregulation ripple through the economy and constraints on capital flows ease, such disparities between investments in many asset classes are likely to widen, not narrow.

A relatively lenient regulatory code, accelerating economic growth, rock-bottom prices, cheap financing, corporate restructuring, and financial innovation have all supported the rebound in Tokyo commercial property. Any slowing of economic growth going forward could well weigh on prices. In addition, rising interest rates may squeeze margins, especially those at REITs whose holdings are not narrowly focused on prime areas of the city. Desirable properties are often located in the arc stretching from Marunouchi to Shinagawa. However, some developers are already positioning themselves for rising capital costs, striving to add value to the properties they hold. Tokyo Mid-town, with its lofty ambitions of becoming an international showcase of Japanese design, is one such example. Tokyo's real estate market should be considered as a regional play, capable of attracting businesses from across Asia and likely to benefit from the rapid growth of China. Needless to say, the attractions of Tokyo real estate are magnified, in relative terms, by the dramatic run-up of prices in the United States.

Investors should carefully examine the holdings of REITs listed on the TSE. Spatial diversity among trust property holdings is not necessarily desirable. Indeed, the greater concentration of holdings in hot neighborhoods, the better.

References

"Beyond the leafy red canna ...." This statement and following quotes are from an interview conducted by the author on 15 December 2005.

"...which is modeled after a first-century Roman house..." facts on the Getty Villa from the museum website http://www.getty.edu/visit/see_do/art.html.

"Closed for renovations in 1997 ...." Belgum, Deborah. "Getty Legal Victory Could End Villa Limbo." *Los Angeles Business Journal.* 30 September 2002.

"$275 million ...." Cost of renovation cited from Ourousoff, Nicolai. "In New Getty Villa, a Nod to Old World." *New York Times.* 20 November 2005.

"A prolific scholar, he co-wrote ...." Mera, Koichi with Bertrand Renaud. *The Asian Financial Crisis and the Role of Real Estate.* Armouk, New York: M.E. Sharp, 2000.

Mera, Koichi. "Making of the Failed Land Policy." In *Unlocking Bureaucrat's Kingdom: Deregulation and the Japanese Economy.* Frank Gibney, ed. Washington, D.C.: Brookings Institute, 1998. p. 178–203.

"Mera wrote an influential paper ...." Mera, Koichi. "On the Urban Agglomeration and Economic Efficiency." *Economic Development and Cultural Change* 21, no. 2 (January 1973): 309–324.

"Now most in policy making circles ...." Numerous scholars have referred to Mera's work. Two examples are:

> Renaud, Bertrand. *National Urbanization Policy in Develop-ing Countries.* A World Bank Research Publication. Oxford University Press, 1981.

> Bertaud, Alain and Stephen Malpezzi. *The Spatial Distribu-tion of Population in 47 World Cities: Implications for Economies in Transition.* Center for Urban Land Economic Research. Madison: University of Wisconsin, December 2003.

"The Ministry of Land, Infrastructure, and Transport announced in November 2005 ...." *Nikkei Net Interactive.* Nihon Keizai Shimbun, Inc. "Building Assessment Fraud Shatters Public Confidence System." 22 November 2005.

"A snowman in the downtown ...." Author attended the opening.

"About 240,000 people work ...." Mitsubishi Estate Co., Ltd. *Annual Report 2005.* See esp. p. 9.

"After the Meiji Restoration, their estates ...." Interview with Masahiro Kobayashi conducted by the author on 11 November 2005. Also, company video.

"In addition, inspections following the Kobe earthquake of 1995 …."
Interview conducted by the author on 11 November 2005.

"In principle, firms were allowed to have a total area 1000% …."
*Otemachi Marunouchi Yurakucho Saikai Hatsu Keikaku Suishin
Kyougi Kai.* December 2004. p. 10, 11. Also, interview conducted by
the author on 11 November 2005.

"In 2003, the Shiodome area, which boasts 3.23 million square feet
…." Kamata, Satoshi,. "Government-Business Collusion and Land
Giveaways in Central Tokyo." JapanFocus.org, 2004.

"Firms such as Dentsu …." Hornyak, Tim. *If You Build It, They Will
Come.* Japan, Inc., August 2003.

"Even farther on …" Bremner, Brian. "Rethinking Tokyo: Can
Minoru Mori Make It More Livable?" *Business Week* online. 4
November 2002.

"However, the Shiodome and Roppongi Hills developments are full
…." Interview conducted by the author on 11 November 2005.

"This firm was formed …." Mitsubishi UFJ Securities. "History."
www.sc.mufg.jp/english/e_company/history.html.

"We have little choice but to rely …." *Nikkei Net Interactive.* Nihon
Keizai Shimbun, Inc. "Law Firms Cashing in on M&As." 8 August
2005. Article also has number of Mori Hamada & Matsumoto
lawyers.

"Clouds of toxic gases engulfed Tokyo in the 1970s …." Interview
conducted by the author on 3 March 2006. Also, Marunouchi Heating Supply Co. DVD.

"The headquarters of firms such as Mizuho Bank …." Interview conducted by the author on 3 March 2006.

"Akira Mori, one of the largest landlords in Tokyo …." This statement
and following quotes are from an interview conducted by the author
on 1 March 2006.

"Indeed, widespread demolitions ...." *Nikkei Net Interactive.* Nihon Keizai Shimbun, Inc. "Asbestos-Related Deaths May Rise as More Buildings Demolished." 11 July. 2005

"Akira Mori is the third son of the late Taikichiro Mori ...." Takagi, Jun. "Families That Own Asia." *Time* Asia. 16 February 2004.

"... Mori Trust, which expects to sales to rise ...." Mori Trust Holdings. *Financial Report for the Fiscal Year Ended March 2005.*

"Tofflemire spent a year ...." Interview conducted by the author on 29 June 2005.

"Commercial land prices in Tokyo rose 0.6% ...." Ministry of Land, Infrastructure, and Transport. Heisei 17 Nen Todoufuken Chika Chousa. http://tochi.mlit.go.jp/chika/chousa/2005/02_h02.htm

"Tokyo was cited in a 2004 survey ...." 2004 Association of Foreign Investors in Real Estate (AFIRE) 2004 Annual Survey.

"Morgan Stanley Real Estate Fund is one ...." Interview conducted by the author on 10 November 2005.

"The central European capital ...." Schorske, Carl E. *Fin-de-siécle Vienna, Politics and Culture.* Vintage Books Edition. New York: Random House, 1981. See esp. p. xviii.

"Indeed, when developers brainstormed ...." Interview conducted by the author in November 2005.

"Up to 1 out of every 6 of the 10,000 people living ...." Mitsui Fudosan Co., Ltd. *Tokyo Mid-town Project.* Handout. See esp. p. 7.

"Reporters gazed down on the area ...." Author attended 8 November 2005 press conference.

"The skeleton of the Tokyo Mid-town Tower, which was already almost fully leased ...." Confirmed by Mitsui Fudosan on 11 April 2006.

"Fuji Photo Film Co., Ltd.," Mitsui Fudosan. Press Release dated 14 July, 2005

"However, Nakayama is anticipating ...." Misui Fudosan. Press release dated 14 July 2005.

"In their internal discussions ...." Interview conducted by the author in November 2005.

"The National Art Center is scheduled to open here in 2007 ...." National Art Center, Tokyo. http://www.nact.jp/index.

"The complex, which is Japan's answer to the radiant cities ...." Bremner, Brian. "Rethinking Tokyo: Can Minoru Mori Make It More Livable?" *Business Week* online. 4 November 2002.

"In the nearby Tokyo Mid-town Tower ..." Interview conducted by the author in November 2005.

"Meanwhile, a sleek building ...." Mitsui Fudosan. Press release dated 14 July 2005.

"Motohisa Furukawa, a lawmaker in the Diet, says Tokyo ...." Interview conducted by the author on 3 March 2006.

"Some of the first irrigation channels in the country's flat ...." Taeuber, Irene. *The Population of Japan.* Princeton: Princeton University Press, 1958. See esp. p. 12.

"The Tokyo Stock Exchange plans to ...." *Nikkei Net Interactive.* Nihon Keizai Shimbun, Inc. "TSE to Open Beijing Office, Focus on Recruiting Chinese Firms." 4 April 2006.

7

BIRTHRATES AND
BUSHIDO

Market Watchers See Opportunities in Upcoming Demographic Shifts

Tama New Town has missed its chance, according to the 71-year-old retiree, sitting along the covered walkway near the city's Nagayama housing complex. "The development of this place is finished," he flatly asserts.

Tama New Town, a suburban community on the outskirts of Tokyo, suffers from an image problem. The New Town is perceived to be getting old and is often cited in discussions of Japan's demographic woes. The population of Tama City peaked in 1993 at 145,659 and then fell steadily until hitting 141,119 in 2001. To be sure, Tama New Town is somewhat of a special case. In the 1960s, the Tokyo Metropolitan government decided to build an entirely new community to prevent ill-planned land development and ease housing shortages in the city, enacting the New Residential Area Development Act.

Housing sites were built, along with roads, parks, and schools. The first settlement occurred about 30 years ago in Tama City.

This generation of residents is now entering its sunset years. The housing units they live in were built in the 1960s and are tiny by today's standards, so young people have little interest in moving in. Thus, some feel pessimistic regarding the outlook for their city.

However, Mika Fukuda, Head of the Planning Division in Tama City Hall, has a strikingly different story to tell. In her eyes, a continuation of the recent decline in population is not inevitable, but could even reverse in the years ahead. Indeed, in 2002, despite the negative hype surrounding her city, its population rose slightly for the first time since 1993.

Fukuda acknowledges that the population in some parts of the city is aging rapidly. However, these sections have special characteristics that suggest such trends will not necessarily become general. For example, as part of the government's development plan, housing blocks were built on hilly ridges that ran through the area. Nagayama was one of the first to be completed and thus among the first to be occupied. About 16% of the population there is now 65 or over. However, housing projects finished in subsequent years have younger populations. The quality of construction steadily improved as well, as development progressed, suggesting that later housing units are not as grim as the Nagayama ones.

Riding out on the train from Tokyo, the forested hills of the city resemble green alpine ridges jutting through a gray glacier of urban sprawl. Fukuda notes that Tama City enjoys more park land per resident than any other city in the Tokyo metropolitan area.

In addition, the city planners allowed the owners of rice paddies in the valleys between the hills to keep their land during the development. Such owners have built new homes and apartment buildings, and these properties are attracting younger residents, Fukuda points out. With several universities nearby, many apartments are leased to students.

In a valley to the east of the aging Nagayama housing unit runs the Kamakura Kaido road, an ancient street that originally served as a military route for the Kamakura *bakafu* more than 1,000 years ago. Now it is lined with plane trees, and a hedge sprouts white flowers in the median during the summer. Alongside the road snazzy BMW and Mercedes Benz dealerships host car buyers near apartment buildings and homes apparently built much later the gray concrete towers just to the west. Turning off the Kamakura Kaido road leads to the Vita Commune, built in 1999. When I visited the futuristic eight-story public hall with a round, glass-enclosed observation deck, young couples relaxed at tables in front of a Starbucks on the ground floor. A stream of subway passengers ebbed and flowed into the nearby train station. Tama City appeared a far cry from a city in decline.

The grim statistics are familiar to many market observers, echoed in most discussions of Japan's outlook for economic growth. In 2006, the Japanese population is expected to peak at 127.7 million people, according to projections of the National Institute of Population and Social Security Research. From then on, inexorable decline sets in. Mainline projections put the number of Japanese in 2013 at 126.9 million, the same level as the 2000 census. By 2050, the population is expected to shrink to 100.6 million, down by one-fifth from current levels.

Although Japan's demographic problems are perceived to be severe, they are shared more or less with many Organization of Economic Cooperation and Development (OECD) member countries. Indeed, Ignazio Visco of the OECD has observed that in almost all OECD countries, fertility rates are now at or below the 2.1 children per family needed to stabilize population levels, and life expectancy has risen because of improvements in health care, nutrition, and living standards. The old-age dependency ratio—the number of 65-year-olds and older relative to the number of 20- to 65-year-olds— is expected to reach nearly 50% throughout the OECD area, he observes. A "considerably sharper" increase is expected for Japan; Visco says this country's old-age dependency ratio is forecast to reach 65% by 2050. Such high dependency ratios are expected to strain societies because fewer workers are forced to support an increasing number of elderly.

Japan's imminent demographic demise is widely accepted by market participants. But is it really inevitable? Increasingly, skeptics are questioning the extremely pessimistic numbers put out by the Japanese government. Although they are not taking issue with the fact that Japan, like other mature societies across the globe, is aging, some critics are questioning the severity and immediacy of Japan's projected plunge in population. Some even argue that a significant decline could be postponed by a decade or more.

John Tofflemire, who is president of Sapient Real Estate Consulting, doubts the government's numbers have much validity. Tofflemire is keenly interested in demographic trends because they are useful in forecasting land prices.

Breaking down the Japanese population into 5-year cohorts, Tofflemire argues the number of births in the 1985–1990 period was fairly reasonable. Demographic trends, however, suddenly turned downward in the 1990–1995 period and plunged downward further in 1995–2000. This period, the "lost decade" of Japan, was marked by economic stagnation and lack of job opportunities. Young people did not merely struggle to find work; they apparently put off marrying and raising families as well.

The government forecasts appear to extrapolate the declining trend of the last two periods, Tofflemire observes. "Perhaps it is a call to arms to show people what would happen if present trends continue; however, it is difficult for me to take this seriously as a forecast," he says.

Tofflemire notes that even a slight increase in the expected trend line would push any significant population decline out to 2015 or even beyond. His research points to a potential "multiplier effect" of good policy, where improvement in economic conditions could lead to a recovery in the fertility rate, further supporting demand through population increases. Importantly, such a viewpoint suggests that demographics are not a current that the policymakers have to fight against to support growth, but a variable that may possibly be influenced.

Japanese government forecasts tend to be more pessimistic than those based on economics or data, observes David Weinstein. Weinstein is an economics professor at Columbia University as well as the Director of the Japan Project at the National Bureau of Economic Research and a Member of the Council on Foreign Relations. Using methodology adopted by the Japanese government leads to the forecast that the last Japanese baby will be born in about 1,000 years, he wryly observes.

Although Japanese fertility rates have been falling fairly substantially, they will likely rise at some point in the future with further per-capita income growth, says Weinstein, who recently edited *Reviving Japan's Economy: Problems and Prescriptions,* with Takatoshi Ito and Hugh Patrick. Rising wages, coupled with a drop of fertility, is seen in many countries as couples realize that the benefits of having two spouses work outweigh the benefits of having large families, he notes.

"When wages rise enough, there is a second effect, which economists call the income effect," he points out. The value of earning an additional dollar or additional yen starts to fall, while the value of having that second child rises.

If you are very wealthy, you may not care about having more money, but you may want that second child, he notes. He forecasts a similar shift in priorities in Japanese households in the future.

Against a backdrop of the expected aging of Japanese society, the Ministry of Finance has warned that a fiscal deficit is a "major obstacle to the realization of a dynamic economy." A rising fiscal deficit may lead to rigidity in government spending, reduced spending by households, investment cutbacks by companies, and possibly even a loss of confidence in government bonds.

Japan's fiscal balance deteriorated sharply during the 1990s as the government greatly expanded its role in the economy. Such a resurgence of the public sector in Japan was in sharp contrast to trends elsewhere on the globe. The fall of the Berlin Wall in 1989 was heralded as not only marking the end of the Cold War, but also a triumph of market-oriented policy making. Many countries spent the 1990s making the difficult transition from centrally planned to more open economies.

Despite such a growing consensus overseas, Japanese policymakers charted their own course during the decade. Blessed with ample savings and obeying a universal human tendency to put off painful decisions as long as possible, bureaucrats and politicians in Tokyo tried to have it all—profound restructuring of the economy without any bloodletting. The result—piecemeal reforms accompanied by public sector spending and a bizarre, creeping nationalization of the country's assets.

Japanese policymakers may have also made the decision, implicitly, to protect Japanese intangible assets, including the know-how accumulated by firms in various industries. Because many of the intangible assets of a firm are held by its employees, this meant protecting jobs and vulnerable firms. This was a rejection of the "creative destruction" approach advocated by many, in which weaker firms would be left to fend for themselves and often go bust, while newer, stronger firms in high-growth industries would be allowed access to more capital. Kasumigaseki officials may have felt that there was inherent value—intangible asset value—in weaker firms as well and that they should not be allowed to go belly up.

Regardless of their motives, Japanese policymakers faced a fundamental, chronic problem when the bubble collapsed. Returns on

Japanese assets were falling, threatening a drop in Japanese living standards at the same time the country's population was aging. Asset deflation was threatening to wipe out household savings, which was primarily invested in the nation's capital stock.

Japanese policymakers could have adopted policies to facilitate the flow of capital from dying industries to faster-growing sectors. The fundamental reason returns on assets were falling was the rigidity of factors of production markets. The land, labor, and capital markets in Japan were fossilized, and entrepreneurial risk-taking was not being rewarded. Excessive regulations, high barriers to entry, and other factors increasingly hindered reallocation of capital and stifled the formation of new businesses. However, adopting aggressively pro–free market policies to stimulate liquidity in the factor markets was also problematic for policymakers. Capital flows between industries would have sparked wealth redistribution, which could have destabilized the existing political order. Jobs would have been lost and intangible assets at firms destroyed as well.

Instead, the government took a more incremental approach throughout the 1990s. Monetary policy was eased, at times dramatically, to support demand. Deregulation was attempted only gradually, and at times when worries about its effect on employment and asset allocation (and, therefore, on wealth distribution) were allayed. Intangible assets were protected as much as possible. Major capital market reforms were not undertaken until late in the decade under Prime Minister Ryutaro Hashimoto's administration.

Meanwhile, to protect Japanese savings at the same time returns on Japanese assets continued to tumble, the government endeavored to support asset prices—by buying them up. The share of the public sector in total Japanese assets rose to 26.5% by 2003, up from only 16.8% in 1989. With the amount of assets managed by the public sector increasing sharply, arguably, this meant that efficiency in the economy was falling. Public sector officials were not under pressure to generate profits like private managers, so overall return on investment probably fell when their share of the economy rose. Bond issuances and government debt also ballooned. When Koizumi took office, he decided something had to be done to rein in the growth of the central government balance sheet.

"We call this the 'mouth of the crocodile,'" says Yuji Baba from the Research Division of the Budget Bureau of the Ministry of Finance. He points to a line chart showing general account expenditures and revenues from the early 1980s to the present. A widening gap from 1989, the peak of the bubble, has resulted in a flood of bond issuances and rapidly deteriorating fiscal balance.

With the mountain of long-term public debt reaching ¥774 trillion in the fiscal year 2005 budget, many worry about how long such profligacy can continue. The Ministry of Finance looks closely at the primary balance, which strips out financial components of the budget, such as interest payments and bond issuances, and measures only the difference in revenues, primarily taxes, and expenditures on social security and the like. Japan has been running a primary deficit on a national accounts basis, which includes both central and local governments, from the early 1990s. The government hopes to return to the black by the early 2010s.

"Some people misunderstand and think if we achieve a primary balance, we are finished," says Baba. The Japanese government does not think that, he notes. Achieving primary balance is just the first step in bringing down the country's debt-to-GDP ratio, taking into account Japan's severe fiscal situation, he adds.

The Council of Fiscal and Economic Policy, which is chaired by Prime Minister Koizumi, is discussing ways to reduce the recent flood of debt and plans to release a list of options by June 2006. In addition to ongoing reductions of discretionary spending, the council is likely considering tax hikes to improve the country's finances.

Corporate tax revenues will probably remain depressed for years, as firms write off losses from previous periods to reduce their upcoming tax obligations. That raises the possibility of consumption or income tax increases.

Local government allocations are also being reconsidered. Currently, the government guarantees that local governments can meet their budgets and makes up for any revenue shortfall. This raises the issue of moral hazard, notes Baba, because even projects unsubsidized by the government and local debt service payments are guaranteed. The Ministry of Finance reduced national subsidies to the regional governments, which total more than ¥4 trillion, and cut tax sharing as well. In addition, the government boosted local tax revenues by shifting part of the national individual income tax to local inhabitant tax. As revenue sources are transferred to local governments, they will increasingly decide for themselves how to spend their money.

The primary balance is expected to improve in the current fiscal year, as both tax revenues rise and expenditures are slashed. However, even with reforms, further improvement in Japan's fiscal situation will require extreme discipline. The Koizumi administration has already dramatically reduced discretionary government spending in recent years. To achieve a primary balance by fiscal year 2011, the cabinet office estimates that discretionary expenditures will need to be pared to the bone and be cut another 30% or so.

Ballooning social security payments make the dynamics of debt reduction even more difficult. An increase of inflation, although helping to support tax revenues, is unlikely to ease the government's plight. In fact, a 4% nominal growth rate would be worse than a 3% rate for the government, says Baba. Although tax revenues would indeed rise, inflation-adjusted social security payments would also increase, and debt payments would jump as well, according to a study by the Ministry of Finance.

Indeed, some believe that the tide is turning against the government and see no improvement in the fiscal deficit for the foreseeable future. Interest rates on 10-year bonds issued in the mid- to late 1990s were at historical lows. If these are rolled over, and indeed they must be if the country is running a primary deficit, then eventually debt will have to be reissued at higher rates, thus boosting the interest rate burden on the government further even if no new bonds are issued.

Thomas Byrne, who writes the Japan country reports for Moody's Investor Service, suggests that the government may be targeting the primary balance rather than the overall deficit because the primary deficit is poised to shrink faster for this very reason. Because the primary deficit does not measure interest payments, rising coupon levels on reissued bonds would not impact this ratio.

Moody's series of downgrades of Japanese local currency government debt from Aaa in 1998 ultimately to A2 by May 2002 has been interpreted by some market watchers as a warning that risk of default has become imminent. That is simply not the case, says Bryne. "The message we were signaling was that Japan's credit fundamentals had deteriorated with high debt, large government deficits, deflation, and very anemic growth," he explains.

The risk of a default within the next 5 years still remains less than 1%, according to Moody's analysis. While Moody's 2002 Japan downgrade resulted in the country's local currency debt rating falling below Botswana's, Byrne notes that the African nation has a small population and a lot of diamonds resulting in much better measures of fiscal stability. Japan has a gross government debt–to–GDP ratio of 170%, and Botswana fares much better, with only a 9% ratio. The gross debt–to–GDP ratio, when central bank holdings are stripped out, is used to ascertain the crowding out of the private sector by the government in the debt markets. Another measure of the sustainability of the fiscal balance, government debt to revenue, measures the ability of the government to repay its obligations using current revenue streams. Japan had a relatively high level of about 570% in

2004; other countries with levels in this range include Argentina and Lebanon. Botswana's measure is only 21%.

"There is a lot of renewed optimism regarding the Japanese economy in recent months, but most of this is still forward looking, in the sense that deflation isn't ended," Byrne observes. Although modest price increases are forecasted to appear within upcoming quarters, "no one is talking about decent inflation, something about the 2% range, which certainly wouldn't be alarming for any other economy, which would just help in terms of government debt dynamics," he adds, noting that almost a "quantum leap" is necessary in terms of end of deflation and continued underlying real growth. Nominal GDP growth of at least 4% is needed to get improvement in key ratios, he stresses.

Although some Ministry of Finance officials and bond analysts worry about Japan's debt ratios, Weinstein's research suggests that Japanese government bond (JGB) holders do not have to be concerned about a fiscal crisis.

In fact, his view is so encouraging that some JGB salesmen take his reports along to client presentations. "The fiscal situation in Japan, especially after the 2004 pension reforms, is either sustainable or very close to being sustainable with minor adjustments," he concludes.

A long-term view is necessary when assessing the dynamics of Japan's fiscal balance, he stresses. Governments calculate pension plan financing based on payments spanning the 40- or 50-year careers of workers. Substantial deficits may temporarily emerge that do not threaten the overall solvency of the social security system, he notes.

"The really important [pension] reform was a .354 percentage point per year increase in the social security contribution rate that will continue until 2017," he explains, "resulting in the rate rising from 13.6% to 18.3%."

"That is [effectively] a very big tax increase, almost 5 percentage points," he observes. Coupled with a number of smaller tax increases, this will result in a radical increase in the amount of revenues going into social security.

The Japanese government also changed the indexing formula that links past and future earnings, he notes. Authorities collect data on each individual's compensation over the course of his or her life and then multiply that compensation figure by a number to compute the payout in any particular year, he explains. The government has revised this number downward as life expectancy rises and the number of people paying into the system falls over time.

"Those are pretty big adjustments, roughly 0.9% per year reduction in the payout ratio through about 2023," he stresses.

The reduction in the pension payment ratio coupled with rising contributions will have a dramatic effect over the long term, he argues.

"If you're looking over a very short horizon, you are not going to see a big effect," Weinstein concedes. "Over a long horizon, these really do add up, and that's going to make the system solvent."

While some are concluding that the outlooks for population growth and public finance are not as grim as generally supposed, some hedge fund managers see demographic trends that may even support corporate performance. Simon Ross notes that the 28- to 35-year-old generation is 80% of the size of the senior citizen age group. "Japan's demographic spread looks like an hour glass, instead of a reverse pyramid like everybody thinks it looks like," he stresses.

He even sees a "potential wind in the sails of the economy" as this 28- to 35-year-old generation grows older and spends more. "In the next 10 to 15 years, we will have a window of opportunity."

"I am not a 50-year demographer, but the opportunity in Japan is this hourglass dynamic," he continues. This is true, he argues, not only in terms of consumption, but in terms of corporate governance and policy making as well. The current generation of business and government leaders rose through the ranks during the 1960s and 1970s, he observes, when capital was scarce. As a result, there is a tendency among corporate leaders either to hoard capital and retain excessive earnings or to rely excessively on debt financing.

"As the generations change, we should have an incremental increase in capital efficiency," he expects.

Overall, the percentage of those becoming presidents in their fifties and sixties fell in the first half of 2005, while those in their forties rose by 2.1%, according to Nihon Keizai Shimbun, Inc. More than 600 major companies replaced their presidents during this time, a sixfold increase from the same period the previous year.

Perhaps the most dramatic change in management prompted by a younger leader is at The Daiei, Inc., whose restructuring by Richard Folsom and his Advantage Partner colleagues was discussed in Chapter 4, "The Future of Japanese Management." They brought in 47-year-old Yasuyuki Higuchi from Hewlett-Packard Japan. However, Sanyo Electric Co., Ltd.; Marui Co., Ltd.; Aoyama Trading Co., Ltd.; and CSK Corp. also recently promoted executives who had not reached the half-century mark yet to president.

A changing of the guard is occurring in the Diet as well. The 80 new Liberal Democratic Party (LDP) members of the Diet elected in September 2005 greatly accelerated an ongoing generational shift, resulting in 70% of Lower House LDP members now being born after World War II. In spring 2006, the front-runner for the LDP presidential race in September was Chief Cabinet Secretary Shinzo Abe, who was born in 1954. If Abe wins the election, he would not only be the youngest prime minister in the post-war period, but he would also be the first to be born after August 15, 1945.

It remains unclear how these leaders, many of whom have no personal recollections of the wartime period, will change Japanese

politics. However, they are clearly a different breed than their predecessors. "This is a generation that is not ignorant of history but never-
theless has a different view of it," observes Brad Glosserman,
executive director at Pacific Forum CSIS, a foreign policy research
institute based in Hawaii. "They believe Japan's record since 1945 is
more important than its record up to 1945. Consequently, this is a
generation that believes ... that Japan has earned the right to be recognized for its achievements. Much of what is perceived as nationalism, I think, is merely a search for status and prestige internationally,"
he adds.

This striving for respect abroad is manifested in the campaign for
a United Nations Security Council seat, growing support for a constitutional revision permitting greater defense capabilities, and a willingness on the part of political leaders to stand up to perceived slights
by other countries, especially China. On the domestic front, a broad
consensus on how to address such critical issues, such as a widening
disparity in incomes, the graying of society, and increased job uncertainty, has been harder to achieve.

However, investors should not misread Koizumi's resounding
mandate for postal savings reform. Part of this generation's pride in
Japan's post-war success stems from the socially equitable distribution of its fruits, Glosserman notes. "I don't think they're prepared to
... embrace Western, frontier capitalism, which has profound winners and losers," he warns.

In addition, politicians face immense difficulties in drafting
reformist legislation. Glosserman warns that the resources available
to politicians interested in crafting policy remain meager compared
with what their U.S. counterparts have. U.S. Congressional staffs
dwarf those of Diet members, which often consist of only a couple
people, he stresses.

Nonetheless, these harried politicians are confronting widespread anxiety about social inequity and job insecurity, he says.

"These issues become more real over time, and the need to come up with answers becomes far more compelling," he observes.

New ideas are percolating in the murky, opaque world of Japanese politics. Faced with a different set of challenges than their predecessors, some farsighted politicians are pushing innovative policies that will increase Japan's competitiveness. LDP lawmaker Yasuhisa Shiozaki, who was born in 1950, has urged measures to prevent auditors and accountants from establishing cozy ties with their clients. "I can't think of any other lawmaker who has shown an interest in accounting as I have," he told the Nihon Keizai Shimbun, Inc. Meanwhile, Motohisa Furukawa, age 40, served as general counsel to the Intellectual Property Rights Strategy Team of the Democratic Party of Japan. They published an extensive report on IP in September 2000, well before Prime Minister Koizumi declared the importance of IP to his administration. Furukawa notes that Koizumi's policies are "basically the same direction" as his party's recommendations about a year and a half before.

"There is a great significance to generations," notes Motohisa Furukawa, who was first elected in 1996 to the lower house at the age of 30. Furukawa participated in the founding of the Democratic Party of Japan (DPJ) the same year. This party joined with several other opposition parties in 1998 to form a new Democratic Party of Japan, and in 2003 also merged with the Liberal Party. Even after the setback in the September 2005 elections, it is the largest opposition party in Japan, with 113 seats in the lower house and 83 seats in the upper. Rather than depend on bureaucrats for drafting legislation, many members of the DPJ, which include former ministry officials, lawyers, and bankers, introduce their own independent bills.

An animated speaker, Furukawa's ready smile and quick laugh suggest that he is a die-hard optimist. Indeed, in the face of the ruling party's dramatic victory in the last lower-house elections, such a temperament is undoubtedly a comfort to his supporters. Furukawa shifts gears while speaking quickly. Quick to raise his voice in indignation at ruling party policies, he turns quieter, more pensive, when discussing what he sees as threats to the traditional sense of community in Japan.

Furukawa did not initially intend to be a politician. In fact, his life was a typical Japanese success story. Having graduated from prestigious Tokyo University in 1988, he entered the Ministry of Finance (MoF) and thought he was set for life.

The stock market collapsed in 1990, and everything changed. "My superiors at the Ministry of Finance were arrested and sent to jail," he notes. Not only bureaucrats, but senior managers at top corporations were also imprisoned. Many were fellow alumni, he observes. Three years later, when he went to Columbia University on an exchange program, he was severely criticized by outspoken U.S. students. They complained that Japan was dominated by bureaucrats and would never change.

That started him thinking about his chosen path in life. The ministry officials he spoke to realized they were being criticized for being conservative and doggedly pursuing old policies. However, his colleagues said that the reason they persisted is that no politicians would steer the government in a new direction.

"Bureaucrats are like train engine operators," Furukawa says. "They are good at guiding policies along existing tracks." However, in the 1990s, Japan had reached an impasse where old policies no longer generated growth. There were no rails for the train to ride on going forward.

"If the train continues, it will crash," he continues his analogy. "There is a need for new rails to be laid. Bureaucrats cannot do this. That is a job for politicians."

Bureaucrats should not be involved in deciding fundamental policy directions for several reasons, Furukawa notes. First of all, the mindset of bureaucrats is narrow—other than the affairs of their own particular offices, they are not well informed. They also lack authority. "If they change policies, then this is not democracy because they are not elected." Furukawa notes.

It is up to the politicians to propose new directions. However, those types of politicians were not around in the early 1990s, Furukawa was told.

"So I quit MoF," he said. After being elected to the Diet, he sponsored 13 bills as a freshman legislator. He helped establish the Committee on Audit and Oversight Administration in 1997 and introduced a financial reform plan the following year. He has been reelected twice.

"The biggest problem facing the country is the aging of Japanese society," says Furukawa. In addition, the country faces resource constraints and must deal with energy and environmental problems.

"Since the Meiji Restoration, Japan has looked abroad for models to see how other countries have modernized or developed their industries," he notes. Japan adopted other countries' approaches. Now Japan is facing new issues, such as climatic change and the graying of society. Although other countries are grappling with similar problems, Japan is now a "front-runner," Furukawa notes ironically.

The opposition politician is critical of the administration, arguing that Koizumi is attempting to shrink government without any consideration of its proper role in society. "Just 'Shrink government!' 'Shift to private sector!'" Furukawa summarizes the market fundamentalist's view.

For example, in addressing fiscal problems, Furukawa argues that the Ministry of Finance and Koizumi are only trying to reduce the burden on the central government rather than consider the finances of the regional governments as well. Kasumigaseki officials are trying to reduce general expenditures and shift burdens to the regions. "It's as if MoF is worried only about cleaning its own garden," Furukawa says, comparing bureaucrats to someone sweeping the garbage in front of his own house into his neighbors' yards.

"In the current period of social and corporate upheaval, the government's first priority should be providing a safety net to the country's citizens," he urges.

"Now individuals must take on more risk. Give them more courage to take risks. The reason that circus acrobats perform on the flying trapeze is [that] there is a safety net below," Furukawa argues.

"Now, Koizumi is telling NEETs [vernacular for young people with No Education, Employment, or Training] to swing on the trapeze and try new things, but if they fall, they will die." The government should provide a minimum pension guarantee as well as health care. Education should also be provided, he adds.

If the administration focuses only on shrinking government, companies will get smaller as well. Trust between people will erode, and employees will start thinking, "If he gets fired, I will survive." Sense of community will deteriorate, he warns.

This sense of community is essential for the welfare of Japanese, he argues. Furukawa discovered the big difference between living in New York and living in Tokyo when he returned to Japan. "When you walk along the street in Japan, you can relax."

"In New York, you cannot relax until you arrive back at your apartment—and lock your door," Furukawa says.

"Companies can churn employees, getting rid of them when they are no longer suitable for their jobs. Countries, however, cannot do this. Politicians must consider those people whose skills do not match current needs."

As the security of old Japan erodes, people are looking for new values to guide their lives. "Old values are destroyed, but new values have not appeared."

Furukawa believes that people should find value in discovering one's inner voice, finding one's own path in life. "Not being told by other people what to do, but deciding for one's self. This is reflected in an old Buddhist saying, *Ware tada taru shiru,*" he notes, which equates contentment or acceptance with limits of knowledge.

The debate has not ended between market fundamentalists, personified by those in the Koizumi administration, and more liberal backers of a larger role for government as Japan makes its transition into a post-industrial society. Indeed, during the grim days of the bank failures and rising unemployment of the 1990s, there was some worry among foreign researchers about a potential destabilization of the country's politics.

Exiting Shinkiba subway station, I stumbled smack into a noisy political demonstration on a May day in the late 1990s. Rows of black *uyoku* trucks of ultranationalist groups clogged the roads. Lines of helmeted police, armed with shields and batons, separated the trucks from a crowd of Communists that had come together along the edge of the park. Party members had gathered to celebrate their organization's roots in the international workers movement. Long banners emblazed with Communist party slogans hung from balloons drifting high in the air, and martial songs blared from loudspeakers mounted on the black trucks.

Skirting between the *uyoku* trucks, cutting in between police wearing riot gear, and plunging into the noisy crowd of Communists, I had a quick tour, up close and personal, of the far extremes of the Japanese political spectrum.

Edging through the groups wearing an uneasy grin, I felt conspicuously bourgeois. Indeed, since I was an American working at a foreign bank, dislike of me would be probably one of the few things the protesters facing each other could agree on that day. Nonetheless, bemused onlookers politely made way for the jaywalking foreigner. Not for one second did I feel threatened. In a surreal moment, I thought I heard the strains of *L'Internationale* wafting through the air.

The resilience of Japanese society as it struggles through its current round of restructuring, unprecedented since the early decades of the Meiji Era, should not suggest to observers that voters here are docile and indifferent to how their country is run.

Japan has a long tradition of mass protest. Many peasant revolts occurred during the Tokugawa Period. Some of the larger ones, such as the *Sanchu* Rising during 1726 to 1727, and the *Ueda Horeki* Rising of 1761 to 1763, involved entire fiefdoms. Although famine and hardship were often the cause of feudal protests, later in the nineteenth century, many revolts were sparked more by economic insecurity than hunger. Herbert Bix noted in his 1987 study of peasant revolts that awareness of later peasant uprisings is vital to understanding the subsequent constitutional movement in Japan in the late nineteenth century. He observed that the "last great wave of peasant protests … prepared rich soil for the freedom and people's rights movement." Such societal pressures for human rights safeguards helped lead to the adoption of the Meiji Constitution in 1889.

Anarchists plotted to assassinate the Meiji emperor in 1910 but were arrested by police before being able to lob a bomb into his carriage. The authorities, "eager to stamp out socialism," responded by making 26 arrests, jailing defendants only remotely connected to the crime, wrote Donald Keene in *Emperor of Japan, Meiji and his World*. With the far left wiped out, two mainstream precursors to the current Liberal Democratic Party dominated the ballot box from 1912, but political turbulence continued to threaten government stability. In 1918, the prime minister resigned after calling in troops to quell rioting over high rice prices in hundreds of towns. A Communist Party was established in 1922, but it was outlawed within 2 years. The government took further steps to suppress dissent in 1925, when it passed the Peace Preservation Law, which forbade advocating significant changes in Japan's political system. After the military consolidated its control over the cabinet in 1937, all political parties were dissolved in 1940 and entered the Imperial Rule Assistance

Association, an organization established to support the war effort. Such government actions appear to have played a role in limiting protests during the prewar period.

With the adoption of a more liberal constitution during the U.S. occupation, protest movements once again resurfaced. Student federations formed a radical nationwide association that would cause headaches for authorities for years. Mass demonstrations against the Japan-U.S. Joint Security Treaty began in the 1950s, and in the 1960s, protests continued against the Vietnam War and other issues. Social unrest escalated with the occupation of Tokyo University and riots in Shinjuku.

As was the case in Europe and the United States, the student protest movement died out as popular support waned because of violent acts by militant students and other groups. In the 1970s, the more radical members of the student association formed splinter terrorist organizations. One group, the Red Army, took hostages and robbed banks. Assailants bombed the headquarters of Mitsubishi Heavy Industries, killing eight people and injuring hundreds in 1974. Stepped-up government repression, commercialization of the counterculture, and the end of the Vietnam War in 1975 also dampened the enthusiasm of protestors.

Against a backdrop of steadily rising living standards during the last several decades, Japan has been relatively free of significant social and political unrest since then. The country was horrified in 1995 when members of the religious cult Aum Shinrikyo launched a sarin gas attack on Tokyo subway cars, killing 12 and injuring more than 5,000. However, Tokyo has largely been spared the violent antiglobalization protests that have broken out in other world capitals.

Groups of protestors broke through barricades and smashed shop windows in Ottawa, Canada, where the IMF, World Bank, and G20 group of nations held their annual meetings in November 2001. The only sign of unrest outside the IMF offices in Tokyo at the time were a couple of young men dressed in black, apparently loitering outside the building. To be sure, they were outnumbered and watched closely by police. However, most discontented, socially aware young Japanese appear to be engaging in society to bring about change rather than dropping out to violently confront existing institutions.

Some scholars argue that Japanese politics and society are evolving to reflect the changing priorities of the electorate. "That's the Japanese economy," says Jun Nishikawa, pointing to Brugel's painting of the Tower of Babel that hangs in his office. However, Nishikawa, a professor in the economics department at Waseda University, is not worried about his country's future. "I am not a pessimist," he insists.

Mounting fiscal problems and the recent banking crisis have shown the unsustainability of an export-oriented economy where economic planners are focused solely on boosting output levels, he points out. "This is a good opportunity for Japan to choose another type of development—social development, qualitative development of society," he notes.

Previously, family and community life was ignored by salaried workers, he notes. "Now people have more time to consider family life and neighborhood activities," he adds.

He points to the passage of a law legalizing nonprofit organizations as evidence of the rapid development of a civil society. With more opportunities to engage and change their worlds, citizens are unlikely to feel disenfranchised. Marxism, as a nineteenth-century economic model, has naturally lost some of its attraction for radicals as the condition of workers improved in the twentieth century. However, Nishikawa notes that part of the reason the Communist Party has not attracted more followers, even during the grim days of bank failures and arrests of bureaucrats and senior company officials, is that Japanese society is basically inclusive. "Marx teaches us how to criticize social society," he notes. Few Japanese feel so isolated as to reject mainstream political participation.

Indeed, the Law to Promote Specified Nonprofit Activities, enacted in December 1998, is widely anticipated to further promote grassroots activism. Only about 26,000 groups gained legal status as nonprofit Public Interest Legal Persons under the previous system, observes Robert Pekkanen in *Japan's Duel Civil Society: Members Without Advocates.* In contrast, the Internal Revenue Service in the United States has granted nonprofit status to more than one million American groups, he notes. The Japanese government has forecasted that the number of nonprofit groups will likely increase by almost 40%.

Although opposition parties are widely perceived not to wield significant power in policy making, the non-profit legislation is one area in which they made a difference. "The writing of the law saw Dietmen wrest legislation away from bureaucrats and the LDP make concessions to small coalition parties (Social Democratic Party and Sakigake) in the face of electoral pressure from a viable opposition (New Frontier Party)," Pekkanen wrote.

One example of grassroots organizations making a difference in Japan's political landscape is the *Seikatsu* Consumers' Club Co-op, notes Nishikawa. Originally founded by a small circle of Tokyo housewives in 1965, the co-op now serves 230,000 households. More than 100 members of the *Seikatsu* Club have been elected to municipal offices. Indeed, Nishikawa sees an elemental shift in the awareness of citizens, arguing that they will change from *shohisha* (consumers) to *seikatsusha* (those concerned with quality of life).

The memories of the horrors suffered by victims of mercury poisoning in Minamata City, on Kyushu Island, linger. In one of the most infamous cases of environmental pollution in the world, a company dumped methyl mercury into a nearby bay for years, and locals who ate seafood from the area were exposed. The town's name became synonymous with environment degradation.

What the emergence of a stronger civil society means for Japan can perhaps best seen here. In a stunning reversal of priorities, Minamata City is now near the forefront of environmental protection. In 1992, the city announced its plans to become a model environmental city. In particular, its waste-management efforts are among the most rigorous to be found anywhere on the globe. Although many Japanese municipalities divide trash into various categories for recycling purposes, Minamata residents separate their garbage into no less than *twenty-one* types. From December 2002, the city even started collecting food scraps from households to be composted at private plants.

"Citizens are taking the lead," says Kazushi Kaneto, an associate at the Matsushita Institute of Government and Management. He points to Minamata as an example of the decentralization of power, which will likely accelerate in the years ahead.

The Matsushita Institute has become a magnet for those like Kaneto who aspire to lead Japan to better days. Of 213 graduates of Matsushita Institute over the last quarter-century, 64 have been elected to public office. Seiji Maehara, the former president of the Democratic Party of Japan, is its most famous graduate. He was on the verge of resigning his leadership when I visited the campus in March 2006; a party member had accused an LDP lawmaker of taking funds from Livedoor's Horie, and the e-mail that the charge had been based on turned out to be fake. Still reeling from its loss in September, this came as a body blow to the country's main opposition party. Indeed, even before the e-mail scandal, some in Tokyo compared LDP supremacy to the 1940s, when all political parties were absorbed into the Imperial Rule Assistance Association.

Despite visiting during some dark days for the institute's alumni, I found its current students upbeat about prospects for change. Kaneto aspires to become a community activist. "Citizens should not delegate all politics to politicians," the graduate of Tokyo University adds. "Each citizen should design his own way of living and try to improve society." He wants to return to Shikoku Island, known for its *hachiju-hachi*, or 88 holy places. Pilgrims from time immemorial have circumambulated the island, visiting each temple in turn. Locals have a tradition of supplying food and assistance to the pilgrims, free of charge. Kenato, who also plans to complete a pilgrimage before he graduates, says such generosity shows that a "volunteer mindset" is deeply rooted in the region.

The ink brush calligraphy of the legendary Konosuke Matsushita, the founder of the institute, can be seen hanging in the tea room on the institute grounds. Matsushita Electric Devices Manufacturing Works, which he founded in 1918 at the age of 23 to market a light socket, eventually grew to become a giant global manufacturer, known by its trademark names National, Panasonic, Technics, and JVC.

The tea room faces out onto a garden, where water trickles melodiously into a stone washing bowl, surrounded by black pines and sasanqua bushes. The characters painted on the scroll, *sunao*, were very important to Matsushita, who founded the institute at the age of 83 in 1980 to train the leaders of twenty-first-century Japan. The term roughly means, "a mind that is docile in the face of truth, enabling one to see things as they truly are."

"We just met with some people from the Mansfield Foundation … it appears that there is nothing like this institute in America," says Kazuhiro Furuyama, who is the director of the institute's training program. Competition to enter the program is extremely fierce; about 200 people applied for next year, and the institute will accept only 7 or 8. Although academic qualifications are considered, more important is whether an applicant has *kokorozashi*, or determination, Furuyama says. The admissions committee is looking for people who will make a difference.

Gemma Kentaro is an aspiring politician who made the cut. After spending years in war-torn Cambodia, working with an organization collecting handguns from villagers, he is convinced that Japan should

take a larger role in international affairs. However, he is not hoping
for a career at the Foreign Ministry. The lack of vision among bureaucrats limits what they can do, and besides, intelligence in Japan
regarding foreign countries is weak, he notes. "Politicians must fix
this," he argues.

Taiwan-born Shoichiro Chida, another associate, argues that
Japan should prepare for the day that the Communist Party in China
loses power and the massive country splits apart. The fluent Man-
darin speaker visited Beijing and Northeastern China in late 2005 and
is convinced that Japan will face a surge of refugees within 15 years.
"Taiwan can be our card," Chida argues. He wants to run for the Diet
as well.

"Philosophy, religion, and history are prioritized," says Furuyama
of the curriculum. While the twentieth century was the age of Amer-
ican-led globalization, Furuyama says the twenty-first century will be
marked by a greater focus on local concerns. "At the same time you
take a global perspective, awareness of Japanese culture becomes
much more important," he notes, adding that associates practice
zazen (zen meditation) and *kendo* (Japanese swordsmanship).

"Our founder believed that if you have an Asian mindset, seeking
harmony with nature, managing human relationships well, and
understanding yourself are all important for a leader." Although
awareness of traditional Japanese morals may have weakened in the
years after World War II, the ethics outlined in *Bushido*, written by
Inazo Nitobe in 1898, still have relevance today, he argues. This book
has resonated among U.S. political leadership in the past; President
Theodore Roosevelt liked the book and gave copies to his friends.

"Either in industrial or post-industrial society, fundamentals of
human existence do not change. Man is by nature a political animal,"
Furuyama observes, citing Aristotle's dictum. "He must live in society. How one manages human relationships is important."

Investment Implications

Japan's demographic woes are often cited in discussions about the future of its financial markets. Some observers worry that a shrinking population will stifle growth and could even lead to a fiscal crisis. Such fears appear to be overblown. The government bases its demographic projections on extremely low birthrates extrapolated into the distant future; these gloomy assumptions appear increasingly unrealistic. In addition, significant reforms enacted in recent years should contribute to fiscal stability over the long term.

On the other hand, investors are ignoring an arguably much more important near-term demographic shift. A younger generation of politicians, executives, and policymakers is poised to take charge. These people are familiar with markets and less enamored with state-directed development and bank financing than previous Japanese leaders. In the corporate world, dramatic restructurings such as that witnessed at Daiei appear to reflect the *modus operandi* of the new elite. Future political trends are much more murky, but recent initiatives concerning the commercial code, accounting, and intellectual property suggest that younger policymakers are increasingly willing to grapple with societal problems in novel ways. In addition, the emergence of a newly invigorated civil society will help check efforts by the bureaucracy to reassert its dominance. Though policymakers will not completely abandon the traditional emphasis on socially equitable distribution of income, increasingly investor-friendly corporate governance and economic policies are likely.

References

"Tama New Town has missed its chance ...." Author interviewed resident on 10 August 2005.

"The New Town is perceived to be getting old ...." Yoshida, Reiji. "Tama's Population Fall Shows How Baby Boom Is Bust." *Japan Times*. 1 January 2005.

"Indeed, the population of Tama City ...." Tama City statistics.

"In the 1960s, the Tokyo Metropolitan government ...." *Tama New Town*. Tama Shi Toshizukuribu Toshikeikakuka, 2004. See esp. p. 30, 31.

"However, Mika Fukuda, Head of the Planning Division ...." This statement and following are from interviews conducted by the author on 10 August 2005 and 18 July 2006.

"In 2006, the Japanese population is expected ...." National Institute of Population and Social Security Research. *Population Projections for Japan: 2001–2050*. May 2002. See esp. p. 2.

"Indeed, Ignazio Visco of the OECD ..." Visco, Ignazio, *The Fiscal Implications of Ageing Populations in OECD Countries*. Oxford Centre on Population Ageing Pensions Symposium, 7 June 2001. See esp. p. 2, 3.

"John Tofflemire, president of Sapient Real Estate Consulting ...." Interview conducted by the author on 29 June 2005 and other conversations.

"Japanese government forecasts tend to be more pessimistic than those based on economics ..." Weinstein, David, Takatoshi Ito, and Hugh Patrick, eds. *Reviving Japan's Economy: Problems and Prescriptions*. MIT Press, 2005. See esp. Ch. 2, p. 39–78. Also, the author conducted an interview with David Weinstein on 4 April 2006.

"The fall of the Berlin Wall in 1989 was heralded ...." Shipley, Andrew. "The Nationalization of the Japanese Economy." *Asian Wall Street Journal*. Op-ed page, 9 June 1999.

"Against a backdrop of the expected ageing ...." Ministry of Finance. *Current Japanese Fiscal Conditions and Issues to be Considered*. 2005. See esp. p. 14.

"We call this the 'mouth of the crocodile.'" This and following statements are from an interview on 3 March 2006.

"To achieve a primary balance by fiscal year 2011…" Cabinet Office, *Kouzoukaikaku to Keizai Zaisei no Chuukitenbou – 2005 Nendo Kaitei,* 18 January 2006. See esp. p. 5 footnote 2.

"With the mountain of long-term public debt reaching ¥774 …." Ministry of Finance. *Current Japanese Fiscal Conditions and Issues to be Considered.* 2005. See esp. p. 6.

"The Ministry of Finance looks closely at …." Ministry of Finance. *Current Japanese Fiscal Conditions and Issues to be Considered.* 2005. See esp. p. 15–16.

"The Council of Fiscal and Economic Policy …." *Nikkei Net Interactive.* Nihon Keizai Shimbun, Inc. "Fiscal Rebuilding Plan Seeks 2% Primary Balance Surplus by FY15." 15 March 2006.

"Thomas Byrne, who writes the Japan country reports …" This and following statements are from an interview conducted by the author on 13 September 2005.

"While Moody's last Japan downgrade …," Clifford, Bill, "Credit where it's due", CBS MarketWatch.com, 2 September 2002.

"…" Weinstein, David, Takatoshi Ito, and Hugh Patrick, eds. *Reviving Japan's Economy: Problems and Prescriptions.* MIT Press, 2005. See esp. Ch. 2, p. 39–78. Also, the author conducted an interview with David Weinstein on 4 April 2006.

"Simon Ross notes that the 28-to-35…." Interview conducted by the author on 7 November 2005.

"Overall, the percentage of those becoming …." *Nikkei Net Interactive.* Nihon Keizai Shimbun, Inc. "Companies Tap Younger Leaders." 13 June 2005.

"However, Sanyo Electric Co., Ltd.; Marui Co., Ltd.;" *Nikkei Net Interactive.* Nihon Keizai Shimbun, Inc. "Companies Tap Younger Leaders." 13 June 2005.

"The 80 new Liberal Democratic Party (LDP) members …." Nishida, Mutsumi. "Generation, Popularity Swing Race." *Nikkei Net Interactive.* Nihon Keizai Shimbun, Inc. 27 February 2006.

"If Abe wins the election …." Nishida, Mutsumi. "Generation, Popularity Swing Race." *Nikkei Net Interactive.* Nihon Keizai Shimbun, Inc. 27 February 2006.

"This is a generation that is not ignorant of history …." Interview conducted by the author on 7 April 2006.

"LDP lawmaker Yasuhisa Shiozaki …. *Nikkei Net Interactive.* Nihon Keizai Shimbun, Inc. "Politicians: Intellectual Property Nation Still Far Off." 4 February 2006.

"There is a great significance to generations," notes Motohisa Furukawa …." This quote and statements that follow are from an interview conducted by the author on 3 March 2006.

"Some of the larger ones, such as the *Sanchu* Rising during 1726 to 1727, and the *Ueda Horeki* Rising of 1761 to 1763, involved entire fiefdoms …." Bix, Herbert P. *Peasant Protest in Japan, 1590–1884.* New Haven and London: Yale University Press, 1986. See esp. Ch. 3–8.

"Although famine and hardship were often the cause of feudal protests, later …." Bix, Herbert P. *Peasant Protest in Japan, 1590–1884.* New Haven and London: Yale University Press, 1986. See esp. p. 223.

"Herbert Bix noted in his 1987 study of peasant revolts …." Bix, Herbert P. *Peasant Protest in Japan, 1590–1884.* New Haven and London: Yale University Press, 1986. See esp. p. 228.

"He observed that the last great wave …." Bix, Herbert P. *Peasant Protest in Japan, 1590–1884.* New Haven and London: Yale University Press, 1986. See esp. p. 228.

"Anarchists plotted to assassinate the Meiji emperor …." Keene, Donald. *Emperor of Japan, Meiji and His World, 1852–1912.* New York, Chinchester, and West Sussex: Columbia University Press, 2002. See esp. p. 691, 692.

"… eager to stamp out socialism …." Keene, Donald. *Emperor of Japan, Meiji and his World, 1852–1912.* New York, Chinchester, and West Sussex: Columbia University Press, 2002. See esp. p. 692.

"… two mainstream prewar precursors …." Reischauer, Edwin O. *The Japanese.* Harvard Press, 1981. See esp. p. 276.

"In 1918, the prime minister resigned …." Oka, Yoshitake. *Five Political Leaders of Modern Japan.* University of Tokyo Press, 1986. See esp. p. 104.

"A Communist Party was established in 1922, but it was …." Reischauer, Edwin O. *The Japanese.* Harvard Press, 1981. See esp. p. 277.

"The Peace Preservation Law, passed in 1925 …." Reischauer, Edwin O. *The Japanese.* Harvard Press, 1981. See esp. p. 97.

"… all political parties were dissolved in 1940 …." Reischauer, Edwin O. *The Japanese.* Harvard Press, 1981. See esp. p. 277.

"In the 1970s, more radical members of the association formed splinter …." Box, Meredith and Gavin McCormack, "Terror in Japan." *Critical Asian Studies* 36, no. 1 (March 2004): p. 91–112.

"Assailants bombed the headquarters of Mitsubishi Heavy …" Asai, Yasufumi and Jeffrey Arnold, "Terrorism in Japan." *Prehospital and Disaster Medicine.* April–June 2003: p. 106.

"The country was shocked and horrified …." Asai, Yasufumi and Jeffrey Arnold, "Terrorism in Japan." *Prehospital and Disaster Medicine.* April–June 2003: p. 106.

"Groups of protestors broke through barricades …." *CBC News.* "Security Tight as G-20 Meeting Begins in Ottawa." 16 November 2001.

"'That's the Japanese economy,' said Jun Nishikawa …." Interview conducted by the author on 28 June 2005.

"Only about 26,000 groups gained legal status …." Pekoe, Robert. *Japan's Dual Society: Members Without Advocates.* Stanford: Stanford University Press, 2006. See esp. p. 30.

"The writing of the law saw Dietmen wrest legislation ...." Pekkanen, Robert. *Civil Society and its Regulators: Nonprofit Organizations in Japan.* Prepared for Energizing Japanese Politics: New Tools for Citizen Participation. 24 April 2001. Washington, D.C. Japan Information Access Project. See esp. p. 4.

"One example of grassroots organizations making a difference ..." Interview conducted by the author on 28 June 2005.

"Originally founded by a small circle of Tokyo housewives in 1965 ...." Institute for Sustainable Development. www.iisd.org/50comm/commdb/desc/d08.htm.

"Indeed, Nishikawa sees an elemental shift in the awareness ...." Interview conducted by the author on 28 June 2005.

"In one of the most infamous cases of environmental pollution in the world ..." Ministry of the Environment. http://www.env.go.jp/en/chemi/hs/minamata2002/index.html.

Minamata City. http://www.minamatacity.jp/eng/history.htm

"In 1992, the city announced its plans to become a model ...." Minamata City. http://www.minamatacity.jp/eng/index.htm.

Yagi, Kazumi, "Getting Over Minamata Disease," *Association for Asian Research,* 29 November 2004. www.asianresearch.org/articles/2324.html.

"'Citizens are taking the lead,'" says Kazushi Kaneto ...." Interview conducted by the author on 27 February 2006.

"Of 213 graduates of Matsushita Institute over the ...." *Asahi Shimbun* Weekend Beat. "Lavish Perks Spur Interest in Political Careers." 12–13 November 2005. p. 34.

"He was on the verge of resigning his leadership ...." *Nikkei Net Interactive.* Nihon Keizai Shimbun, Inc. "DPJ Chief Maehara Announces Resignation," 3 April 2006.

Nikkei Net Interactive, Nihon Keizai Shimbun, Inc. "DPJ in Turmoil over E-mail Fiasco." 1 April 2006.

"Indeed, some in Tokyo have even compared LDP ...." Ishizuka, Masahiko, "A Search for a Tenable Opposition," *Nikkei Net Interactive*. Nihon Keizai Shimbun, Inc. 19 September 2005.

"However, Kaneto aspires to become a community ...." Interview conducted by the author on 27 February 2006.

"Kaneto wants to return to Shikoku Island ...." Statler, Oliver. *Japanese Pilgrimage*. New York. William Morrow and Co., 1983.

"Matsushita Electric Appliance Company, which he founded in 1918 ...." Panasonic. http://panasonic.net/history/founder/chapter1/story1-04. html.

"The characters painted on the scroll, *sunao*, were ...." "Overview of MIGM," handout.

"We just met with some people ...." Interview conducted by the author on 27 February 2006.

"Gemma Kentaro is an aspiring politician ...." Interview conducted by the author on 27 February 2006.

"Taiwanese-born Shoichiro Chida ...." Interview conducted by the author on 27 February 2006.

"Although awareness of traditional Japanese morals may have weakened in the years after World War II ..." Nitobe, Inazo. *Bushido*. Tenth edition. New York and London: G. P. Putnam's Sons, Knickerbocker Press, 1905.

"U.S. President Theodore Roosevelt liked the book ...." Keene, Donald. Emperor of Japan, Meiji and His World, 1852–1912. New York, Chinchester, and West Sussex: Columbia University Press, 2002. See esp. p. 611.

(and) Nitobe, Inazo. *Bushido*. Tenth edition. New York and London: G. P. Putnam's Sons, Knickerbocker Press, 1905. Preface to the tenth and revised edition.

8

THE CHINESE PARADOX

Japanese Firms Face Conundrum in Crucial Chinese Market

Workers in Xi'an, China, stunned both Japanese and Chinese scholars in 2004 when they unearthed a stone marker containing the haunting epitaph of Jing Zhencheng. The discovery of the burial memorial, dated 734 A.D., shed new light on the ancient ties between the two largest nations of East Asia. The stone recorded the last wishes of a young Japanese student. He had traveled to Changan, the capital of imperial China from the seventh to the tenth centuries, to study Tang civilization.

In summer 2005, the Tokyo National Museum featured this artifact in a special exhibit on *kentoshi,* Japanese missions to the Tang court. These envoys would brave high seas and unpredictable winds during their ocean crossings, and shipwrecks were common. However, their contribution to Japanese culture was enormous. The scholars transmitted Buddhist and Chinese teachings—as well as a strategic awareness of the behemoth that dominated the mainland.

Jing Zhencheng died before completing his overseas studies, broken-hearted over his inability to return to the country of his birth. His sad words are etched in ancient Chinese on the gray stone block— "My body is buried in foreign soil, yet I earnestly pray my soul may return to its homeland." Banners in the park outside the museum greeted the relic with the simple phrase *Okaeri* (translated as "Welcome home").

No investor in Japan can ignore its economic ties with the emerging powerhouse on the mainland. Although Sino-Japanese trade has been subject to prolonged interruptions throughout history, Japan's economic ties with China have often shaped its relationship with the rest of the world. The two countries have alternatively been fierce competitors and mutually dependent on each other for growth. This complex relationship has been strained by brutal military conflict and Japan's prewar imperialistic record. Chinese poverty and political factors have resulted in Japan's economic relationship with the United States eclipsing that with the mainland in the post-war period. However, no one should doubt that such a state was transitory. Given the rapid growth of the Chinese economy and the proximity of Japanese ports, trade and investment have begun to surge. The origins of such huge trade flows can be traced to the ancient past.

More than 1,000 years ago, Jing Zhencheng and other Japanese strolled Chinese city streets with silver jingling in their purses. Visitors to the *kentoshi* exhibit saw one such Japanese coin dating from the eighth century that had been found in the Tang capital. Traders plied the seas between the shores of the two countries in the following centuries as well, and, even in feudal times, Japanese industries faced competition from Chinese artisans. Although many American and European managers have only recently become aware of the looming threat of low-cost production from China, some Japanese businesses have raced against mainland producers for centuries.

The China that awed Japanese nobility throughout premodern history was, for the most part, rich, powerful, and huge. Japanese feudal rulers and elites knew that they lived in its shadow. When Jing Zhencheng visited Changan, the Chinese population was about 14 times larger than the number of residents on the Japanese archipelago, according to estimates provided by Carl Haub at the Population Reference Bureau in Washington, D.C. Jing Zhencheng's views of crowded, prosperous Chinese cities must have been nothing short of a revelation. Except for a period during the Ming Dynasty, Japan's population has hovered at a mere one-tenth that of China's for the past 10 centuries, according to Haub.

As is often remarked, the British are similarly outnumbered by Europeans on the continent. However, there is a crucial and often overlooked difference between the strategic positions of the two island nations. The English have rarely faced a unified threat on the mainland. The empires of Charlemagne and Napoleon were the only semblances of a European-wide power in history, observes Charlie Steen, an associate professor at the University of New Mexico. Indeed, the English have joined forces with European allies whenever necessary to head off that ultimate nightmare—a unified European empire confronting them from across the channel. "Everyone spoke longingly of Christendom, but it was never a reality and never an institutional form," Steen observes. Japan has faced a unified Chinese civilization for centuries.

Because Japanese rulers and merchants have long been aware of the enormous threat that unified Chinese power presents, many have strived to distinguish their own activities from those of China, to avoid direct competition whenever possible, notes Ricciardi, founder of Light Year Research (Japan) K.K. "It is viscerally, implicitly, and intuitively more aware of that than many other countries, especially those outside Asia," he stresses. Japanese companies are keenly aware of the ability of Chinese firms to continue to erode pricing margins and manufacture commodities far more cheaply than they can. As a result, they strive to create high-value products and harder-to-imitate businesses or services.

"They realize that the minute their business is easily replicable, it's going to become commoditized on the mainland and they will not be able to compete," Ricciardi notes. Sensitivity to the Chinese threat, he adds, is in the DNA of Japanese firms.

Even Tokugawa artisans, despite the shogunal decrees against overseas trade, had exposure to Chinese goods. Chinese and Dutch traders carried sufficient Chinese products to designated ports to support a relatively large Chinese population in at least one coastal town. Marius B. Jensen noted in *The Making of Modern Japan* that almost 5,000 Chinese were housed in Nagasaki in 1689. At the same time Christianity was barred from Japan, this Chinese community during the seventeenth century was served by up to four temples, staffed by priests and abbots from China, he observed.

Feudal Japan should not be viewed as a modern nation-state, and domestic trade between daimyo territories was much more important than overseas exports and imports, says Michael Smitka, an economics professor at Washington & Lee University. However, demand for Chinese goods among the Japanese elite was not negligible. "Until about 1720, there was a fairly vigorous export trade in Japanese silver for Chinese luxury goods," notes Smitka. China was a silver-based monetary system, and Japan had silver mines, which it used to purchase goods such as silk and porcelain.

Developing an indigenous pottery industry was a strategic priority for feudal Japanese rulers. Korean potters were forcibly relocated to northern Kyushu following the peninsular invasions by the shogun Toyotomi Hideyoshi in 1592 and 1597. Chinese refugees fleeing the collapse of the Ming dynasty in 1644 also raised the quality of domestically made porcelain, says Smitka.

Sakaida Kizayemon lived from the end of the sixteenth century through the first half of the seventeenth century. He eventually took the name Kakiyemon and created the porcelain style bearing this nomenclature. These delicate dishes and the work of other Japanese craftsmen became highly prized among Western royalty, such as August II of Poland. Overseas shipments of Chinese porcelain dropped off sharply because of political upheaval in the mid-seventeenth century, and Japanese porcelain soon made inroads into the European markets. Kyushu potters fired dishes in their kilns to be shipped on Dutch boats.

Perhaps Japan's first experience with low-cost Chinese production flooding a strategic market came when its rival's porcelain shipments recovered toward the end of the seventeenth century. The re-emergence of lower-price Chinese products for the European market prompted traders from the Dutch East Indies Company to lose interest in Japanese porcelain, notes professor Dr. Christiaan Jörg at Lieden University. Interest in expensive Japanese ceramics among the wealthy in Europe remained. Japanese potters were left to supply a high-end, niche market, relying solely on private Dutch traders for orders, says Jörg, who wrote *Fine & Curious: Japanese Export Porcelain in Dutch Collections.* Eventually the Chinese targeted this high-end market as well, changing their styles to compete with Japanese goods, Jörg adds. However, the "Chinese Imari" that mimicked Japanese wares was just one of many styles exported by the Chinese to Europe, he notes.

Japanese merchants probably heard about the lucrative Chinese trade in the foreigners' quarter of Nagasaki. However, they were prohibited from sailing to the Chinese coastal towns where Qing authorities had opened customs offices in 1685. Many in Edo watched with dread as Western powers scrambled to force unequal treaties on the tottering Chinese court following its defeat by the British in the Opium War. Residents were further horrified by the sudden appearance in Edo Bay of the huge black ships of Commodore Matthew C. Perry in 1853.

To avoid China's grim fate, the Japanese government frantically struggled to modernize the country in following decades. Japan did not emerge as a major player in the unequal treaty system until it defeated the Chinese navy in the Yellow Sea in 1894. The Treaty of Shimonoseki granted most favored nation status to Japan the following year. The Chinese court also agreed to cede Taiwan and recognized the right of Japanese nationals to open factories and engage in industry on the mainland.

"Britain was the 800-pound gorilla in the nineteenth century [in the China trade], but by the 1930s, the Japanese had become King Kong by comparison," says Peter Duus, professor emeritus of Japanese history at Stanford University and co-editor of *The Japanese Informal Empire in China, 1895–1937* (with Ramon H. Myers and Mark R. Peattie). Japanese traders, who had always been aware of the large market in China, felt they had natural advantages vis-à-vis their European competitors, he notes. The proximity of Osaka and Tokyo to Chinese ports reduced shipping costs, and cultural similarities, such as related writing systems, worked to the benefit of Japanese traders. Europeans usually had compradors, or Chinese agents, to act as go-betweens for treaty port merchants and interior markets in the nineteenth century. The Japanese went directly into distant cities to market their goods. Indeed, the Japanese government even used its consulates in cities outside the treaty ports to hold trade exhibitions, Duus notes. The traveler Everard Cotes, who wrote *Signs and Portents in the Far East* in 1907, observed "kimono-clad merchants have started shops and banking houses and are hawking the wares of Kobe and Osaka in every considerable Chinese City from Canton to Mukden."

Japan wrested control of Manchurian assets from the Russian government in a bloody conflict from 1904 to 1905. The victors of the epic Battle of Tsushima transferred the spoils of war, including the Russian leasehold in the Liaotung Peninsula and the Tsarist regional railway, to the South Manchuria Railway Company. The profitable firm's total investment likely grew to more than $570 million by 1931, wrote Myers in *Japan's Informal Empire in China,* and members of the Kwantung Army guarded its possessions. The South Manchuria Railway was probably the leading foreign investor in China by the early 1930s, he observed.

Japanese trade with China soared during this period. Exports increased thirtyfold, in real terms, between the 1890s and 1930s, and imports increased tenfold, said Mizoguchi Toshiyuki in *Japan's Informal Empire in China*. China became an important market for Japanese textiles, a major engine of Japanese development, Toshiyuki noted.

Japan's second experience with low-cost Chinese production threatening to drive them out of a key export market probably took place during World War I. This time, well-capitalized Japanese firms fared better than the isolated Kyushu craftsmen of the Tokugawa period. Skyrocketing textile prices because of wartime demand resulted in rising profits and prompted Chinese entrepreneurs to enter the industry. At home, Japanese managers reacted to the threat from low-cost Chinese producers by establishing integrated spinning-weaving operations, shifting from steam to electrical power, and diversifying into the manufacturing of wool, silk, or artificial fibers, according to Duus. Intensifying competition, as well as a hike in the tariff rate on Japanese imports to the mainland and rising costs at home, also prompted Japanese firms to aggressively invest in textile mills on the mainland, he adds. In 1916, Chinese firms owned 4,052 cotton looms, while Japanese firms had 886. Although the whole industry grew in subsequent years, by 1936, the Japanese owned more looms than Chinese firms, he notes.

The rise of Chinese nationalism in the 1920s threatened Japan's huge investment holdings and the massive trade flows between the two countries. Faced with boycotts of foreign goods and protests, Western powers ultimately agreed to rewrite unequal treaties and award numerous concessions. Japan had much more to lose than other foreign powers by such measures, and policymakers in Tokyo were paralyzed as discussions of the "China Problem" dominated political talks, Duus said.

Eventually, the Kwantung Army took matters into its own hands by assassinating a Chinese warlord and installing a puppet regime in Manchuria in 1931. The army planners, who viewed private capitalists suspiciously, attempted to implement a massive program of state-directed development on the vast, sprawling territory of Manchukou, observed Nakagane Katsuji in *Japan's Informal Empire in China*. Their industrialization efforts continued even as volleys of gunfire erupted on the banks of the Marco Polo Bridge in 1937, ushering in the second Sino-Japanese War.

The recent economic advance of China can be seen as the recovery of the Chinese state from its traumatic encounters with Western and Japanese imperialism over the last 2 centuries and a shifting toward a more equitable distribution of global resources commensurate with the country's tremendous population.

Indeed, future historians will likely view Japan's post-war dependence on the United States as an export market as a temporary phenomenon. China is resurfacing as a major trading partner for Japan. For the first time since the late 1940s, Japanese trade with greater China surpassed that with the United States in 2004. Ultimately, much Chinese production is still destined for the United States, so reliance on the U.S. economy is only partially eased. However, the anticipated rapid growth of the domestic Chinese market in the longer term contrasts favorably with the likely slower expansion of the mature U.S. economy.

Political barriers, as well as China's relative poverty, have hindered growth in trade with Japan for much of the post-war period. Japan had no diplomatic relations with China until 1972, when Prime Minister Kakuei Tanaka visited the country in the wake of the "Nixon Shock." Japan's bilateral trade with China accelerated following the signing of a long-term trade agreement in 1978. At first, China shipped coal and Japanese firms exported machinery, notes Hiroshi Kadota, executive counselor for international affairs at Nippon Keidanren. Nippon Keidanren is an influential body of both private companies and industrial and regional associations. Most big companies are members.

Many in the Japanese business community long feared competing with low-cost Chinese production. "The emergence of China as an economic power was initially viewed cautiously by Japanese business executives," he remembers. "Several years ago, Japanese business thought the Chinese economy was a kind of threat .... They thought investment in China would cause a hollowing-out of Japanese industry," he adds.

"Recently, those ideas have changed completely," he stresses. Kadota points to China joining the World Trade Organization (WTO) in December 2001 as the reason for the change in attitudes regarding the country in Japanese business circles. Business leaders now view China not only as a production base, but as a big market as well.

Trade with China has exploded since China's entry into the WTO. From 2002 to 2004, exports from Japan to China surged 61% to ¥8 trillion, and imports climbed 32% to ¥10.2 trillion—Japan has a trade deficit with the country. The two countries are planning to sign a free trade agreement in 2010, which should bolster trade flows even further.

To date, China's importance as a production base far outweighs its importance as a final market for Japanese firms, according to an analysis by Cameron Umetsu and Colin Asher at Nomura Securities International. Shipments of production goods and, to a lesser extent, capital goods account for most of growth of shipments, not consumer items. "Simply put, China still serves primarily as an assembly and manufacturing base for Japanese companies," they conclude.

Reflecting China's importance as a production base, direct investment by Japanese firms in the country is rising. The number of cases has climbed steadily since 1999, from 78 to 332 in 2003, according to the 21st China Research Institute. Annual investment more than quadrupled, from $745 million in 1999 to $3.6 billion in 2003. Electrical machinery makers make up most of the institute's 2003 ranking of the top 50 firms in China with Japanese participation. Of these, Dairen Toshiba Television Co., Ltd., a subsidiary of Toshiba Corp. that had 4.2 billion *renmimbi* in sales, is the largest. Matsushita Electric Industrial Co., Ltd., had invested in 60 firms in China (including Hong Kong) and employed 60,000 people as of June 2004.

Not only electrical machinery makers are investing in China. Makers of automobiles and auto parts had eight firms in the institute's top 50 as well. The largest Japanese-invested Chinese auto firm was Guangzhou Honda Automobile Co., Ltd., which was ranked eleventh of all foreign participating firms and enjoyed sales of 13.6 billion *renmimbi* in 2002. In 2003, China ranked fourth, after the United States, Germany, and Japan in passenger vehicle output, producing 4.4 million units, including buses and trucks. Although this is only half of Japan's output, capacity is increasing rapidly. The institute forecasts overall production to rise to 7.5 million by 2010.

Meanwhile, service sector companies, such as banks and insurance firms, are also looking to expand into the Chinese market. Trading companies, which have been in China for more than 30 years, are rethinking their businesses. "Trading companies are interested in distribution in China," Kadota noted. They are setting up companies to help automakers and other firms establish networks for parts and finished products. Financial companies also plan to expand. Nomura Securities Co. Group aims to set up a financial holding group in China.

Eisuke Sakakibara at Keio University sees an epochal shift in the global economy because of the rise of China. The former Vice Minister for International Affairs at the Ministry of Finance is quick to laugh during an interview in his office. He wears an elegant tailored suit, but his clear glasses rest on the chiseled features of a boxer. Even in academia, he has not lost the assertive, rough-and-tumble speaking manner he used to keep often cantankerous journalists and investment bank analysts in line during briefings on fiscal policy in the 1990s.

"The center of gravity of the world economy is shifting from West to East," he observes. Trading patterns shifted several times in recent centuries, and each shift brought about a new balance of power and distribution of wealth among nations. The Venetian Empire controlled the European distribution of the overland Asian trade riches until the circumnavigation of Africa brought its monopoly to an end. Eventually, Amsterdam emerged as the global center for trade and finance because of the city's success in controlling the spice trade and credit markets. British hegemony of the sea lanes in the nineteenth century and its extensive overseas colonial empire resulted in the dominance of London in the financial markets.

"The 1920s and 1930s were a transition period from British hegemony to U.S. hegemony. Now it is a transition period to someone else's hegemony—to China," Sakakibara notes.

Japan's proximity to Chinese ports ensures that it will enjoy close economic ties with the emerging Asian powerhouse in the future. However, the emergence of a new generation of Japanese politicians, focusing more on Japan's post-war accomplishments than wartime actions, suggests that ties could be strained between these rivals for dominance in East Asia. To be sure, the ultimate cause of such contemporary tension is probably not the rise of new leaders in Tokyo who lack personal memories of World War II. Friction was bound to arise between the two incompatible political systems. The oppressive communist giant and the established democracy with increasingly free-wheeling capital markets were certain to make each other nervous. Strains are also more keenly felt with the need for closer political interaction accompanying the surge in bilateral trade after China's WTO entry.

As Japanese corporate leaders and policymakers become aware of the importance of the country's intellectual assets, they take tougher stances in protecting such prized possessions. As we saw in Chapter 2, "Intellectual Property Wars," corporations are increasingly willing to litigate to ensure that their IP rights are not violated. Meanwhile, the Ministry of Economy, Trade, and Industry (METI) is planning to double prison sentences and fines for IP violations to up to 10 years in jail and ¥10 million, which would make Japanese penalties for such infractions the most severe in the world. Such a hard-line stance will likely raise eyebrows in Beijing; many Chinese firms have developed a reputation as raiders of intellectual property.

METI found that half of the Japanese firms in China responding to a survey conducted in Spring 2005 had pursued administrative, criminal, or civil procedures to fight off intellectual property right infringements. Electronics makers felt the most vulnerable; fully 90% were petitioning authorities to move against violations of their IP property rights. Japanese firms applied to get counterfeit goods confiscated more than 3,000 times in 2003 and 2004, and asked for manufacturing operations and sales for such goods to be halted in almost 780 cases during the same period.

Many Japanese companies appear to be dissatisfied with the response of the Chinese government to such law-breaking. Most of those firms petitioning authorities had difficulties when seeking a response or sensed a lack of smooth progress. More than one-third had specific complaints against authorities, such as IP cases being handled unfairly, with Chinese officials demanding unnecessary documents and failing to initiate legal actions simply because the accused were absent. Half of the companies petitioning government authorities had repeatedly experienced IP rights infringements, METI stressed.

"I think in the last year, people have been really ticked off by the lack of actual progress," said Mike Kaminski, a patent attorney at Foley & Lardner LLP, in early 2006. Japanese firms have been doing an end run around Chinese authorities by going to the customers of the infringers, he observes. They force these firms to change their suppliers to those who are not violating IP laws.

Japanese firms are perhaps weakly positioned to protect them-selves from IP encroachments. The U.S. government still has the trade and military strength to push the Chinese government much more strongly in patent infringement issues, notes Professor Hiroyuki Itami at Hitotsubashi University. "Japanese firms cannot rely on their govern-ment to do much," he concedes. On the other hand, the intellectual assets at U.S. firms tend to be more portable than that those of Japan-ese ones, he observes. Many Japanese intangible assets are intimately tied to production know-how and manufacturing processes and, as such, are much harder to steal. Companies are also rethinking their shift to production on the mainland. Canon Inc., is bringing production back home to partly ensure that such knowledge stays in-house.

In the high-stakes Sino-Japan trade game, political theater can threaten corporate survival. Following Prime Minister Koizumi's visit to Yasukuni Shrine in August 2005, Japanese bank managers started worrying about the launch of their financial derivative products in China, reported Nihon Keizai Shimbun, Inc. China has long protested such visits by Japanese political leaders to the shrine, which honors Japan's war dead, including World War II war criminals. Now Japanese bank managers fear that such events may result in China discriminating against Japanese financial groups when the country opens its banking sector to foreign companies at the end of 2006. Not only could approvals of derivative products be delayed, but bank managers fear that Chinese authorities could stall on new branch applications as well.

Mutual visits by both countries' leaders have been suspended as a result of Koizumi's repeated pilgrimages, and the Japanese Foreign Ministry is apparently nervous about their economic fallout. The anti-Japanese demonstrations that erupted across China in spring 2005, reflecting opposition to Japan's bid for a permanent seat on the UN Security Council, also spread uneasiness in the business community. From April 2006, the ministry announced that an in-house team specializing in the Chinese economy will be formed, providing macroeconomic analysis and studying intellectual property violations.

Opposition party lawmaker Motohisa Furukawa also worries about the direction of Sino-Japanese relations. Furukawa is not just concerned about a few bank branch applications. The farsighted politician, who has worked on intellectual property policy reports for his party, frets about the eroding of Japan's intellectual asset base as a result of the intransigence of ruling party officials.

He suggests that the government and companies should not only be focused on legal protection of Japanese IP rights. Although he acknowledges that imitation by Chinese firms of IP developed elsewhere is a problem, he argues that Japanese firms must not lose sight of the role China will play in determining which technologies will succeed in the twenty-first century.

Developing the *de facto* standard in growth industries is very important, he points out. "Even if your technology is superior, if it does not become the *de facto* standard, its value decreases," he stresses. Japan had previous experience with the failure of Sony's Betamax video technology, he notes. Even though Betamax was widely perceived to be the better format, VHS went on to become the industry standard.

"Even if you have a lot of patents, if they are not used overseas, it is meaningless," he notes.

To be sure, industry participants are very familiar with the importance of market acceptance of technology. Fujitsu's Masanobu Katoh agrees that information technology is partially led by *de facto* standards. In fact, he believes that "researchers can lead the global trend." Fujitsu researchers and engineers work closely with other companies and participate in international conferences, hoping to influence the future direction of industries. "People have to persuade the world that the world should use a certain technology .... Engineers have to be active in creating the new trend, and they can't just be followers," he stresses.

Furukawa frets that many in government do not appreciate the importance China will play in determining industry winners and losers in the future. "To become a *de facto* standard, you need a big market," Furukawa adds, pointing to the massive number of Chinese consumers. "If your technology is not accepted in China, from now on it will be difficult for it to become a *de facto* standard, he notes. "The China market will become extremely important."

Businesses must not just protect patent rights; they must make technology open for as many market participants as possible. Furukawa stresses that Japan-China relations are extremely important for the development of Japanese intellectual property. "If Japan-China relations deteriorate, this could hurt Japanese potential," he warns.

Japan is facing a paradox in its dealings with China. On one hand, it must continue to defend its interests in the region and stubbornly protect its critical assets, notably intellectual property. On the other, it must generate sufficient goodwill to ensure that its products and services are welcomed by the vast consumer market. As long as China is not threatened by perceived aggressive behavior on the part of Japanese leaders, the situation is far from untenable. Respect for intellectual property rights is in the interests of Chinese citizens and companies as well. Indeed, Chinese consumers are endangered by fraudulent products; a number of deaths resulted from fake baby formula in 2004. Meanwhile, Chinese firms are also becoming aware of the value of their own intellectual property holdings. Shenzhen-based Netac Technology Company, which makes flash-memory products, filed suit against U.S. rival PNY Technologies for patent infringement in a Texas court in 2006 and previously filed suit against Sony Electronics (Wuxi) in 2004. If Japanese political leaders can hold the ghosts of a troubled relationship at bay, their country has much to gain.

References

"Workers in Xi'an, China stunned both ...." *Kentoshi to Tang no Bijitsu (Cultural Crossings—Tang Art and the Japanese Envoys).* Published in conjunction with the exhibition "Kentoshi to Tang no Bijitsu," shown at the Tokyo National Museum. The exhibition ran from 20 July to 11 September 2005.

"More than 1,000 years ago, Jing Zhencheng and ...." *Kentoshi to Tang no Bijitsu (Cultural Crossings—Tang Art and the Japanese Envoys).* Published in conjunction with the exhibition "Kentoshi to Tang no Bijitsu," shown at the Tokyo National Museum. The exhibition ran from 20 July to 11 September 2005.

"When Jing Zhencheng visited Changan, the Chinese population was ...." Interview conducted by the author in January 2006.

"The empires of Charlemagne and Napoleon" Interview conducted by the author in Spring 2006.

"Because Japanese rulers and merchants ...." Interview conducted by the author in November 2005.

"Marius B. Jensen noted in *The Making of Modern Japan* ...." Jensen, Marius B. *The Making of Modern Japan.* Cambridge, MA, and London: The Belknap Press of Harvard University Press, 2000. See esp. p. 87–88.

"Feudal Japan should not be viewed ...." This statement and following quotes are from an interview conducted by the author in September 2005.

"Korean potters were forcibly relocated." Elisonas, Jurgis, "The inseparable trinity: Japan's relations with China and Korea," in *The Cambridge History of Japan*, Vol. 4, edited by John Whitney Hall, Cambridge University Press. 1991. See esp. p. 293.

"Sakaida Kizayemon lived from the end ...." Gorman, Hazel. *Japanese & Oriental Ceramics.* Rutland, VT, and Tokyo: Charles Tuttle Company, 1971. See esp. p. 101-103.

"Shipments of Chinese porcelain dropped off sharply ...." Jörg, Christiaan "The Dutch Connection: Asian Export Art in the Seventeenth and Eighteenth Centuries." *Magazine Antiques*. March 1998.

"The re-emergence of lower-price ...." Interview conducted by the author via e-mail on 2 February 2006.

Jörg, Christiaan J. A. *Fine & Curious: Japanese Export Porcelain in Dutch Collections*. Amsterdam: Hotel Publishers, 2003.

"However, they were prohibited from sailing ...." Hsü, Immanuel C. Y. *The Rise of Modern China*. New York and Oxford: Oxford University Press, 1990. See esp. p. 96.

"Many in Edo watched with dread as Western powers ...." Hsü, Immanuel C. Y. *The Rise of Modern China*. New York and Oxford: Oxford University Press, 1990. See esp. p. 202–219.

"The Treaty of Shimonoseki granted most favored nation ...." Hsü, Immanuel C. Y. *The Rise of Modern China*. New York and Oxford: Oxford University Press, 1990. See esp. p. 342, 345.

"Britain was the 800-pound gorilla in the nineteenth century ...." Interview conducted by the author in January 2006.

"The traveler Everard Cotes, who wrote ...." Cotes, Everard. *Signs and Portents in the Far East*. New York: B. P. Putnam Sons, 1907. See esp. page 203.

"The profitable firm's total ...." Myers, Ramon H. "Japanese Imperialism in Manchuria, The South Manchuria Railway Company, 1906 to 1933." In *The Japanese Informal Empire in China, 1895–1937*, eds. Peter Duus, Ramon H. Myers, and Mark R. Peattie. Princeton, NJ: Princeton University Press, 1989. See esp. the footnote on p. 125 and Table 4.1 on p. 110.

"The South Manchuria Railway was probably the leading foreign investor in China ...." Myers, Ramon H. "Japanese Imperialism in Manchuria, The South Manchuria Railway Company, 1906–1933." In *The Japanese Informal Empire in China, 1895–1937*, eds. Peter

Duus, Ramon H. Myers, and Mark R. Peattie. Princeton, NJ: Princeton University Press, 1989. See esp. the footnote on p. 125.

"Exports increased thirtyfold, in real terms ...." Toshiyuki, Mizuguchi. "The Changing Pattern of Sino-Japanese Trade 1884–1937." In *The Japanese Informal Empire in China, 1895–1937*, eds. Peter Duus, Ramon H. Myers, and Mark R. Peattie. Princeton, NJ: Princeton University Press, 1989. See esp. p. 14.

"China became an important market ...." Toshiyuki, Mizuguchi. "The Changing Pattern of Sino-Japanese Trade 1884–1937." In *The Japanese Informal Empire in China, 1895–1937*, eds. Peter Duus, Ramon H. Myers, and Mark R. Peattie. Princeton, NJ: Princeton University Press, 1989. See esp. p. 30.

"At home, Japanese managers reacted to the threat ...." Duus, Peter. "Zaikkabo: Japanese Cotton Mills in China, 1895–1937." In *The Japanese Informal Empire in China, 1895–1937*, eds. Peter Duus, Ramon H. Myers, and Mark R. Peattie. Princeton, NJ: Princeton University Press, 1989. See esp. p. 81–85.

"Intensifying competition, as well as a hike in ...." Duus, Peter. "Zaikkabo: Japanese Cotton Mills in China, 1895–1937." In *The Japanese Informal Empire in China, 1895–1937*, eds. Peter Duus, Ramon H. Myers, and Mark R. Peattie. Princeton, NJ: Princeton University Press, 1989. See esp. p. 84 and Table 3.5.

"The Japanese had much more to lose than ...." Duus, Peter. "Japan's Informal Empire in China, 1895–1937: An Overview," In *The Japanese Informal Empire in China, 1895–1937*, eds. Peter Duus, Ramon H. Myers, and Mark R. Peattie. Princeton, NJ: Princeton University Press, 1989. See esp. p. xxv.

"... policymakers in Tokyo were paralyzed ...." Duus, Peter. "Japan's Informal Empire in China, 1895–1937: An Overview." In *The Japanese Informal Empire in China, 1895–1937*, eds. Peter Duus, Ramon H. Myers, and Mark R. Peattie. Princeton, NJ: Princeton University Press, 1989. See esp. p. xi.

"The army planners, who viewed private capitalists ...." Katsuji, Nakagane. "Manchukuo and Economic Development." In *The Japanese Informal Empire in China, 1895–1937,* eds. Peter Duus, Ramon H. Myers, and Mark R. Peattie. Princeton, NJ: Princeton University Press, 1989. See esp. p. 141.

"China is resurfacing as a major trading partner ...." Ministry of Finance. Customs Clearance Trade Statistics. Greater China includes Hong Kong.

"Japan had no diplomatic relations with China until 1972 ...." Nippon Keidanren. *Japan-China Relations in the Twenty-First Century: Recommendations for Building a Relationship of Trust and Expanding Economic Exchanges Between Japan and China.* 20 February 2001. p. 5.

"At first, China shipped coal and Japanese firms ...." Interview conducted by the author on 12 August 2005.

"From 2002 to 2004, exports ...." Ministry of Finance. Customs Clearance Trade Statistics.

"To date, China's importance ...." Umetsu, Cameron and Colin Asher, "China Watch," *Japan Insight.* Nomura Securities International, Inc. New York, 9 September 2004.

"Reflecting China's importance as a production base ...." Inagaki, Kiyoshi. *Chuugoku Shinshutsu Kigyou Chizu, Nikkei Kigyou-Gyoushu Betsuhen.* The 21st China Research Institute, 2004. See esp. pp. 33, 59, and 291.

"Trading companies are interested ...." Interview conducted by the author on 12 August 2005.

"Nomura Securities Co. Group will set up ...." *Nikkei Net Interactive.* Nihon Keizai Shimbun, Inc. "Nomura Sec Group to Set Up Financial Holding Firm in China." 8 April 2005.

"Eisuke Sakakibara at Keio University ...." Interview conducted by the author on 5 July 2005. At the time of printing, Professor Sakakibara had moved to Waseda University.

"Meanwhile, the Ministry of Economy, Trade, and Industry is planning ...." *Nikkei Net Interactive.* Nihon Keizai Shimbun, Inc. "METI Seeks Stiffer Penalties for Intellectual Property Violations." 28 February 2006.

"METI found that half of the Japanese firms in China ...." METI. *Field Survey for Infringement of Intellectual Property Right in China (Final Report).* 23 June 2005. www.meti.go.jp/english/report/data/050623ChinaIPR.html.

"Most of those firms petitioning authorities ...." METI. *Field Survey for Infringement of Intellectual Property Right in China (Final Report).* 23 June 2005. www.meti.go.jp/english/report/data/050623 ChinaIPR.html.

"I think in the last year, people have been really ...." Interview conducted by the author on 15 February 2006.

"The U.S. government still has the trade and military strength ...." Interview conducted by the author on 1 March 2006.

"Canon, Inc., is bringing production back home, to partly ensure that such knowledge stays in-house ...." *Nikkei Business.* "Looking to the future after China's Yuan Revaluation."1 April 2005.

"Following Prime Minister Koizumi's visit to Yasukuni Shrine ...." *Nikkei Net Interactive.* Nihon Keizai Shimbun, Inc. "Shrine Dust-up May Keep Japan Banks from Opening China Branches." 18 October 2006.

"Mutual visits by both countries' leaders have been suspended ...." *Nikkei Net Interactive.* Nihon Keizai Shimbun, Inc. "Foreign Ministry to Form Special Team to Assess China's Economy." 17 February 2006.

"From April 2006 the ministry ...." *Nikkei Net Interactive.* Nihon Keizai Shimbun, Inc. "Foreign Ministry to Form Special Team to Assess China's Economy." 17 February 2006.

"Fujitsu's Masanobu Katoh points out that …." Interview conducted by the author on 16 March 2006.

"Furukawa frets that many in government …." Interview conducted by the author on 3 March 2006.

"Indeed, Chinese consumers are endangered …." Goto, Yasuhiro. "Japan Firms Rethinking China Role." *Nikkei Net Interactive*. Nihon Keizai Shimbun, Inc. 2 May 2005.

"Shenzhen-based Netac Technology Company, which …." Kurtenbach, Elaine. "Netac Files Suit Against PNY Technologies." Associated Press, 17 February 2006.

Tan, Xiao, "Shenzhen's Netac Technology Sues Sony." *Beijing Review*. 9 December 2004. www.bjreview.com.cn/200449/Business-200449(A). htm.

9

HIGH-SPEED
CAPITALISM

Structural Reforms Lead to Stronger
Firms, More Opportunities for Investors

On a pine-covered hill carpeted with bamboo grass at the edge of
Yoyogi Park, the blue tarpaulins of the homeless are rapidly disappearing. A sign of the times in the grim 1990s, such tent villages
reflected the widening gulf between haves and have-nots in Japan as
the economy deteriorated and people struggled to cope with sweeping societal changes. Now the increasingly isolated tents are squeezed
between numerous roped-off areas, which resemble sites primed for
archeological excavations.

City employees marked off the areas to prevent new squatters
from setting up camp. The Tokyo city government is providing public
assistance to the homeless, providing them with cheap housing and
support in getting jobs. On the other hand, they have been said to
engage in more aggressive tactics as well—the *Koen-no-Kai*, made up

partly of homeless, say that authorities have violently removed tents. The number of homeless in Tokyo reached a peak in August 1999 at about 5,800 and fell to 4,600 by February 2005.

James Fiorillo Ortega can see the shrinking tent village from his offices across the street. The road separates two different worlds— men living hand-to-mouth, battling mice and mosquitoes, and a foreign hedge fund advisor picking winners and losers among Japan's corporate giants. The decline in homeless arguably says little about overall economic trends and decidedly more about the city government's desire to clear a tiresome eyesore from public view. However, for Fiorillo, the tents are a reminder, as is the copy of the *Brooklyn Daily Eagle* from October 24, 1929, that hangs on his wall. Its headline declares, "Wall Street in Panic as Stocks Crash."

Fiorillo says these are motivators to himself and his team every day that they "have to work hard, smart, and provide prudent investment advice."

Such a cautious attitude does not lend itself to blind enthusiasm. Indeed, Fiorillo earlier made a name for himself as a prudent and thoughtful analyst for the financial sector, a notoriously difficult industry in Japan to cover. He was pessimistic about the prospects for Japanese banks through much of the 1990s, as they struggled with huge amounts of bad debt, and worried about the economic outlook for the country.

By 2003, however, Fiorillo finally saw signs that politicians, bureaucrats, and corporate managers were coming to grips with the problems they faced. He started setting up Ottoman Capital the same year to take advantage of opportunities in investing in troubled companies.

By then, he had spent more than 15 years in Japan. While putting himself through college, Fiorillo worked at Salomon Brothers in New York for 4 years and received a scholarship for a new MBA program in Japan, offered by The International University of Japan in collaboration with Dartmouth College's Amos Tuck School. He worked for Bank of New York's Tokyo office as head of credit and was also a loan portfolio manager for nearly 4 years. He then went over to Barings, which would eventually become ING Barings and spent a decade as an equity analyst.

Fiorillo is one of an increasing number of foreign investment advisors who believe that dramatic changes to the nature of capitalism in Japan will generate long-term opportunities. Fiorillo argues that these changes, often triggered by policy measures, are evolutionary in nature, suggesting that many Japanese firms will not only survive, but also thrive, even if the economy slows.

To be sure, Fiorillo's strategy is unique. His long-short event-driven strategy focuses on troubled firms listed on the First Section of the Tokyo Stock Exchange, an unusual approach. Most hedge fund managers looking for turnaround plays focus on the Second Section and over-the-counter stocks, believing that these companies are less picked-over by analysts.

Fiorillo believes there is no need to look further than large companies for arbitrage opportunities, noting that brokerage analysts do not even cover many troubled companies on the First Section. He focuses on struggling firms that he believes most other advisors and analysts do not thoroughly understand. Meanwhile, his fund does not just hire analysts and tell them to find ideas. "We have a quantitative process that is the beginning of our stock-selection policy," he notes. His fund also relies on propriety research, including company visits, and assessment of macroeconomic factors as well. They are thorough; they even meet with target company bankers to ensure that the firms in question are adequately supported.

With pictures of Darwin and his ship, the *Beagle*, plastered on investor handouts for the fund, Fiorillo makes a compelling case for dramatic corporate changes in Japan that offer opportunities for investors. As deregulation and other spurs to competition accelerate, he is positioning the Japan Natural Selection Fund to sort out the winners and losers.

Long a skeptic of Japan's ability to handle change, he is now convinced that Japanese firms are being swept along in an evolutionary process that will lead to rising profitability at many. This process is not driven by economic or market forces, he stresses, but by structural changes unlocking the potential at Japanese firms. One of the first things he cites as evidence are the changes in shareholder composition.

Keiretsu groups, each with its own main bank and held together by cross-sharing holding, dominated corporate finance in the past. Banks held shares in group companies and firms held shares in business partners to cement relationships, not to maximize returns. This system is disintegrating. The percentage of shares outstanding held by long-term investors dropped from 46% in 1990 to 27% in 2002, while cross-share holdings fell from 18% to 7% during the same period, according to NLI Research Institute

With fewer shares in the hands of business partners friendly to management and more in the hands of investors focusing on returns, Fiorillo anticipates that corporate governance will improve at Japanese firms.

Such unraveling of cross-share holdings is a direct result of wide-ranging deregulation in the financial sector. "Deregulation of the financial industry and the establishment of financial holding companies enabled firms to more easily spin off unwanted divisions and streamline operations," Fiorillo notes.

Ryutaro Hashimoto, who was then prime minister, got the ball rolling in 1996. That year he announced measures to free the Japanese financial system of regulations designed to protect the traditional dominance of banks. The Diet passed the Financial System Reform Bill, widely referred to as the Big Bang in reference to a reform of the U.K. financial markets in 1986, in December 1998. Federal Reserve Bank of New York First Vice President Ernest Patrikis observed that year that once the reforms were fully implemented, "Japan's cloistered financial system will come to resemble the open, competitive system we know in the United States." Patrikis grouped the reforms into three areas: those breaking down barriers, those freeing prices, and those opening Japan to the world.

As a result of the Big Bang, financial institutions were permitted to establish holding companies, offer new services, and speed rationalization by cutting overlapping operations. The results have been striking. Ten massive bank holding companies, as well as three insurance holding companies, were formed by January 2006. Bad debts have been slashed and weak companies jettisoned.

In addition, banks, trust banks, and securities companies were able to enter each other's markets in fiscal 1999, and, from fiscal 2000, insurance companies and banks started competing as well. Banks started selling their own mutual funds over-the-counter, while securities firms expanded their asset-management services. Brokerage commissions were fully liberalized. The groundwork was laid for banks to expand out of their traditional loan business and generate fees by marketing a broad spectrum of financial products and services.

Banking sector deregulation has also stimulated restructuring in the rest of the economy, as new financial products have enabled dealmakers to engage in a greater array of transactions. Meanwhile, Fiorillo adds that mergers between banks are spurring smaller companies to follow suit, as the traditional ties between banks and firms break down and sources of lending for weak business lines disappear.

"The level of corporate restructuring is much larger now and [is] affecting much larger, headline-grabbing names," he notes. "The lack of outright layoffs does not necessarily suggest that things aren't going forward at a brisk pace." Fiorillo also points to the recent revision of the Commercial Code as encouraging for foreign investors.

Meanwhile, Japanese authorities are more aggressive in enforcing regulations, increasing protection of shareholder interests. The Financial Services Agency is reorienting its inspections on compliance and risk-management issues now that bad debt problems have largely been eased. The agency is taking steps to improve the effectiveness of such audits, including raising the quality of inspectors and improving intra-agency coordination. The introduction of mark-to-market accounting from fiscal year 2001 has made Japanese financial statements more transparent. The Tokyo Stock Exchange also recently delisted Seibu Railway in response to corporate misbehavior, revealing a vigilant stance as well.

Fiorillo is not alone is pointing to the significance of recent changes in the Commercial Code for foreign investors. Born in Argentina into a Japanese diplomatic family and raised in The Hague, Go Kondo speaks with diction suggestive of his years of British schooling overseas. In a conference room at his law firm, Kondo discusses the changes in the Code that passed during summer 2005.

"Key change is not statutory, but understanding," he notes. Spirited discussions of mergers and acquisitions have led many business leaders to conclude that increased market liquidity and fair opportunities for corporate takeovers would benefit the Japanese economy, he observes.

Even 2 years ago, he notes, few in Japan felt that way.

Kondo, who has practiced law for 9 years, graduated from Tokyo University in 1987 and originally worked with The Boston Consulting Group as a management consultant. After a few years, he left to work as a secretary for his father, who had become a Diet member, and also study for the bar. Out of about 24,000 who sat for the exam, only 700 passed the year he was admitted. Kondo then joined Nagashima & Ohno Law Offices, the largest law firm in Tokyo, and later moved to White & Case, where he has focused on equity financing and merger and acquisition deals.

Gendaika, or modernization, is the theme of recent Commercial Code revisions, Kondo notes. The main body of the Commercial Code dates from the Meiji Era, and the Code has been amended several times in the post-war period. However, much of the language was archaic and needed to be updated. Although overall the reform of the Code is neutral to foreign investors, he points to two sections that hold particular interest for foreign firms.

Perhaps the most infamous is Section 821, which deals with so-called pseudo-foreign firms. The activities of foreign firms that have branches in Japan, do most of their business in Japan, and lack any legitimate foreign headquarters are comprehensively barred. Violators of this statute would be held jointly liable with the foreign firm for any obligations arising from the banned trading.

"There is a lot of concern about this in the financial community," notes Tom O'Sullivan, CEO of Gartmore Investment Japan, Ltd. "A lot of the securities companies and banks are branches, not K.K.s [corporations under Japanese law], so if they did have to incorporate here in Japan, that would cause quite a few problems."

Initially catching the attention of the International Banking Association, nonfinancial firms also lobbied against passage of this section of the bill. Many members of the American Chamber of Commerce of Japan (ACCJ) contacted the U.S. Embassy, which quickly alerted Australian and E.U. representatives, says Kondo, who was involved with the lobbying efforts against this statute. Not only foreign firms would be affected—special-purpose corporations, which are used in securitization transactions by Japanese commercial banks, would also be banned. Although the Ministry of Justice initially said that such concerns would be addressed in the wording of the bill, they were not, Kondo observes. Many policy-conscious LDP members raised their concerns in committee meetings, and even Mikio Aoki, the leader of the LDP in the upper house, admitted that the Ministry of Justice made a mistake in drafting the bill, recounts Kondo. However, if the bill was redrafted, it would have had to go back to the lower house, and that could require another 20 to 30 days. For the Koizumi administration, which was pushing hard for passage of postal savings reform, this delay was undesirable.

Since a redrafting looked increasingly unlikely, the ACCJ and other representatives of foreign interests decided their next-best option was a question-and-answer session in the Diet, says Abby Pratt, associate director for external affairs at the ACCJ. Diet members asked Ministry of Justice officials which companies would be liable in what situation. "We provided a long list of questions to friendly Diet members ... a very long list. It went down, category by category. 'What about this case? What about this case?' And the answers were all, 'It wouldn't apply, it wouldn't apply,'" says Donald Westmore, executive director of the ACCJ.

"It was a classic case of Japanese. It didn't matter if you read it fairly. You could see that it did apply, but they said it didn't, so it didn't," he added. It was the understanding of ACCJ members that the legislation was drafted in an academic vacuum with no consultation with the private sector. They drafted it with blinders on.

This is not unusual. In many policy discussions, "you don't get an early warning [or] heads-up [on] what direction they are going so you can submit the input [on] what the needs are from the investor end of the stick," notes Benes, chair of the Foreign Direct Investment Committee of the ACCJ.

Kondo also points to the legalization of *sankakugappei* —triangle mergers —as being of interest to foreign investors. Previously, if a foreign company established a 100%-owned subsidiary in Japan to merge with a Japanese firm, cash had to be paid out for shares in the domestic company. The new law permits shares, including those of the foreign parent company, to be used for takeovers.

Not all market watchers are convinced that this legislation will have a major impact. Peter Espig, who has worked in both the leveraged finance and private equity fields in Japan, says flat out that the legalization of *sankakugappei* will not bring in foreign investment. He notes that, under U.S. law, when shareholders exchange shares in one company for another company's shares in a merger deal, the shares are not taxed. Japanese tax law is much different for such share exchanges. "It's a just paper transaction, but it's done as a selling of shares and a purchase of shares," he observes. Japanese shareholders have to pay tax on their gains, a huge disincentive.

In addition, the introduction of triangle mergers will be delayed because of misled concerns by those who did not understand that such takeovers were possible only under mutual agreement. Although the rest of the Commercial Code revisions went into effect April 2006, triangle mergers will not be permitted until 12 months later.

Deregulation has not been limited to the financial sector. The Japanese economy is often described as two-tiered—a competitive manufacturing sector and an uncompetitive, overly regulated services industry. As late as 1995, approximately 44% of Japanese industry was at least partially regulated, according the Economic Planning Agency. Only 7% of U.S. industry was regulated after the move to deregulation in the late 1970s and early 1980s, according to Clifford Winston. Deregulation is an area attracting the attention of foreign investors— as rules that limit business activity are dropped, inefficiencies in the economy can be targeted. Those investors anticipating at least partial convergence between U.S. and Japanese business practices look to arbitrage current asset prices with the likely value of winners and losers in the wake of less public sector interference.

Since the mid-1990s, there have been sweeping measures to limit government interference in business, and the Koizumi administration has reiterated its commitment to further deregulation.

The Japanese government has taken steps to dismantle controls and open the services sector to competition. Perceived inefficiencies in retailing and wholesaling—bloated distribution channels that boost final prices, as well as selling practices that downplay consumer desires—are seen as a potential opportunity by some foreign investors.

For them, the government's decision to scrap the Large Store Law in 1998 is epochal, likely to change the retailing landscape. The Large Store Law, enacted in 1974, required Ministry of International Trade and Industry (MITI) approval for all large stores. The approval review incorporated hearings before local panels that included small business owners threatened by the establishment of the larger stores. These panels tended to either recommend against approval or propose onerous restrictions on the new stores, such as limiting the hours that they could operate, notes David Flath, a researcher at Kyoto University. Under intense outside pressure from the United States, which claimed the Large Store Law was a structural impediment to the sale of imports from the United States, the government eased restrictions under the law in 1994 and scrapped it in 1998. A new law, the Large Scale Retail Store Location Law, now puts the regulation of large stores under the auspices of prefectural governments, which are mandated only to consider environmental factors such as noise and traffic, not the impact on local retailers.

To be sure, some researchers such as Flath are skeptical that the restrictions on large-scale stores were the main limitation on the building of such stores. He sees the lack of car ownership and small dwellings as stifling the need for such stores; people could not drive to large stores, and in any case, they had little room in their homes for storage of cheap items bought on bulk. Indeed, the high density of stores in urban areas made their supply and operation relatively efficient, he observes. However, the condition of households has changed. Rising car ownership and the moving of Japanese households to suburban areas are making larger stores in Japan a much more viable business, he notes.

If anything, the passage of the new Large Scale Retail Store Location Law sparked a flood of overdevelopment, notes Seth Sulkin,

CEO of Pacifica Malls K.K. His company was the first foreign firm to develop shopping malls in Japan without a domestic partner. Fears that municipalities would turn down many applications triggered a flurry of new developments not justified by demand or rents, he says. These worries proved groundless, and the pace of development has continued to accelerate. Meanwhile, the increased sophistication of Japan's financial markets has created new financing opportunities for both retailers and developers. Sulkin notes that he was able to get a nonrecourse loan from Shinsei Bank, a product not previously offered by other domestic banks in 2002, although it is now widely available. Nonrecourse loans are desirable for developers because banks do not put a lien on the developer's other assets; they do so only on the single property to be developed.

The track record of foreign retailers taking the plunge is decidedly mixed. Boots of the United Kingdom and both Sephora and Carrefour of France have all pulled the plug on Japanese operations in recent years. Meanwhile, Costco of the United States, Metro of Germany, and the U.K.'s Tesco remain. Japanese consumer tastes are widely perceived to be finicky and hard to predict. In addition, the country is no stranger to discounting, suggesting that foreign mass-merchandisers can gain no advantage by merely slashing prices. Many are now watching Wal-Mart Stores, Inc., which boosted its holdings in struggling retailer Seiyu, Ltd., to a majority share in December 2005. Seiyu announced another loss for fiscal year 2005 and has continued to struggle since Wal-Mart initially took a stake in the company in 2002.

Other sectors have seen less dramatic regulation, but even entrenched fortresses such as construction, long immune to market pressures, are coming under siege. The government privatized the Japan Highway Corp. and three other public road construction firms in fall 2005. Skeptics were quick to call the reform toothless; no new construction will be cancelled by the firms, which have often been derided for building roads to nowhere. In addition, taxpayers remain on the hook—a new administrative agency will take over the firms' debts, totaling ¥40 trillion, and the government will finance some toll-free roads.

However, public indignation at corruption in this sector is rising, which hints of further reforms. In summer 2005, several former executives of Japan Highway were arrested for alleged bid-rigging along with officials of bridge-building firms as well. A revision to the Anti-Monopoly Law in January 2006, aimed at this industry, increases penalties and is designed to prevent even suspected violators from bidding on new projects. Meanwhile, Koizumi is pushing forward a plan to change tax revenues specifically earmarked for road construction for general use, attacking the special funding system that ensured the power of LDP politicians with close ties to the industry for decades.

The lower house was also debating government plans in spring 2006 to consolidate publicly financed lenders. It plans to privatize the Development Bank of Japan and the Shoko Chukin Bank, dissolve the Japan Finance Corp. for Municipal Enterprises, and join five others with the international finance operations of the Japan Bank for International Cooperation, creating a new institution. Through this reduction in the number of public lenders, wasteful financing is expected to be curtailed, especially in the previously well-connected construction industry.

But that is not all. The Koizumi administration is permitting some firms to apply for exceptions to onerous regulations that hamper their growth. Companies such as Tmsuk Co. now collaborate with local governments to bypass such rules and are enjoying a new freedom to develop their businesses as a result. Although robots are banned on city streets elsewhere, this Kyushu Island firm was able to work on a security patrol robot project because this law was lifted in Fukuoka. Similarly, Kanagawa Prefecture applied to the central government to allow a plastic surgery clinic to be operated by Biomaster Inc., in May

2005. Previously, the Ministry of Health had barred for-profit hospitals and clinics.

In a troubling nomenclature more evocative of a closed communist economy than a free-wheeling, capitalistic one, the government has designated such territories *tokku*, or Special Zones. A total of 475 Special Zones, enjoying regulatory exemptions, had been created by December 2004. The national government also decides whether to reform regulations in response to such applications. A total of 188 regulatory changes had been made in Special Zones, and 285 had been enacted nationwide as a result of the program by the same date.

This program has gotten mixed reviews from observers. Reforms in the zones should be applied on a national basis as quickly as possible, avoiding extended evaluation periods, said the Organization of Economic Cooperation and Development (OECD) in its *Economic Survey of Japan 2005*. The organization also argued that the national government should not depend solely on the initiative of local government to implement changes. With such an approach, the program should be an effective tool for accelerating regulatory change, was the OECD's upbeat assessment. Foreign participants, perhaps among those with the most to gain from an elimination of rules hampering start-ups, are much more skeptical of this approach.

"Koizumi was elected because the power bosses did not realize there was so much unhappiness with the LDP out there," observes Westmore of the ACCJ. "The *tokku* (Special Zones) were sops—they were the usual 'We're going to do something, and make it look like we're doing something.'"

"What they didn't realize was, by God, there was unemployment out there!" he adds. The local politicians had to deal with this problem. "Proposals for Special Zones came in out of nowhere." Requests continued to mount.

"At first they said, 'No, no, no,' but it was so overwhelming that they had to do something," Westmore observes.

To some cynics, the Special Zone system appears to be just an excuse to deregulate specific, small regions, enabling the government to put off doing the same reforms nationwide.

Postmaster Hiroshi Ueno is about to face the challenge of his life. Although his post office in Katsushika Okudo, near the Kiowa Station on the Sobu line in eastern Tokyo, has been in operation for more than half a century, some feel that the days of operations such as his may be numbered. On a weekday morning in February 2006, Ueno was darting between counters, helping local residents buy stamps and mail parcels, as he has done since 1988, when he took over the office from his wife's uncle, who initially founded the branch in 1947.

Takashi Hamada, a postmaster in Nagoya, says that small operations such as Ueno's will face increasing competition because of the scheduled privatization of Japan Post. The government has pledged to provide support to some remote post offices in the countryside so rural residents will not be deprived of services. However, numerous operations in urban areas such as Ueno's will likely receive no such aid. Hamada argues that if such operations are allowed to go under, the elderly and small businesses dependent on them will suffer. Indeed, the concentration of businesses and residents into pockets of the city with good transportation and communication links, as noted in Chapter 6, "The Manhattan of Asia," could well be accelerated by the loss of postal offices in some neighborhoods.

However, such widening disparity in the health of urban neighborhoods is apparently a price the prime minister and his supporters are willing to pay for smaller government. Koizumi submitted six postal-privatization bills to the Diet in April 2005. Although passed by the lower house, the legislation was defeated in the upper house on August 7. As he promised to do if the bills did not go through, Koizumi called snap elections the same day. The September 11 lower house vote, viewed as a referendum on Koizumi's plans, resulted in an overwhelming victory for the pro-privatization LDP and handed the prime minister his desired mandate. Both houses passed the privatization bills in October.

As a result, Japan Post is scheduled to be divided into four entities in October 2007, one each for mail delivery, banking, insurance services, and administration of postal payrolls and properties. These will be owned and managed by a holding company, initially presided over by Yoshifumi Nishikawa, former president of Sumitomo Mitsui Banking Corp. By 2017, the holding firm must sell off its shares in the banking and insurance firms.

Koizumi apparently hopes to achieve two major goals by privatizing Japan's postal system. First, the move is in line with his objective of shrinking central government. Three hundred thousand employees will be taken off the national administrative payrolls and transferred to the Postal Public Corp. In addition, because the ¥203 trillion in postal savings deposits and another ¥112 trillion in insurance funds will eventually be managed by the private sector, resource allocation is expected to be improved in the economy as well.

Currently, some of the postal savings deposits are made available to the Fiscal Investment and Loan Program, a government program designed to funnel funds to infrastructure projects and loans to public corporations. It is widely believed that there is waste in such spending with politicians and their supporters benefiting from pork-belly projects. If postal savings funds are shifted out of the program and managed instead by private-sector funds, which are exposed to market pressures to invest in profitable enterprises, returns in the economy could arguably rise. Heizo Tanaka, the minister in charge of postal savings privatization, argues that even if households started buying Japanese government bonds directly rather than indirectly through postal savings accounts, it would force the government to pay market rates on debt, raising the cost of capital and imposing fiscal discipline, reported the *Financial Times*.

About 65% of postal saving funds and 55% of postal insurance funds were invested in Japanese central and local government bonds at the end of February 2006. Even after the Japan Post's split-up into different entities, many postal savings time deposits and insurance funds will still be parked in these sort of secure investments. Savings time deposits accounted for about 75% of all postal deposits in fiscal year 2004. Some market watchers hope that when such accounts mature, some of these funds could flow into equities as a result of the privatization of Japan Post. Some bulls project that such investment will help support Japanese share prices for years to come.

However, investor behavior in recent years suggests that Japanese households are unlikely to pour money into financial products they are unfamiliar with. In 2001 and 2002, about $1 trillion in 10-year fixed-term postal savings deposits matured. Many market observers expected that much of this would flow into the equity market. After all, the funds had been held in postal savings accounts since the early 1990s. Yields had since fallen sharply, so many expected that depositors would shift funds into higher-risk investments with the potential for higher returns.

Of course, the stock market fell both years, disappointing those who expected a stream of money from postal savings to bolster share prices. Many have downplayed the attractiveness of postal savings accounts because of the low nominal yields that they offer. However, because many prices in Japan have been falling, the purchasing power of depositors had been protected even with such low yields. In fact, discounted for deflation, interest rates were comparable with those overseas. In addition, postal savings offered government-backed safety desired by aging Japanese households approaching retirement.

Both education and inflationary expectations probably played a role in the rising allocation for stock investment in household portfolios overseas. Japanese investors, on the other hand, are relatively unfamiliar with many investment strategies and, in any case, have little incentive to chase yields as long as falling prices support their standard of living. Barring a jump in consumer prices, it is unlikely that the appetite for risk in Japanese households will change overnight, and money flowing out of the postal entities into financial products other than Japanese government bonds will probably increase only gradually over time.

Foreign investors are increasingly encouraged by these sweeping privatization efforts and moves to deregulate industries. However, such promising developments should not blind investors to still-present dangers. The Japanese economy remains heavily dependent on overseas shipments for growth, suggesting that if the U.S. or Chinese economy slows, investments in Japan may also get hit. Kaneko's scenario of a "slow panic" could well materialize if conditions destabilize overseas.

In the realm of intellectual property, arguably one of the most promising areas for investors to hunt down bargains, information disclosure remains weak by most firms. Indeed, Japanese firms themselves are often only starting to extract financial value from their IP holdings. Hedge funds face rising insistence by their investors on extensive risk-management controls. The sharp increase in the number of funds in Asia suggests that the talent pool for running money is getting squeezed as well. The outlook for private equity is extremely bright, but competition, from both domestic and international players, is heating up. Corporate governance is evolving, but investors still often rank low on the priority list of management. Boards often lack independence. Meanwhile, a strategic awareness that firms must start growing organically to remain competitive in this global age is spreading among policymakers and corporate leaders. Yet Japanese firms are still shy regarding tie-ups with foreigners.

Tokyo real estate players have enjoyed fair weather for years—rising rents and rock-bottom financing costs have helped fuel the recovery. They are finally seeing storm clouds on the horizon. An eventual increase in interest rates could roil funds with property holdings in undesirable locations. The Bank of Japan announced in March 2006 that it is shifting its target for money market operations from liquidity measures back to the overnight call rates. Although any significant hikes could be still well off, this reorientation of central bank policy is the first step toward raising borrowing costs.

Foreign investors cultivating their own businesses in Tokyo believe opportunities outweigh such risks. Importantly, Japan's focus on intellectual asset cultivation suggests that it is well positioned for business in the twenty-first century, when the bulk of enterprise value is likely to be generated by such holdings. Japanese firm strength in this area will likely become increasingly obvious as the dust settles from the drastic restructuring of the banking sector over the last decade. Japanese companies are becoming more much aggressive in defending their IP turf, vastly improving their competitive positions in the process. Investors will probably become much more focused on such assets in the future as well. Indeed, the foreign investment community could be on the brink of reassessing Japanese management based on its strengths in cultivating such intangibles. The pendulum of investor perceptions, as Roehl described in Chapter 2, "Intellectual Property Wars," could well swing back toward respect for the first time since the 1980s.

Meanwhile, as firms become more sophisticated in unlocking financial value from their invisible assets, such as brands and patents, they will increasingly look abroad to leverage such holdings. As a result, tie-ups with compatible foreign firms will probably proliferate.

Japan's proximity to China, as well as the increasing degree to which Japanese firms are integrating their operations with the mainland powerhouse, also bodes well for the country's future. As we saw in the last chapter, Sino-Japanese trade relations can be traced to the distant past. Trade and investment flows, which have surged since China's WTO entry, are likely to continue to increase. Balancing the need to defend Japanese strategic interests, such as intellectual property protection, and maintaining goodwill with customers in this fast-growing market may sometimes be difficult. However, Chinese firms and consumers have a stake in IP protection as well, which suggests the situation is far from untenable.

Of course, a new administration could slow the pace of reform. In addition, maladroit handling of relations with the mainland could hurt Japanese company efforts at expansion into this important market. In addition, the massive privatization and deregulation programs implemented in quick succession are increasing anxieties among voters. Debate between market fundamentalists and more liberal politicians will likely continue. Meanwhile, the rise of a civil society suggests that more people will become involved in governance issues, suggesting that the powers of the once-dominant bureaucracy will be further eroded.

Despite the uncertain political outlook ahead, one thing is clear. Japan must change—the old way of doing things no longer works in the increasingly global economy. Japan is reinventing itself for a new era, and savvy foreign investors are positioning their businesses to benefit from likely changes.

"Prime Minister Kozumi is right," says Masao Igarashi, vice president of the Japan Federation of Service and Distributive Workers Union in November 2005. Some of his union members worked at Seiyu, Ltd. , which was on the verge of being taken over by Wal-Mart Stores, Inc., at the time. Because Wal-Mart shows little tolerance for organized labor in the United States, one would expect him to express dismay at his members' new bosses. However, Igarashi says his union was willing to give Wal-Mart a chance at turning around the ailing retailer.

Through much of the post-war period, Japanese companies depended on banks for financing, and that is strange, Igarashi points out. "Money should flow more freely throughout the economy. Investors taking stakes directly in firms, that is now commonplace throughout the world," he says. In this age of globalization, Japan had to change.

"Japanese will get used to it," he replied, when asked about the stress and anxieties now many feel. "When the *shinkansen* [bullet train] was first built, everybody was worried about the speed of the train," he remembers. Now everyone has become accustomed to the velocity.

With regards to recent structural reforms, "It's the same thing," he asserts. "People will adapt."

Investment Implications

Waves of deregulation and privatization have repeatedly swept through Japan, leaving very few parts of the economy untouched. With the emergence of more than a dozen financial holding companies, the banking system no longer drains the country's economic vitality, but is a force for change. Consolidation among financial giants is forcing many smaller firms to adapt to changing market conditions or perish. Stricter regulatory oversight and accounting improvements are increasing transparency among corporations, making it easier for investors to distinguish between potential winners and losers. The Commercial Code has been modernized. Constraints on successful firms are being lifted, while weaker firms are often left to fend for themselves. Japanese management and employees are still adapting to this new, harsher environment, so in the short run, the results of such change on aggregate corporate profits are likely to be ambiguous. Indeed, this brave new corporate world is sparking fears among some policymakers that many workers are unprepared for a Japanese society that increasingly reflects the forces of globalization. This presents the risk of a political backlash against ongoing liberalization efforts.

Furthermore, some of the optimism regarding some recent policy reforms appears to be misplaced. Efforts at liberalizing mergers and acquisitions are unlikely to stimulate activity without additional tax reforms. The Special Zones programs are inefficient, piecemeal efforts at deregulation rather than a comprehensive approach that would kick-start new businesses throughout the country. Those market watchers expecting a surge of capital from postal savings into Japanese stocks will likely be disappointed, as they were earlier in the decade. Having no fear of inflation and often in need of further financial education, postal account holders are unlikely to dump their life savings into much riskier investments, despite privatization of the postal savings system.

Nonetheless, as a result of recent regulatory reforms, successful risk takers will be more generously rewarded in Japan. This spells good news for entrepreneurs and those foreign investors capable of differentiating between well-run companies and dinosaurs unable to adapt to new market conditions. The premium on picking winners is likely to rise sharply. For years, generous across-the-board financing limited the upside potential of stronger firms as their weaker and subsidized competitors clung, zombie-like, to market share. Now parent firms and banks unsentimentally jettison such deadweight. Importantly, even many vulnerable workers agree that Japan must change to survive in the twenty-first century.

With deflationary fears abating, market winners in Japan will no longer be those who stand to benefit the most from cheap financing, but those who can create the most value for their clients, often leveraging hard-to-measure intangible asset holdings. Those investors who adapt to this landmark change stand to prosper in the years ahead.

THE JAPANESE MONEY TREE

References

"City employees marked off the areas to prevent new squatters …." Author held conversations with residents in March 2006.

"The Tokyo city government is providing public assistance …." Tokyo Metropolitan Government. *2005 Social Welfare and Public Health in Tokyo*. www.fukushihoken.metro.tokyo.jp. See esp. p. 15.

"On the other hand, they have been said to engage in more …." *Housing and Land Rights Network*. Member of Habitat International Coalition. "Japanese Activists Protest Against Tokyo." 11 May 2005. www.hlrn.org/news_show_user.php?id=40.

"In any case, the number of homeless in Tokyo reached a peak …." Tokyo Metropolitan Government. *2005 Social Welfare and Public Health in Tokyo*. www.fukushihoken.metro.tokyo.jp. See esp. p. 15.

"However, for Fiorillo, the tents are a reminder …." Quotes and statements are from interviews conducted by the author on 3 July 2005 and 2 March 2006.

"The percentage of shares outstanding…" Kuroki, Fumio. *The Relationship of Companies and Banks as Cross-Shareholdings Unwind – Fiscal 2002 Cross-Shareholding Survey*. Financial Research Group, NLI Research 18 November, 2003, at www.nli-research.co.jp/eng/resea/econo/eco031118.pdf.

"Federal Reserve Bank of New York Vice President Ernest Patrikis …." Patrikis, Ernest. *Japan's Big Bang Financial Reforms*. Speech for Brooklyn Law School, Center for the Study of International Business Law, at the New York Stock Exchange, 27 April 1998. http://fednewyork.org/newsevents/speeches/1998/ep980427.html.

Ministry of Finance. *Financial System Reform*. 13 June 1997. www.mof.go.jp/english/big-bang/ebb32.htm.

"Ten massive bank holding companies …." List provided by Chiaki Wakazono at Japan Securities Research Institute.

"In addition, banks, trust banks, and securities …." Patrikis, Ernest. *Japan's Big Bang Financial Reforms.* Speech for Brooklyn Law School, Center for the Study of International Business Law, at the New York Stock Exchange, 27 April 1998. http://fednewyork.org/newsevents/speeches/1998/ep980427.html. See esp. Table 3.

"The Financial Services Agency is reorienting its inspections …." Financial Services Agency. *Basic Guidelines and Plan for Financial Inspections in Program Year 2005.* www.fsa.go.jp/news/newse/e20050708-1.html.

"Introduction of mark-to-market …." *Nikkei Net Interactive.* Nihon Keizai Shimbun, Inc. "Analysis: Improving Domestic Economy Lifts Stock Market," 5 April 2004.

"Born in Argentina into a Japanese diplomatic family …." This statement and following quotes are from an interview conducted by the author on 4 July, 2005. At the time of printing, Kondo had left White & Case.

"There is a lot of concern about this …." Interview conducted by the author on 12 August 2005.

"Because a redrafting looked increasingly …." Interview conducted by the author on 12 August 2005.

"We provided a long list of questions …." Interview conducted by the author on 12 August 2005.

"It was a classic case of Japanese …." Interview conducted by the author on 12 August 2005.

"In many policy discussions …." Interview conducted by the author on 12 August 2005.

"Peter Espig, who has worked both …." Interview conducted by the author in July 2005.

"As late as 1995, approximately 44% of Japanese industry …." Economic Planning Agency. *Economic Survey of Japan 1994–1995.*

"Only 7% of the U.S. industry was regulated …." Winston, Clifford. "Economic Deregulation: Days of Reckoning for Microeconomists." *Journal of Economic Literature* 31, no. 3 (September 1993): 1263–1289. See esp. p. 1263.

"These panels tended to either recommend …." Flath, David. *The Japanese Distribution Sector in Economic Perspective: The Large Store Law and Retail Density*. May 2002. For the National Bureau of Economic Research Conference in Tokyo, March 2002. At the time of printing, Flath was at North Carolina State University.

"If anything, the passage of the new Large Scale …." Interview conducted by the author on 27 June 2005.

"Boots of the United Kingdom and both Sephora …." *Nikkei Net Interactive.* Nihon Keizai Shimbun, Inc. "Carrefour Exit Marks Tough Road for Foreign Retailers." 14 March 2005.

"Many are now watching Wal-Mart Stores …." *Nikkei Net Interactive.* Nihon Keizai Shimbun, Inc. "Wal-Mart to Make Seiyu a Group Company." November 2, 2005.

"Seiyu announced another loss for fiscal year 2005 …." *Nikkei Net Interactive.* Nihon Keizai Shimbun, Inc., "Seiyu Reports Net Loss in FY05." 2 November 2005.

"The government privatized the Japan Highway …." *Nikkei Net Interactive.* Nihon Keizai Shimbun, Inc., "Japan Privatizes Four Expressway Public Corporations." 1 October 2005.

"Skeptics were quick to call the reform toothless …." *Nikkei Net Interactive.* Nihon Keizai Shimbun, Inc., "Govt to Build All Highways Listed in National Road Plan." 26 January 2006.

"In addition, tax-payers remain on the hook …" *Nikkei Net Interactive.* Nihon Keizai Shimbun, Inc. "Privatized Highway Firms Lack Logic." 3 October 2005.

(And) *Nikkei Net Interactive.* Nihon Keizai Shimbun, Inc. "Govt to Build All Highways Listed in National Road Plan." 30 September 2005.

"In summer 2005, several former executives ...." *The Japan Times.* "Japan High Retiree, Four Bridge Execs Held in Big-rigging." 13 July 2005.

Nikkei Net Interactive, Nihon Keizai Shimbun, Inc. "Japan Highway Suspects Six More Officials Involved in Big-rigging." 22 September 2005.

"A revision to the Anti-Monopoly Law ...." *Nikkei Net Interactive.* Nihon Keizai Shimbun, Inc. "New Anti-Monopoly Law Kicks Off." January 16, 2006.

"Meanwhile, Koizumi is pushing forward a plan ..." *Nikkei Net Interactive,* Nihon Keizai Shimbun, Inc. "Reform Saps Clout of 'Zoku Giin' Politicians." November 21, 2005.

"The lower house was also debating government plans ...." *Nikkei Net Interactive.* Nihon Keizai Shimbun, Inc. "Lower House Begins Discussing Administrative Reform Bill." 23 March 2006.

"It plans to privatize the Development Bank of Japan ...." *Nikkei Net Interactive.* Nihon Keizai Shimbun, Inc. "Public Lenders Need Tough Oversight." 27 March 2006.

"Firms such as Tmsuk Co. are now collaborating ..." *Nikkei Net Interactive,* Nihon Keizai Shimbun, Inc. "Special Zones Sparking Innovation." 6 September 2004.

"Similarly, Kanagawa Prefecture ..." *Nikkei Net Interactive.* Nihon Keizai Shimbun, Inc. "Government to Okay Plastic Surgery Clinic as First Stock Company Hospital." 19 May 2005.

"A total of 475 Special Zones, enjoying regulatory exemptions, had ..." Cabinet Office. *Cabinet Office Government of Japan,* 2005. See esp. p. 12.

"It should be an effective tool for accelerating ...." OECD. *Economic Survey of Japan 2005.* See esp. the chapter entitled "Removing Obstacles to Faster Growth."

"Koizumi was elected because ...." Interview conducted by the author on 12 August 2005.

"Takashi Hamada, a postmaster in Nagoya, says ...." Interview conducted by the author on 14 March 2006.

"As a result, Japan Post is scheduled to be divided ...." *The Nikkei Weekly*. "Japan Post Pads up Prior to Privatization." 6 March 2006. p. S22.

"These will be owned and managed by a ..." *Nikkei Net Interactive*. Nihon Keizai Shimbun, Inc. "Ex-SMBC Chief Nishikawa to Head Postal Holding Firm." 11 November 2005.

"Three hundred thousand employees will be taken ...." Cabinet Office. *Drastic Streamlining of the Central Government*. www.kantei.go.jp/foreign/central_government/04_drastic.html.

"In addition, since the ¥203 trillion in postal savings ..." Japan Post. *Yuucho Shikin no Unyou Joukyou*. February 2006. www.yu-cho.japanpost.jp/j0000000/ju060200.htm.

Kampo. *Shikin Unyou Joukyou*. February 2006. http://kampo.japanpost.jp/osirase/report/unyou/unyou0602.html.

"Heizo Tanaka, the minister in charge of postal savings ...." Pilling, David. "Postal Privatization, A Welcome Shock to the Old System." FT Special Report Japan. *Financial Times*. 13 December 2005.

"About 65% of postal saving funds and 55% of postal insurance funds..." Japan Post. *Yuucho Shikin Unyou Joukyou*. February 2006. www.yu-cho.japanpost.jp/j0000000/ju060200.htm.

Kampo. *Shikin Unyou Joukyou*. February 2006. http://kampo.japanpost.jp/osirase/report/unyou/unyou0602.html.

"Even after Japan Posts' split-up into different entities ...." Yuusei *Mineika Kanren Houritsu No Gaiyou*. www.yuseimineika.go.jp.

"Savings time deposits accounted for about 75% of all deposits ...." *Yubin Chokin 2005*. www.japanpost.jp/ir/disclo-05c.html. See esp. p. 12.

"In 2001 and 2002, about $1 trillion in 10-year ...." Bremner, Brian, . "Birth of an Investor Class." *BusinessWeek* on line 31 October 2000.

Shipley, Andrew, "A Cautionary Tale: Dramatic Changes in Household Asset Allocation Not Likely Overnight." *Japan Economics Weekly*. Schroders Japan, Ltd., 19 October 1999.

"The Bank of Japan announced in March 2006 that ...." Bank of Japan. *Change to the Guideline for Money Market Operations*. March 9, 2006. www.boj.or.jp/en/type/release/zuiji_new/k060309.htm.

"'Prime Minister Kozumi is right,'" says Masao Igarashi ..." Interview conducted by the author on 10 November 2005.

INDEX